IMAGES
of America

HIGHLANDS RANCH

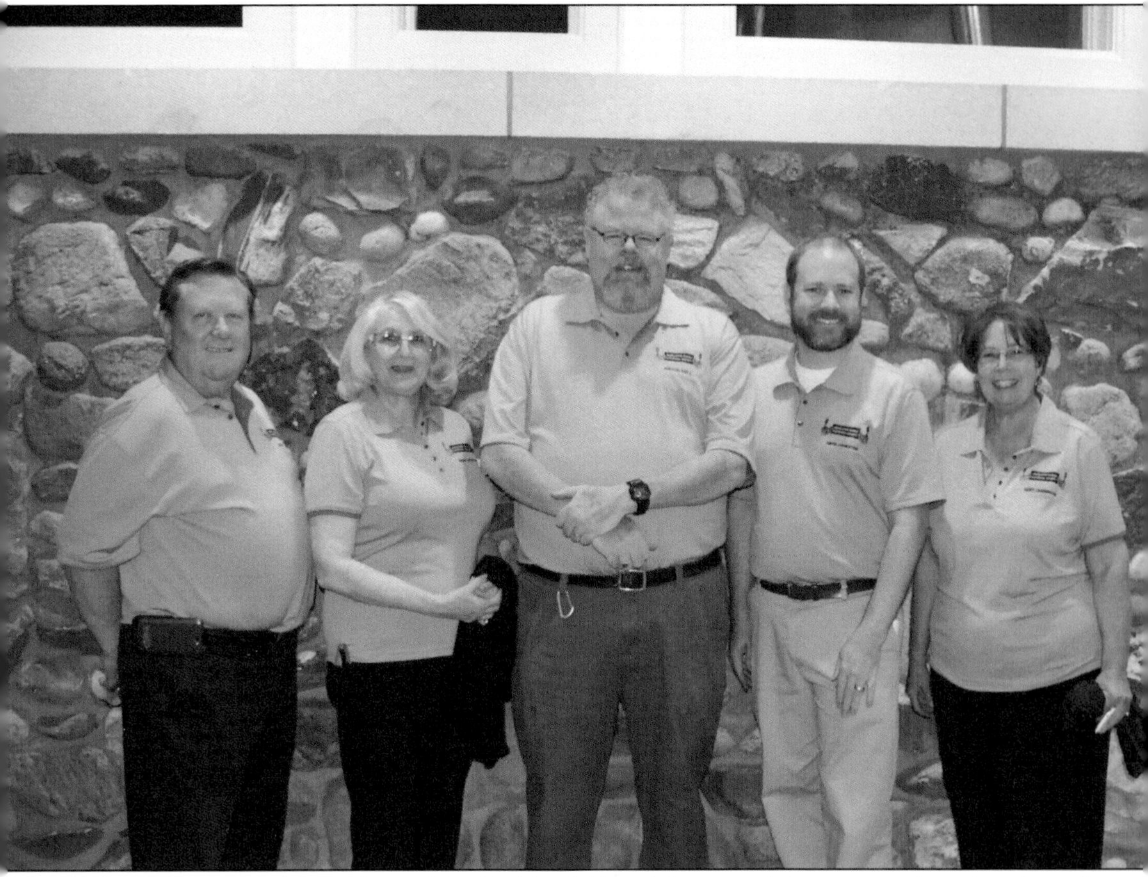

The current board members of the Highlands Ranch Historical Society are pleased to share the community's history through this book, meetings, and other forms of outreach. Pictured from left to right are Paul McKeag, Sara Lebofsky, David Hill, David Johnston, and Nancy Linsenbigler. (Courtesy of the Highlands Ranch Historical Society.)

On the Cover: The Highlands Ranch Mansion is known as the soul of Highlands Ranch. The mansion is currently owned by Highlands Ranch Metro District and is regularly open to the public to experience and develop their own personal connection. The image of the mansion was taken during the Kistler era, from 1926 to 1938. (Courtesy of Kistler Family Photos, the Highlands Mansion, Douglas County History Research Center, Douglas County Libraries, 2011.004.0039.)

IMAGES
of America

HIGHLANDS RANCH

Highlands Ranch Historical Society

ARCADIA
PUBLISHING

ISBN 978-1-4671-1614-5

Published by Arcadia Publishing
Charleston, South Carolina

Printed in the United States of America

Library of Congress Control Number: 2016936364

For all general information, please contact Arcadia Publishing:
Telephone 843-853-2070
Fax 843-853-0044
E-mail sales@arcadiapublishing.com
For customer service and orders:
Toll-Free 1-888-313-2665

Visit us on the Internet at www.arcadiapublishing.com

This book is dedicated to everyone who takes part in making Highlands Ranch history, including all who have lived, worked, visited or taken part in an event.

Contents

ACKNOWLEDGMENTS

Writing a book about Highlands Ranch, Colorado, took the assistance of the whole community. We have written this book to record the history of the community that we call home.

I, David Johnston, would like to acknowledge the other members of the Highlands Ranch Historical Society who helped make this book possible. They are as follows: Nancy Linsenbigler, who believed we could complete this book; David Hill, who aided with the book's images; Sara Lebofsky, who proofread; Paul McKeag, who, in general, supported the project; and Mark Stevenson and Robert Morse, who helped with proofreading and fact-checking.

We also want to acknowledge the help given by the following people and organizations. Blake Graham and Shaun Boyd from the Douglas County Libraries Historic Research Center provided assistance with research, photographs, and encouragement. Terry Nolan, Jeff Case, and Sherry Eppers of the Highlands Ranch Metro District provided photos along with their time and historical insight. Maggie Glass and Susie Appleby of the Highlands Ranch Mansion provided historical reviews and photographs of previous mansion owners. We also want to thank the Philbrook Museum for permission to share their photographs of the Waite Phillips era. Reid Farmer, the chairman of the Douglas County Historic Preservation Board, provided images and text for the pre-homestead history of northern Douglas County. Thank you to the staff at Historic Douglas County, Inc. for their work in the community and photographs of the Grigs homestead today.

I would like to thank my wonderful wife, Nicole, who helped and put up with the long hours that I gave to the creation of this book, which included me taking photographs, coordinating schedules, writing captions, and researching the facts. I thank my father, Robert Van Johnston, for his assistance with the closing photograph. I took all photographs not otherwise credited in this book. I would also like to thank my brother-in-law Mike Littlehorn for assisting in proofreading. Finally, I would like to thank my personal inspiration for writing this book, my daughter Ashley, who has lived in Highlands Ranch her entire life.

Introduction

Welcome to Highlands Ranch, the home on the range for almost 100,000 people. In 1980, there were less than 100 people who called Highlands Ranch home. The goal of this book is to provide the history of the area, as well as its development and growth toward the future. With great outlooks for the future, present-day Highlands Ranch is the nation's largest unincorporated homeowners' association–controlled area.

Around 10,000 years before Highlands Ranch was developed, mammoths and early camels roamed the land. Indians moved through the area for many years but never set up permanent settlements. The Ute Indians moved around this area in the 1500s, migrating up from Southern California. Then, in the 1700s, the Comanche came in from the northern plains. The Cheyenne and Arapaho also moved through Highlands Ranch.

From the time of the earliest European settlements in the 16th and 17th centuries, eastern Colorado was part of the territory of French Louisiana, an administrative district of New France, France's New World colonies. Louisiana essentially comprised most of the drainage basin of the Mississippi River and its tributaries. On the west, it bordered New Mexico, a province of New Spain, which included Spain's colonies in Mexico and the rest of Western North America. After its defeat by Great Britain in the Seven Years War, France ceded all of Louisiana west of the Mississippi River to Spain in 1763 under terms of the Treaty of Paris. Spain governed Louisiana as a Spanish province with its capital in New Orleans.

In 1800, France and Spain were allied against Great Britain's interests, though there was no open warfare at the time. That year, under the Third Treaty of San Ildefonso, Spain ceded Louisiana back to France in return for land in Italy and other considerations. The transfer was kept a secret, and Spain continued to administer the territory. In 1803, France went to war with Great Britain, and First Consul Napoleon Bonaparte, fearing he might lose Louisiana to a British invasion, agreed to sell it to the United States for $15,000,000 in cash and debt cancellations. Spain formally ceded Louisiana back to France shortly before it was sold to the United States.

Early explorers moved through the area setting up the original trails of travel in this region. The Highlands Ranch area is bordered on the west by the historic Santa Fe trail between Denver and Santa Fe, New Mexico, which ran along modern day US 85 also known as Santa Fe Drive. The first homestead was established in 1859 by the "Potato King of Colorado," Rufus "Dad" Clark, who filed a 160-acre homestead. The majority of homesteads in the region sprouted in the 1880s, with the west side of Highlands Ranch being checkerboarded with alternate sections being given to the railroads. Many of the ranchers who purchased smaller homesteads quickly found that Colorado's dry climate required more land. They sold their properties to their neighbors to create several larger ranches. Since the Homestead Act only allowed one limited sized property per person, this prompted homesteaders to purchase adjacent lands under the names of wives, children, and extended family members to gain larger parcels.

The early families were the Grigs, Failings, Weltes, and Plews. The Grigs homestead was on the east side of Highlands Ranch. The Failing homestead, which later became the Douglas Investment Company, was located in the southern part of what is the Highlands Ranch Backcountry. In the northeast of Highlands Ranch was the Welte Cheese and Beer Ranch. Johanne Welte was known nationally for his innovations in dryland farming and was featured in a national magazine. The Plews homestead is now called the Fly'n B Ranch. It is located in the northwest corner of Highlands Ranch and is a property of the Highlands Ranch Metro District. The property is being renovated for multipurpose use, particularly small weddings.

The soul of Highlands Ranch began as a 40-acre homestead by Samuel Long of the Baltimore and Ohio (B&O) Railroad in 1884. He called the ranch "Rotherwood" after his boyhood home. Samuel Long was able to expand his homestead to 2,000 acres, and by 1891, he had built a modest farmhouse, which is still the core of the Highlands Ranch Mansion today. Samuel Long used dryland farming for his crops and orchards.

In 1897, John Springer started the transformation from a house into a mansion. He was a great orator from a family of lawyers and politicians. He ran for Denver mayor in 1904, losing in the most corrupt election in Denver's history. John concentrated on his love of ranching and grew the Springer Cross Country Horse and Cattle Ranch to 12,000 acres. Also around that time, he did the first major remodel of the home and turned it into "Castle Isabel" for his second wife, Isabel Patterson. Isabel would play a central role in a love triangle that led to the infamous murder at the Brown Palace Hotel in Denver, Colorado.

The scandal drove John Springer from the public eye and forced him to sell the ranch to his first father-in-law, Col. William Hughes, in 1913. William Hughes was a colonel in the Civil War and was successful in both law and banking. He changed the ranch name to Sunland Ranch and continued to operate it until his death in 1918, when the ranch passed to his granddaughter Annie, the daughter of John Springer.

The ranch later was sold to Waite Phillips. Waite was the younger brother of the founders of the Phillips Petroleum Company. He made his own money in oil reportedly selling his Waite Phillips Company for $25 million in 1925. Waite purchased ranches from Montana to New Mexico including the Sunland Ranch in 1920, which he renamed Highland Ranch (without the "s" as it is currently spelled). The name came from the Highland Hereford cattle he raised on the ranch. Waite continued the expansion of the mansion and is credited with adding the west wing. Waite also combined the ranch with other nearby ranches he purchased, increasing the total land size.

In 1926, Frank Kistler, who also made his fortune from oil, purchased Highland Ranch. After the purchase, he changed its name to the Diamond K Ranch. Ranch operations flourished with Angus cattle, sheep, chickens, and hogs. Kistler transformed the mansion with a major remodel from the Gothic stone castle look to that of a classic English Tudor, which remains until today.

The last rancher and owner was Lawrence Phipps Jr. He was the son of former US senator Lawrence Phipps Sr., who made a fortune working for Carnegie Steel. Lawrence Phipps Jr. served in both World War I and World War II, managed the National Western Stock Show, and founded the Mountain States Telephone Company, which went on to become Qwest (now Century Link). Lawrence loved horses, and in 1929, he joined the Arapahoe Hunt Club and convinced Frank Kistler to have the club headquarters at the Diamond K Ranch.

When Frank experienced financial problems in 1937, Lawrence purchased the ranch and renamed it Highlands Ranch. He lived at the Highlands Ranch Mansion until his death in 1976. If you are interested in more information on the mansion, we recommend the mansion website at www.highlandsranchmansion.com.

The modern-day Highlands Ranch began with the purchase of the ranch by Marvin Davis in 1976. Marvin Davis marketed and sold the 22,000-acre Highlands Ranch in 1978 to the Mission Viejo Company. Mission Viejo started residential construction in 1980, and in September 1981, the first family moved in.

The community of Highlands Ranch reached many milestones during the 1980s. In 1982, Northridge Park, Northridge Recreation Center, and Northridge Elementary all opened to serve the new community. In 1983, the Centennial Water and Sanitation District and Highlands Ranch Metropolitan District offices opened. 1984 brought the first Convenience Center at South Broadway and Springer Drive. Many of the parks and roads throughout Highlands Ranch have been named after people related to the history of Highlands Ranch.

The second half of the 1980s was defined in 1985 by the largest change to not only Highlands Ranch, but also to all the southwest Denver area with the opening of State Highway 470 (C-470). The new and simple access would open the community for decades of growth that would propel Douglas County to become the fastest growing county in the entire United States. Highlands Ranch added its first golf course, the Links Golf Course, in 1986.

By 1991, Highlands Ranch was 10 years old and had a population that had grown to 17,000. The community was enhanced with the addition of a branch library and soon its own post office. Highlands Ranch continued to grow quickly with new homes, schools, businesses, fire stations, and churches opening regularly. In 1997, the Mission Viejo Company was acquired by Shea Homes. Growth continued with the establishment of the regional offices of Lucent Technologies. In 2000, the Douglas County Libraries opened the Highlands Ranch Library. The library system received the national award, the John Cotton Dana Library Public Relations Award, in 2007.

In 1999, Shea Homes started building the Highlands Ranch Business Park. The next step was the creation of Highlands Ranch Town Center with the first businesses opening in 2004. In December 2013, the Children's Hospital Colorado South Campus, Highlands Ranch, opened to provide service to the region's children.

A key to the growth of Highlands Ranch is its well-planned parks and open spaces, from Northridge Park, the first park in 1982, to Redstone Park, the largest park at 55-acres in 2000, and finally to Civic Green Park in Town Center in 2005. Today, Highlands Ranch has 25 parks that are managed by Highlands Ranch Metro District. Since 2009, Highlands Ranch is also blessed with 8,200 acres of conserved open space and trails, called the Backcountry Wilderness Area, along the south side of the community; the Backcountry Wilderness Area is managed by the Highlands Ranch Community Association. The Highlands Ranch Community Association (HRCA) built, owns, and operates all four recreation centers and provides programs. For more information on HRCA visit their website at www.hrcaonline.org.

Today, Highlands Ranch has received multiple national recognitions for its great quality of life and amenities. Welcome to this journey in images of Highlands Ranch.

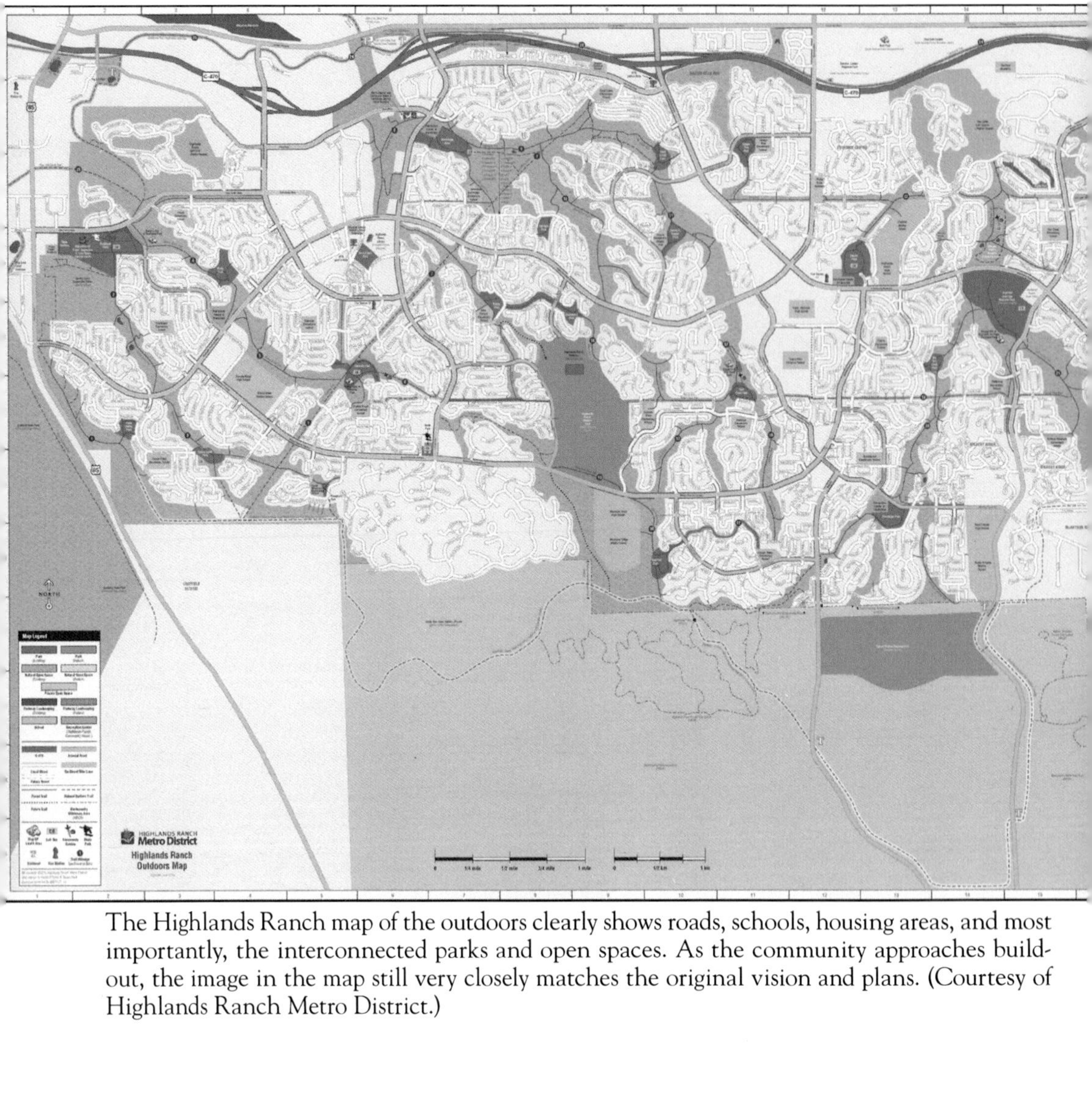

The Highlands Ranch map of the outdoors clearly shows roads, schools, housing areas, and most importantly, the interconnected parks and open spaces. As the community approaches build-out, the image in the map still very closely matches the original vision and plans. (Courtesy of Highlands Ranch Metro District.)

One

Early Homesteads

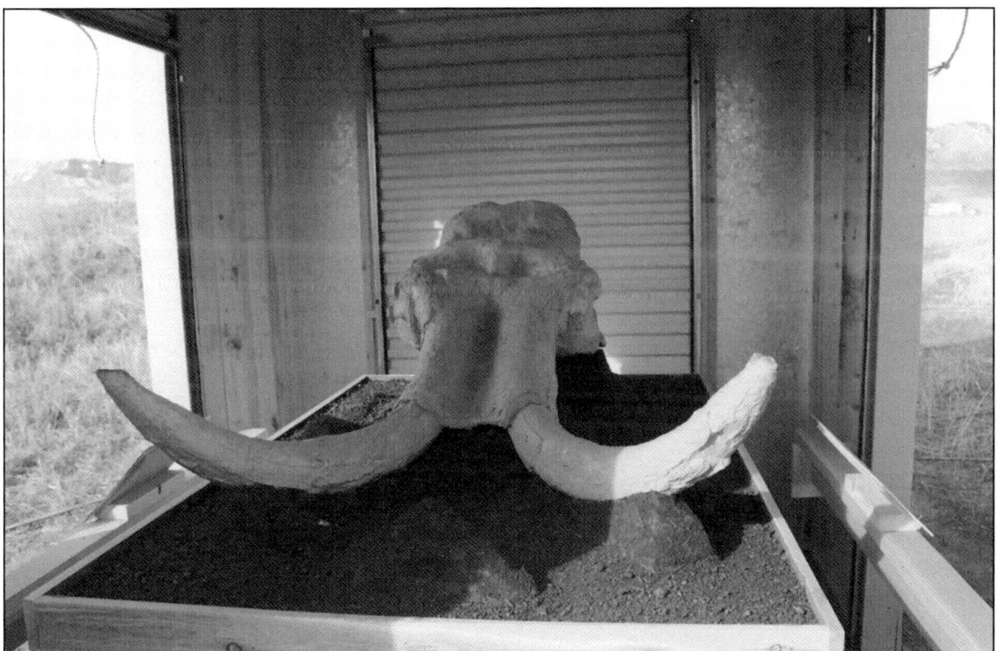

It is not known precisely when ancestors of the modern Indians first came to the New World or to Douglas County specifically, but the earliest evidence dates to 13,000–14,000 years ago. Archaeological investigations at the Lamb Spring Site, just west of Highlands Ranch, have uncovered the oldest evidence of Paleo-Indian activity in the area. A bed of bison bone, with associated stone tools, demonstrates hunting activity dating from about 9,000 years ago. Indirect evidence of flaked and broken bone with mammoth remains, dates to about 13,100 years ago. This picture is of a cast of one of the mammoth skulls recovered. (Photograph and caption by Reid Farmer.)

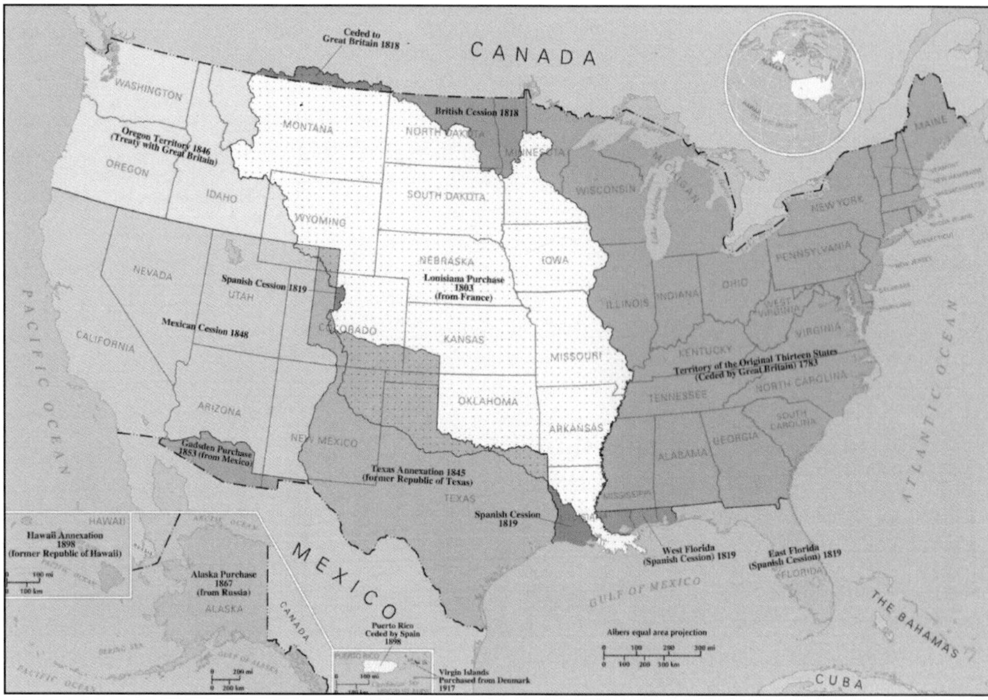

From 1540 to 1803, the area changed ownership back and forth between Spain and France several times. The transitions stopped when Thomas Jefferson negotiated the Louisiana Purchase from France for the United States in 1803. "(Courtesy of the US Geological Survey.)

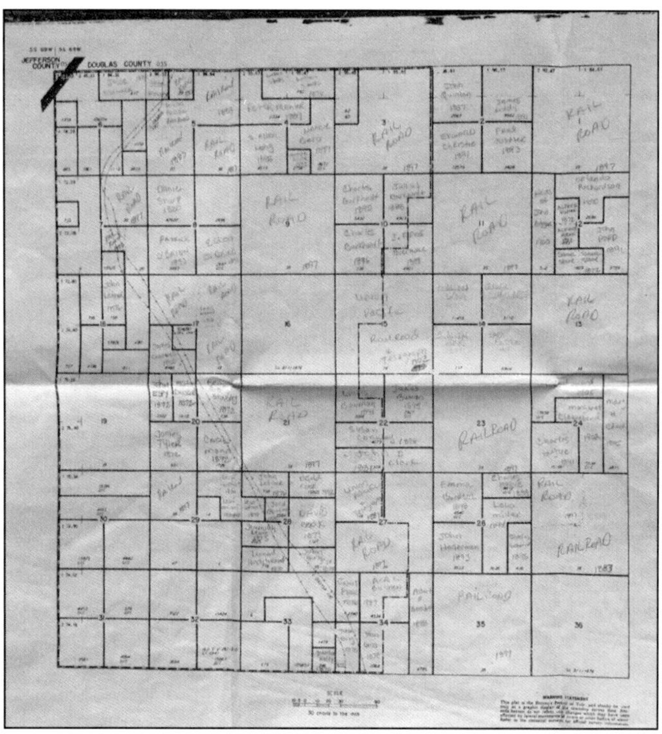

In 1859, a 160-acre homestead was started by Rufus H. "Dad" Clark in the northwest corner of today's Highlands Ranch beginning the conversion from open plains. Clark started his homestead where today's Highlands Ranch Golf Club is located. His first harvest was so abundant that he became known as the Potato King of Colorado.

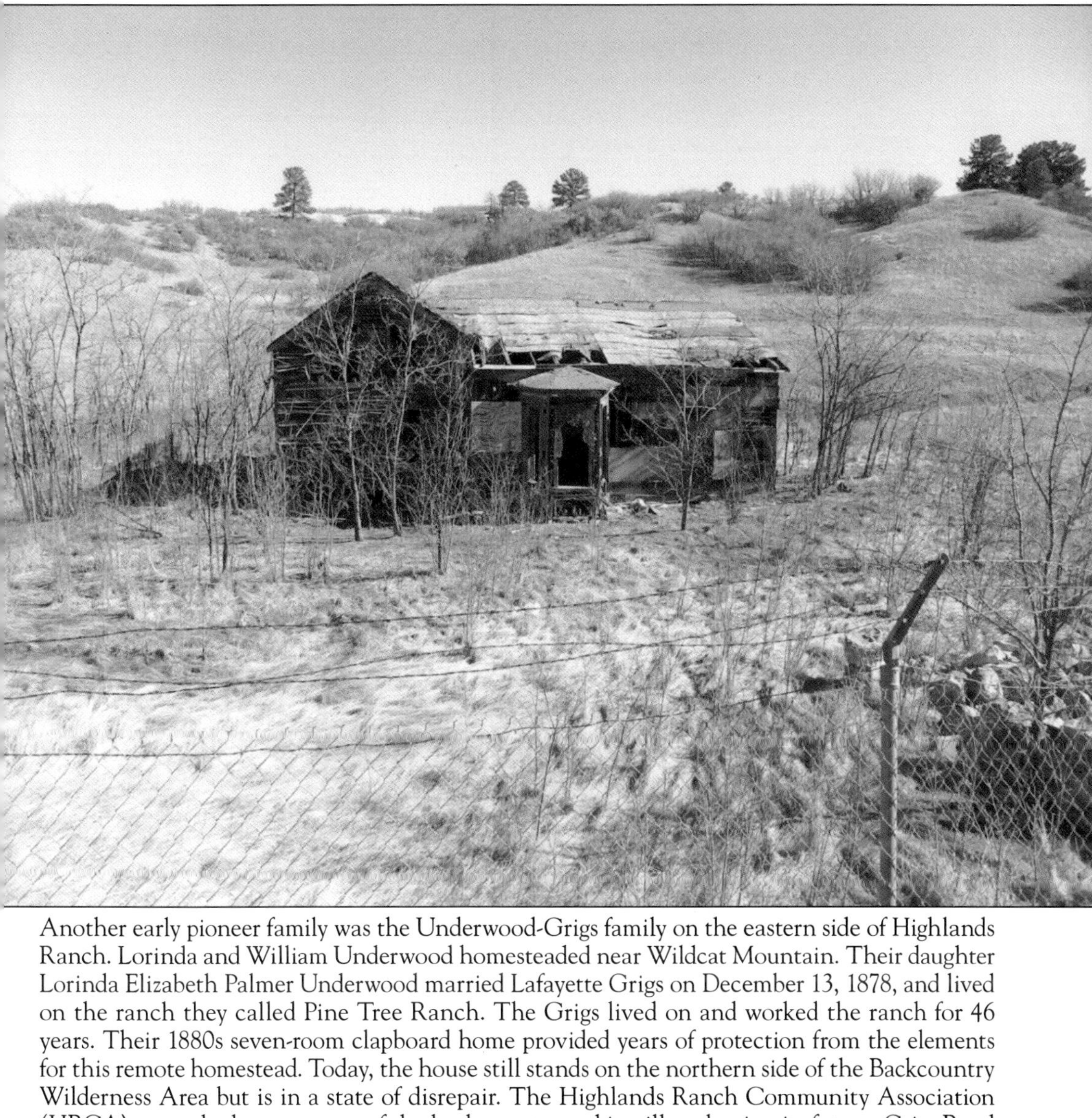

Another early pioneer family was the Underwood-Grigs family on the eastern side of Highlands Ranch. Lorinda and William Underwood homesteaded near Wildcat Mountain. Their daughter Lorinda Elizabeth Palmer Underwood married Lafayette Grigs on December 13, 1878, and lived on the ranch they called Pine Tree Ranch. The Grigs lived on and worked the ranch for 46 years. Their 1880s seven-room clapboard home provided years of protection from the elements for this remote homestead. Today, the house still stands on the northern side of the Backcountry Wilderness Area but is in a state of disrepair. The Highlands Ranch Community Association (HRCA) owns the home as part of the backcountry and is still evaluating its future. Grigs Road that turns into Daniels Park Road passes near the home. The road follows the old Territorial Road. (Courtesy of Historic Douglas County, Inc.)

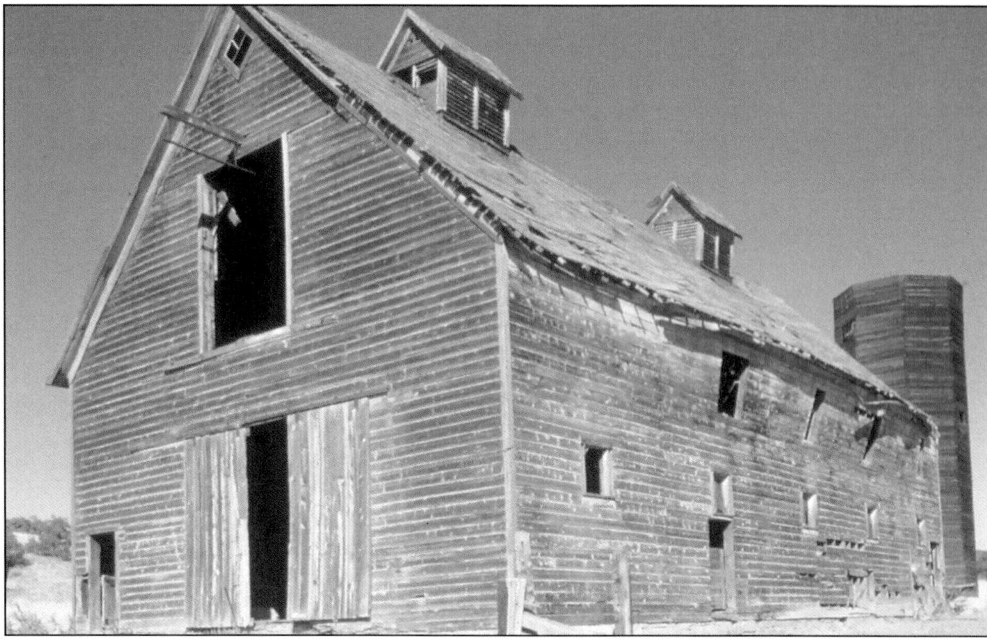

The Failing homesteads on the southern side of Highlands Ranch and the Backcountry Wilderness Area are more good examples of how the ranches came about. Many of the early pioneers quickly found that 40 and even 160 acres of land in Colorado's dry climate was not enough to live on. As a result, claims for neighboring areas were quickly filed by spouses and children of the original homesteaders. The Failings eventually sold the ranch to the Douglas Investment Company, which proceeded to run an active ranching operation at the ranch and most of the current Backcountry Wilderness Area for many years. (Courtesy of Highlands Ranch Metro District.)

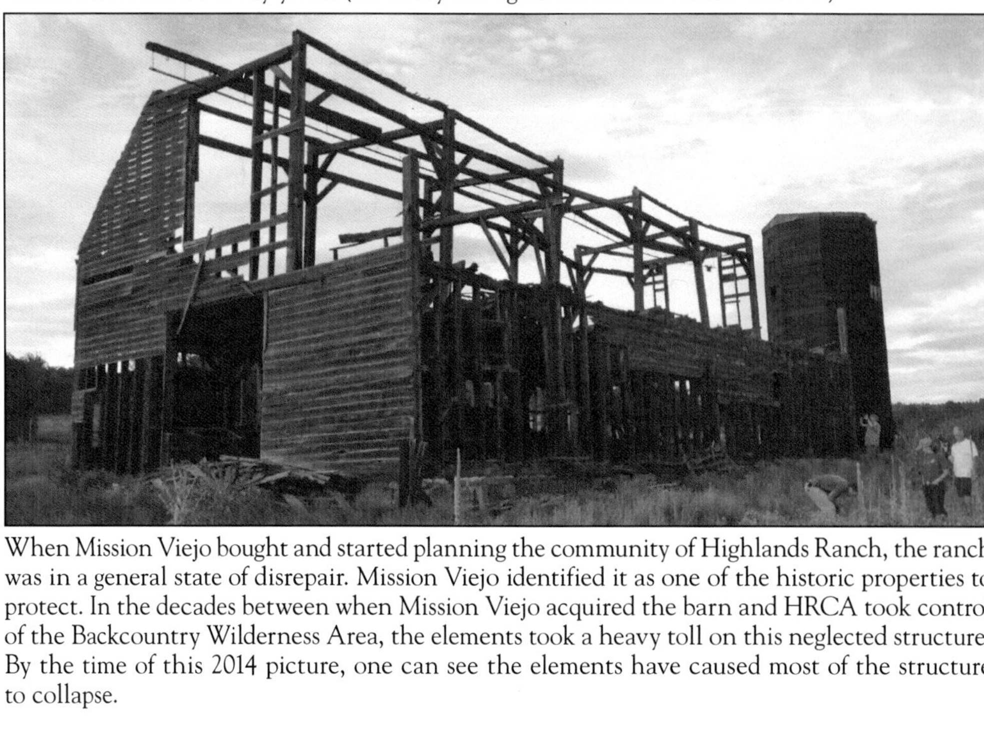

When Mission Viejo bought and started planning the community of Highlands Ranch, the ranch was in a general state of disrepair. Mission Viejo identified it as one of the historic properties to protect. In the decades between when Mission Viejo acquired the barn and HRCA took control of the Backcountry Wilderness Area, the elements took a heavy toll on this neglected structure. By the time of this 2014 picture, one can see the elements have caused most of the structure to collapse.

This unique octagon-shaped silo was built in 1920 and is still standing in good shape today. The good construction allows the silo to withstand the elements with little preventive maintenance.

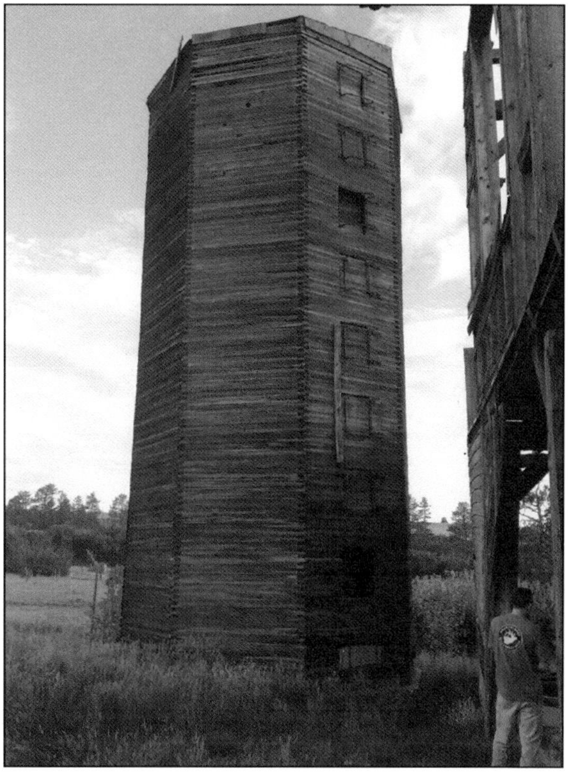

The main Failing's family farmhouse also continues to stand but is in a state of disrepair. The Highlands Ranch Community Association has completed a historic assessment of the property and is trying to determine plans for the home's future. The association could choose to leave it as is, protect just the outside, or even revitalize it as a functioning historic destination.

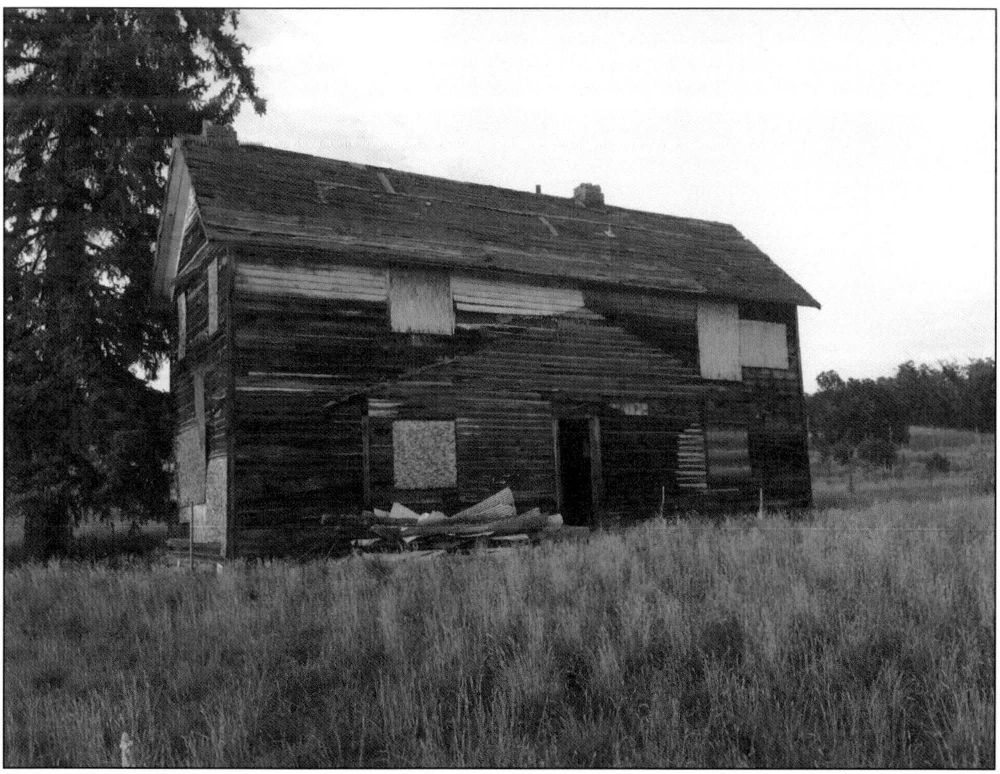

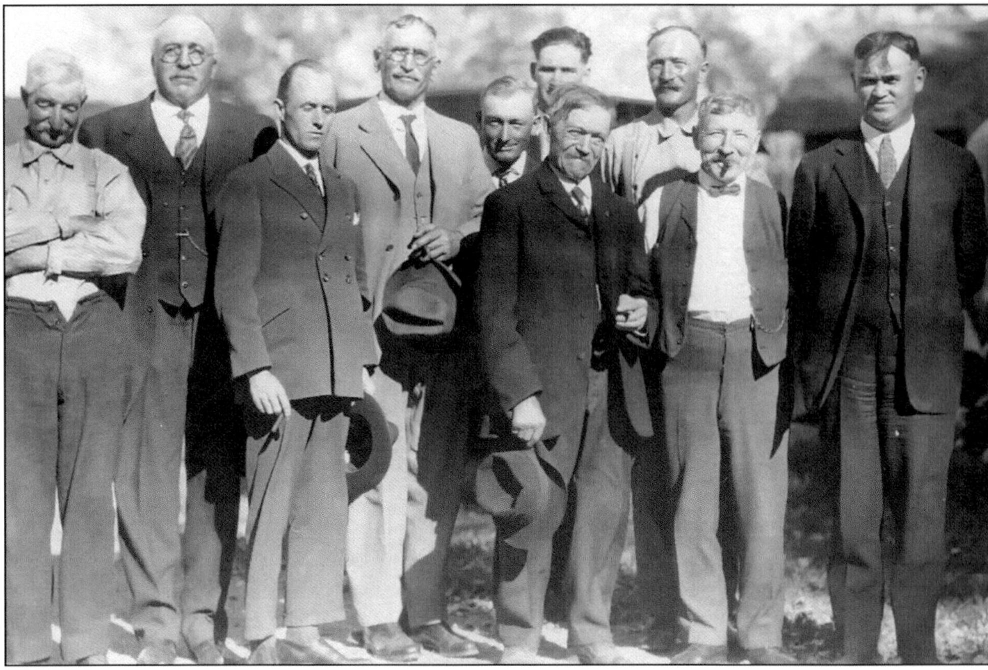

Another important early settlement was the Big Dry Creek Cheese Ranch in the northeast part of Highlands Ranch, settled by Austrian immigrant Johanne Welte in 1879. Johanne is pictured here in the front wearing a dark suit just right of center. He worked with his brother-in-law Plaziduo Gassner to establish the Big Dry Creek Cheese Ranch. The June 1880 census showed 11 people living at the Cheese Ranch. (Courtesy of Scott Terhark Collection, Douglas County History Research Center, Douglas County Libraries, 2011.020.0003.)

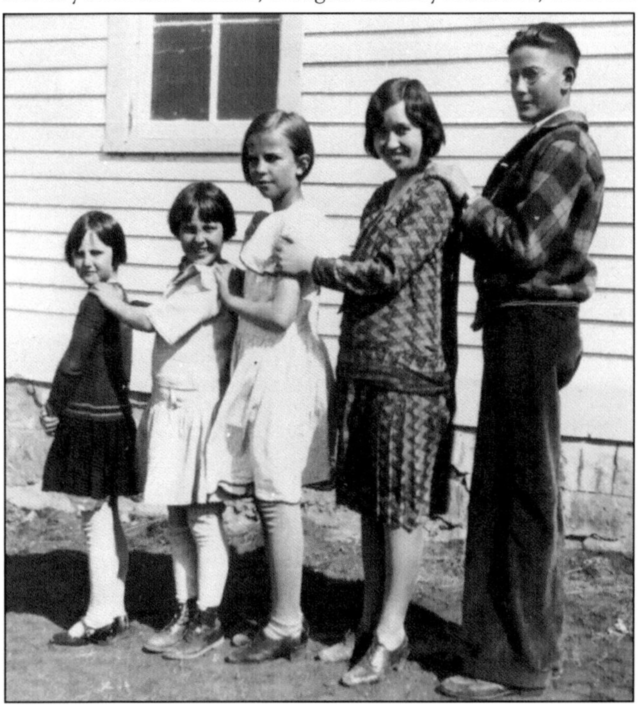

In the remote area of northern Douglas County, a big challenge was educating the children. In 1930, the Welte kids are shown lined up outside the local schoolhouse ready to learn. (Courtesy of the Douglas County Historical Society Visual Materials, Douglas County History Research Center, Douglas County Libraries, 1992.001.0654.0002.)

This 1900 ranch photograph was passed down through the family to Philip Renner, who continued the dairy ranch operation that created butter as well as brick and Limburger cheeses. Johanne Welte planted fields of alfalfa, corn, barley, and beets and eventually cultivated a 10-acre fruit tree orchard. (Courtesy of the Sara Gohr Papers, Douglas County History Research Center, Douglas County Libraries, 2001.020.0118.)

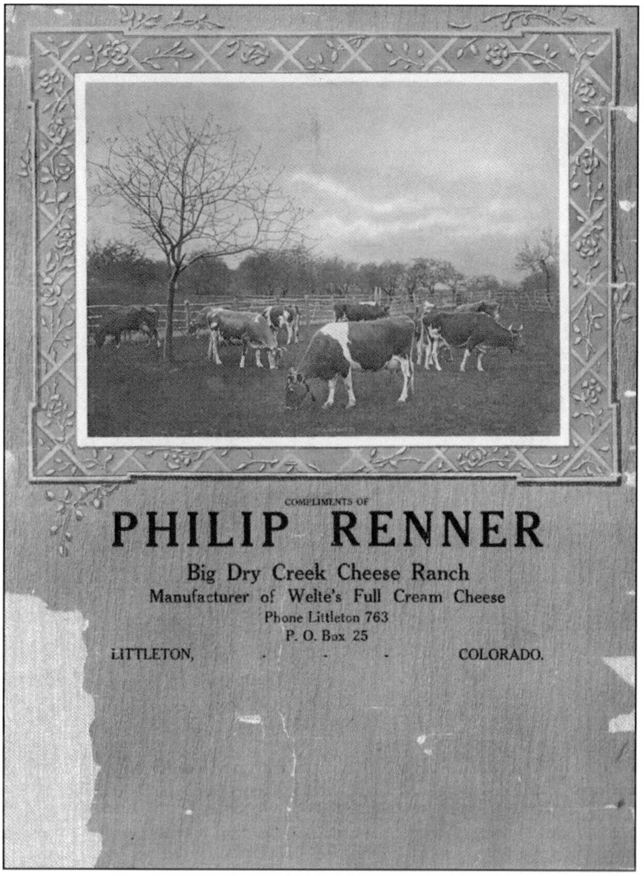

Prior to the development of modern-day Highlands Ranch, the Big Dry Creek Cheese Ranch was about the only thing in northeast Highlands Ranch. This aerial photograph of the "Cheese Ranch" shows many of the open dirt roads and barns that lasted until modern development in the 1980s. (Courtesy of Highlands Ranch Metro District.)

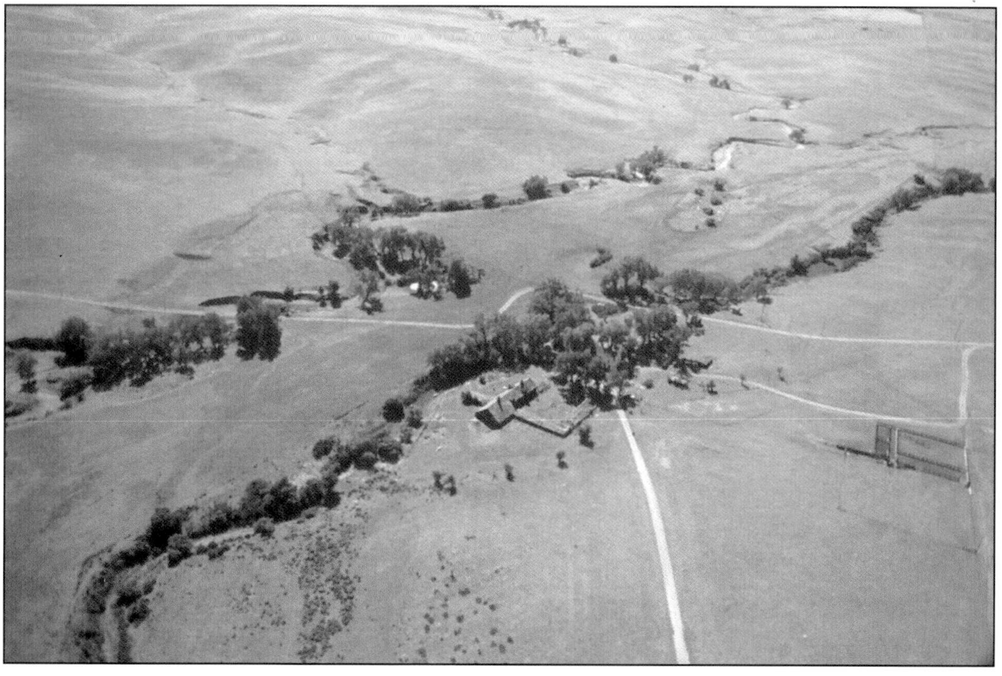

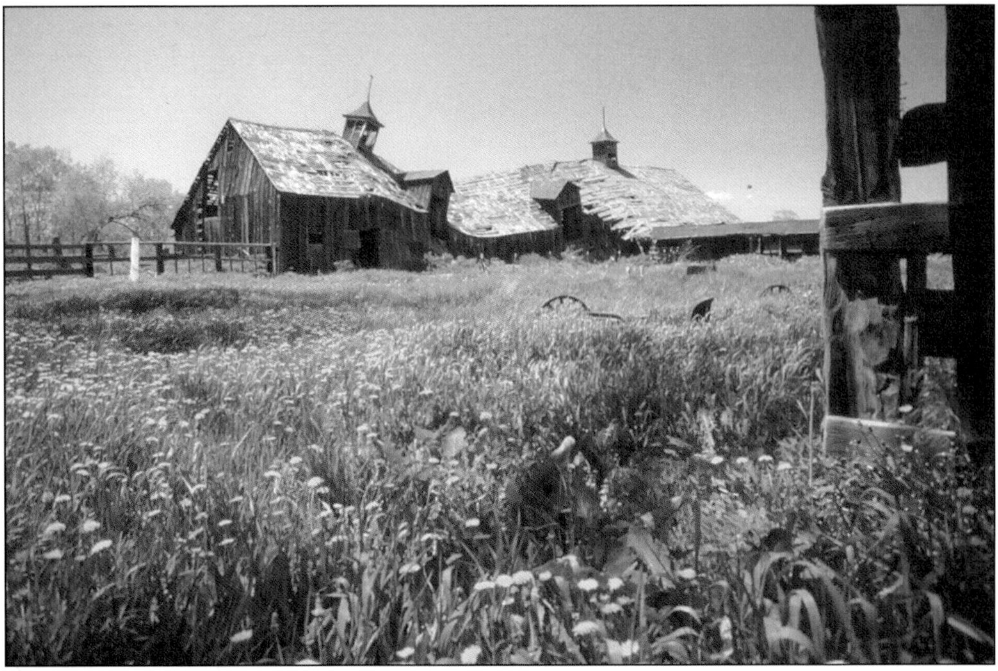

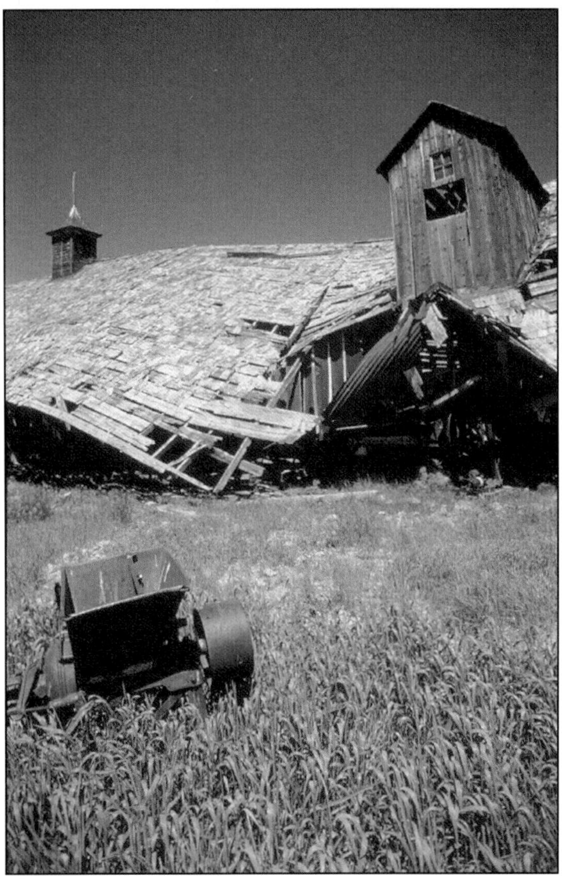

Mission Viejo designated the Cheese Ranch for historic preservation. The buildings were used occasionally as the east ranch after Lawrence Phipps Jr. acquired the land in 1943. Later pictures of the barn show that it had started to fail structurally by the time Mission Viejo took over the ranch. (Both, courtesy of Highlands Ranch Metro District.)

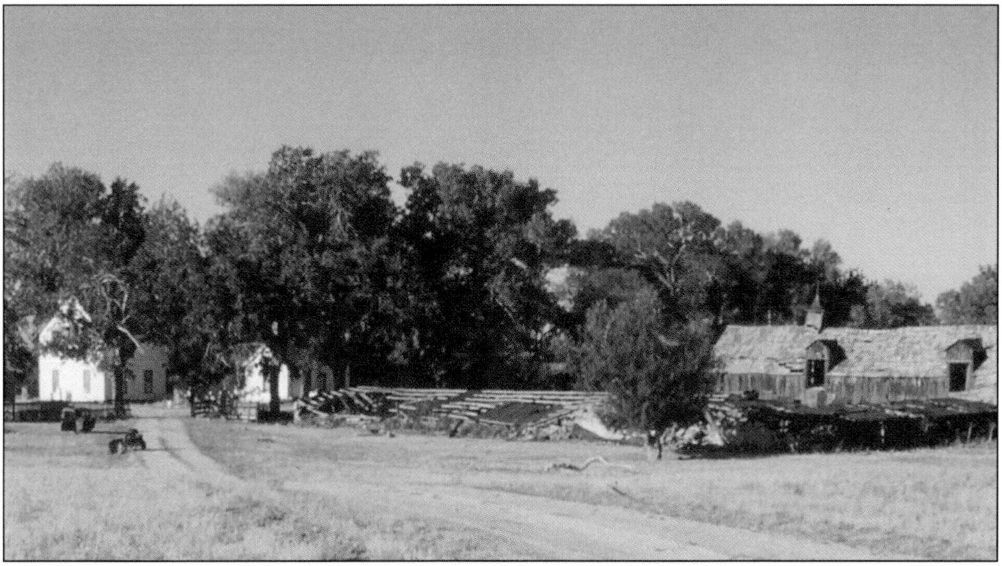

The Cheese Ranch is seen nestled in the trees growing along Big Dry Creek. The Cheese Ranch received national recognition in the *Scientific Farmer* magazine for innovations in dryland farming. In 1985, the buildings were weathered but still standing. (Courtesy of Highlands Ranch Metro District.)

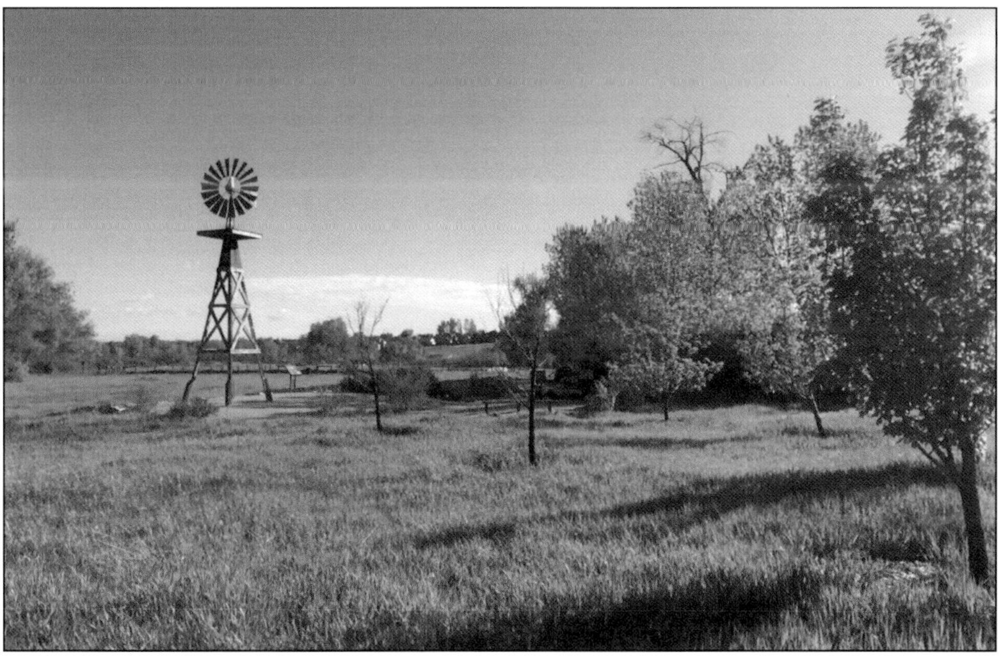

After Dr. Richard Carrillo and staff completed a historical, architectural, and archaeological study of the Big Dry Creek Cheese Ranch, Mission Viejo chose to tear down and completely remove the buildings. Due to the remoteness of the site, Mission Viejo was having problems keeping it safe from and free of local teenagers. The decision did not sit well with Douglas County commissioners who started today's Douglas County Historic Preservation Board. The Cheese Ranch has now been converted into a park and open space that includes a community garden along with the Big Dry Creek Trail.

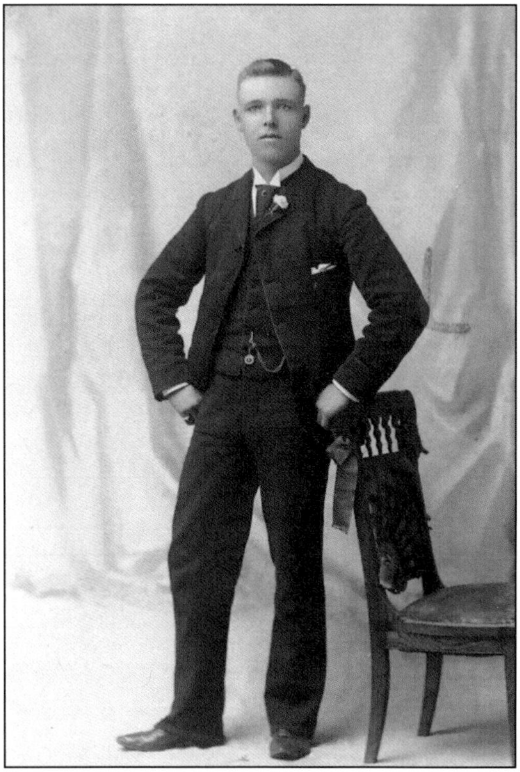

Mathew Plews was another homesteader and a talented horticulturalist. Plews built a home for his family on this land in 1906. The Mathew Plews homestead is located in the northwest corner of Highlands Ranch. (Courtesy of Plews Family Photos, Douglas County History Research Center, Douglas County Libraries, 2008.050.0002.0001.)

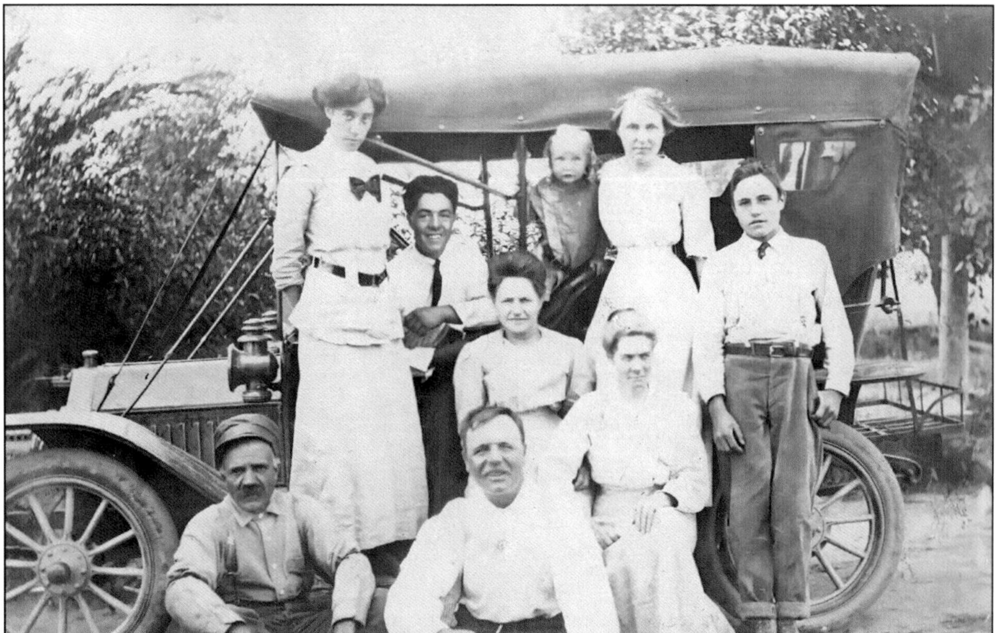

The Plews family was like many other families who moved to this remote area seeking a better life for the whole family. Family members are seen posing in front of their car in 1914–1916. (Courtesy of Plews Family Photos, Douglas County History Research Center, Douglas County Libraries, 2008.050.0001.0011.0003.)

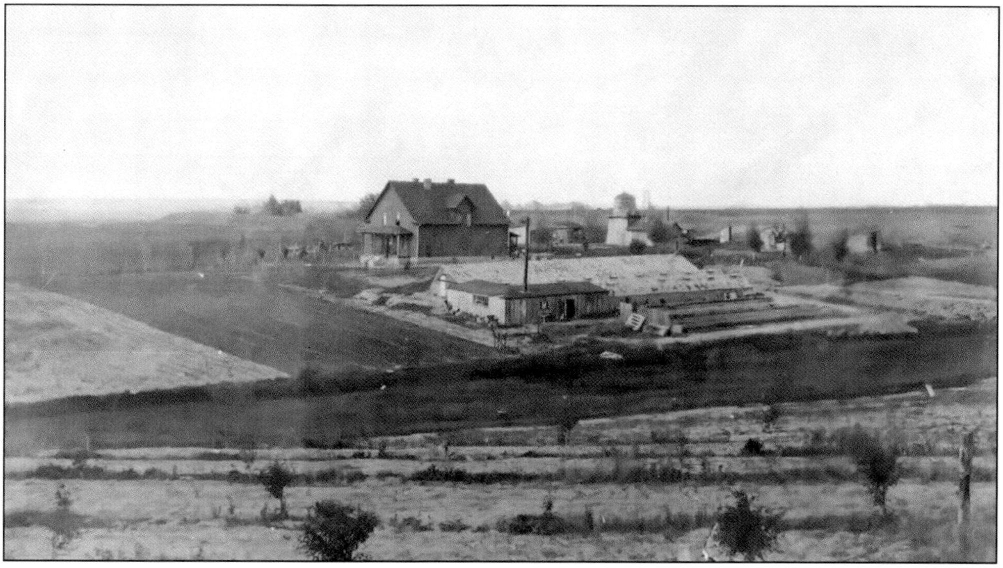

This c. 1910 picture of the Plews house shows the farm without the many trees that surround it today. Plews sold the house in 1937 to O.E. "Smiling Charlie" Stephens, who ran illegal gambling operations. In 1944, the Stephens family sold the property to Fred and Marguerite Eberhardt. In 1967, the property was sold to the Gates Rubber Company, which traded the property to the Bowen family. (Courtesy of Plews Family Photos, Douglas County History Research Center, Douglas County Libraries, 2008.050.0001.0005.0002.)

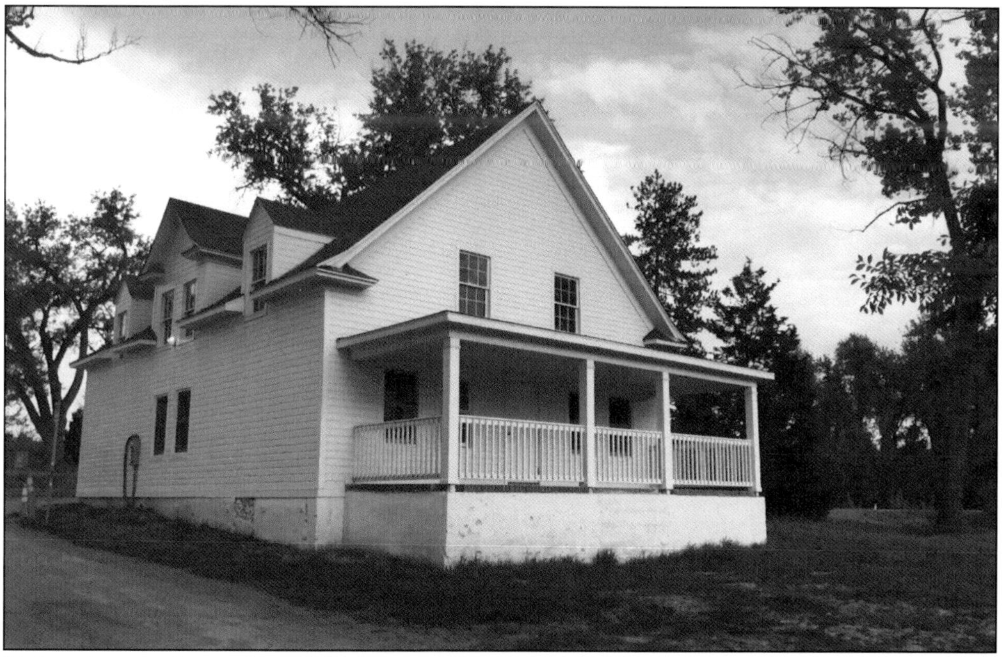

Today, the same house from 1906 is part of the Highlands Ranch Metro District's Fly'n B Ranch. The house and five acres around the property were conveyed to Highlands Ranch Metro District in 2006. The house is currently being secured from the elements for future restoration. After the outside is secured, future renovations are planned for the interior to make the home usable for hosting small- to medium-sized events.

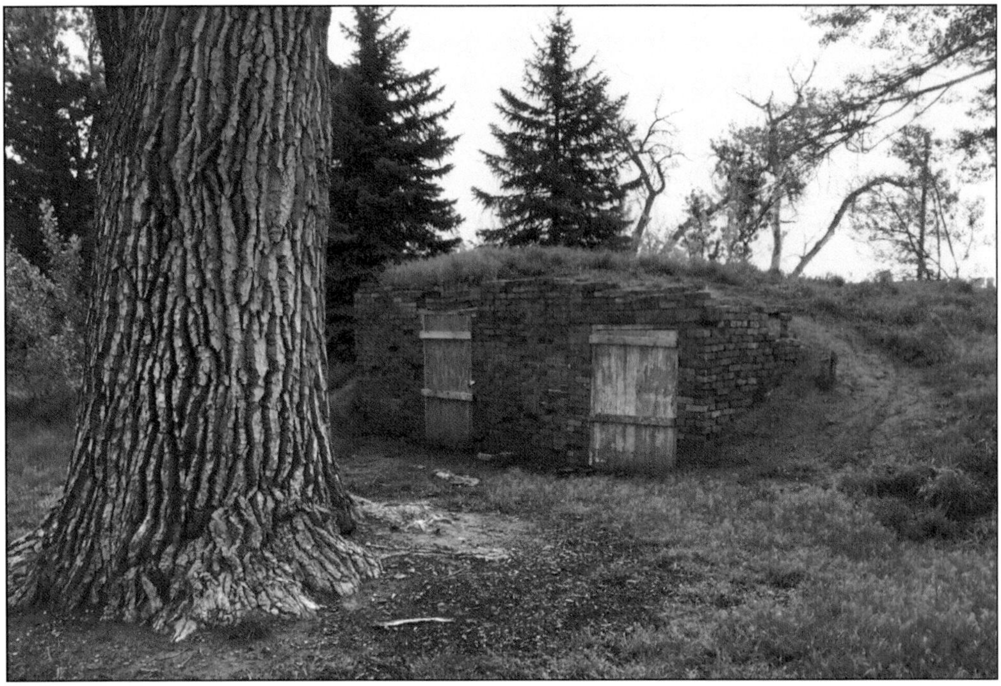

Behind the house and next to the Highline Canal is the historic root cellar. For years, root cellars like these were used to keep food cool and help it last.

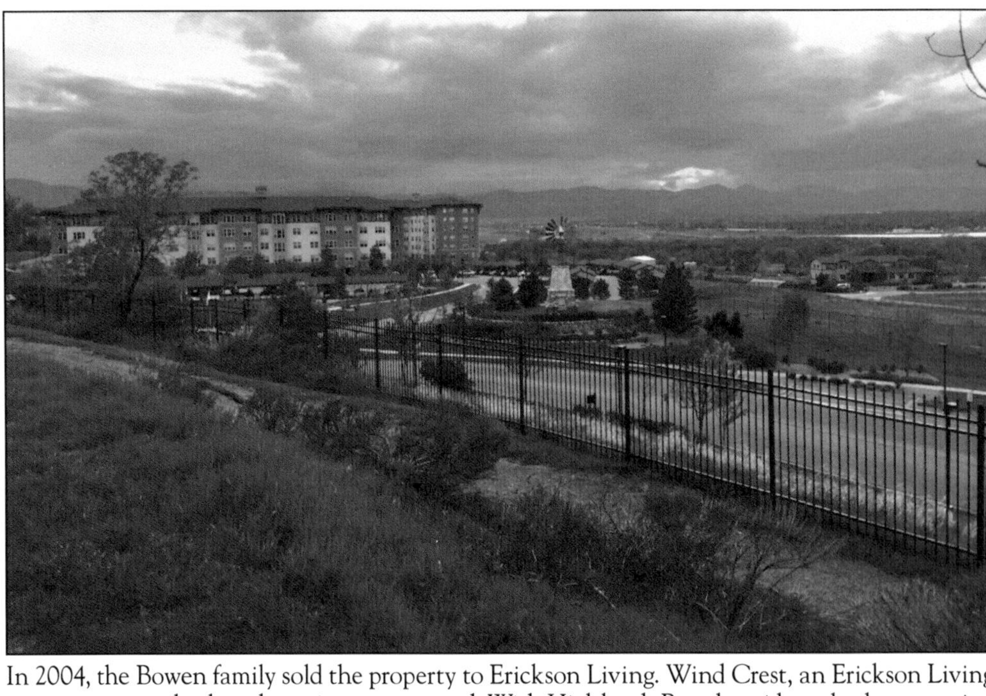

In 2004, the Bowen family sold the property to Erickson Living. Wind Crest, an Erickson Living community, was built and continues to expand. With Highlands Ranch residents both supporting their aging parents and aging themselves, retirement communities like Wind Crest are growing in demand.

Two

Mansion and Ranch History

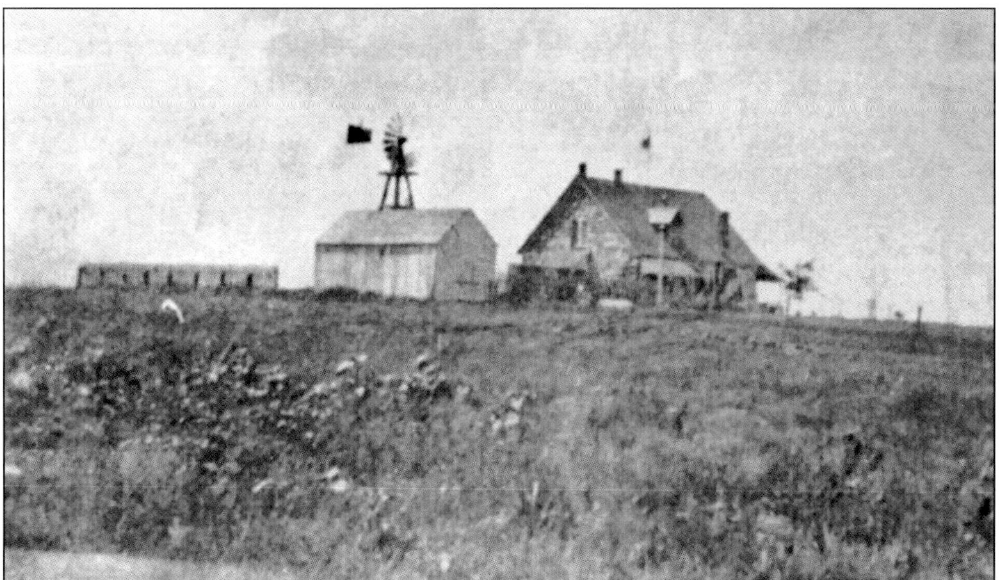

Highlands Ranch's past focuses around the farmhouse that began on the 40-acre homestead and timber culture in the center of Highlands Ranch. A timber culture is the practice of farming trees by planting them so they could be used later for timber. In 1884, Samuel Long started his farm and named it Rotherwood after his boyhood farm in Pennsylvania. By 1891, Long had expanded his ranch to 2,000 acres. (Courtesy of Highlands Ranch Metro District.)

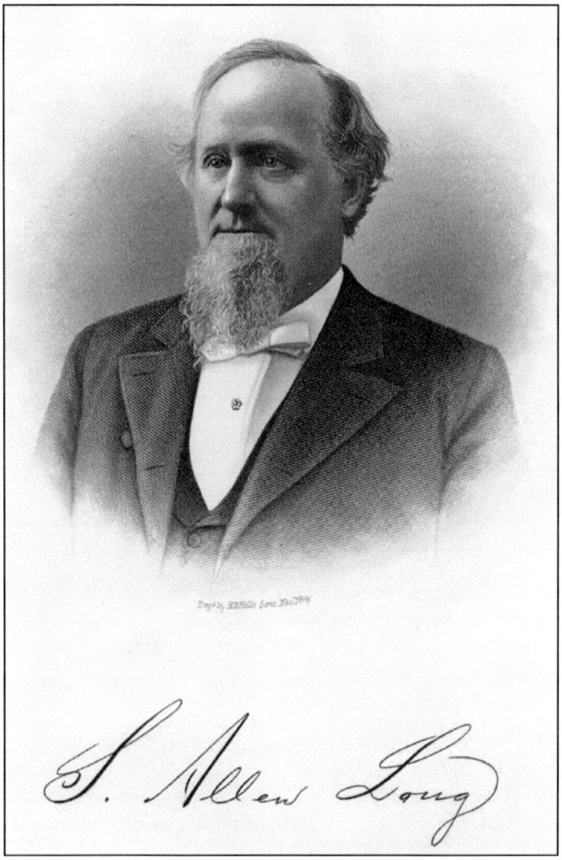

Samuel Long was a petroleum refiner in the Pittsburgh, Pennsylvania, area in 1861 and served on the Pittsburgh City Council. Also, he was a director of the Baltimore & Ohio (B&O) railroad of Monopoly fame. Long was recognized as an innovator in dryland farming and timber planting that required little or no water. (Courtesy of Highlands Ranch Mansion.)

The Rotherwood farmhouse is still a key part of the Highlands Ranch Mansion today. During renovations, a stone inscribed with an 1891 date was found below the upstairs window. This wall shows the variation of the stones' size and color. (Courtesy of Highlands Ranch Metro District.)

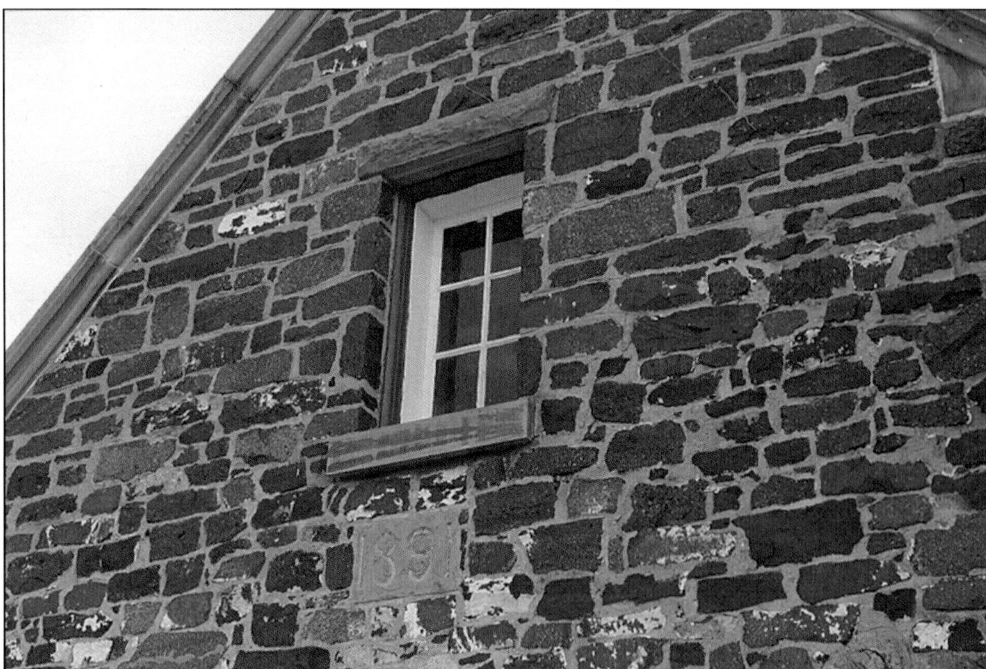

John Springer, owner from 1897 to 1913, was a wealthy and ambitious lawyer with ties in law, banking, and politics. His wife, Eliza Clifton Hughes, suffered from Tuberculosis. John, Eliza and his daughter Annie moved to Colorado because the sunny and dry environment is beneficial of Tuberculosis sufferers. (Colorado is also known for National Jewish Health, a leading research institution on the disease since 1899.) Springer became president of Continental Trust Company and the National Livestock Association. He ran for mayor of Denver in 1904 and lost in what is known as the most corrupt election in Denver's history. Eliza died days after the election The Western Cattlemen named him as someone that should be nominated for vice president of the United States. (Courtesy of Highlands Ranch Mansion)

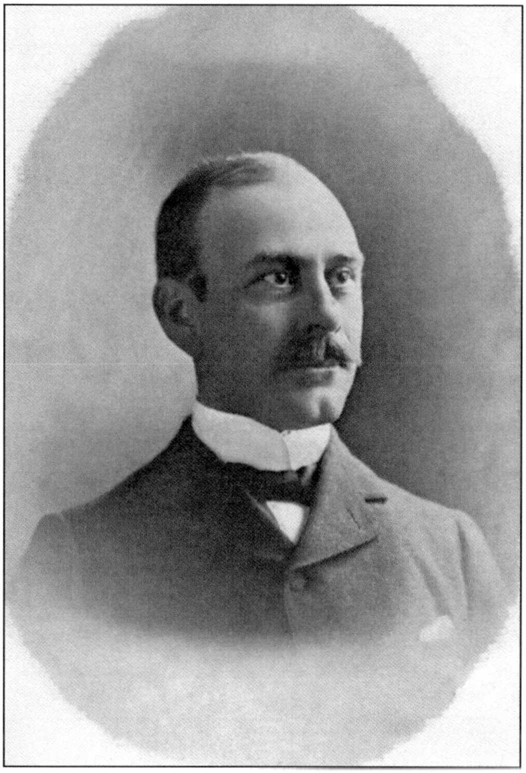

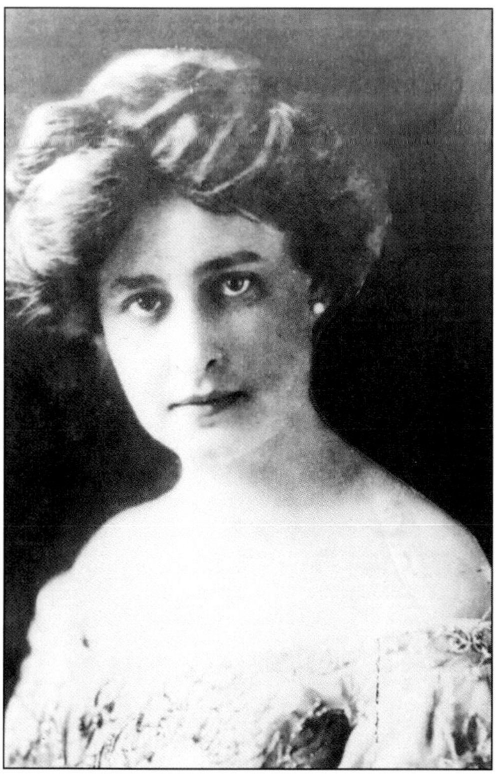

John Springer's second wife, Isabel Patterson, was 20 years his junior. John Springer renamed the mansion, Castle Isabel, in the hope that it would make her happy to live on the ranch. Isabel did spend time at the ranch and kept a room at the Brown Palace in downtown Denver. Isabel was involved in a love triangle with two other men that led to the murder at the Brown Palace on May 24, 1911, and the subsequent trial of the century. (Courtesy of Highlands Ranch Mansion.)

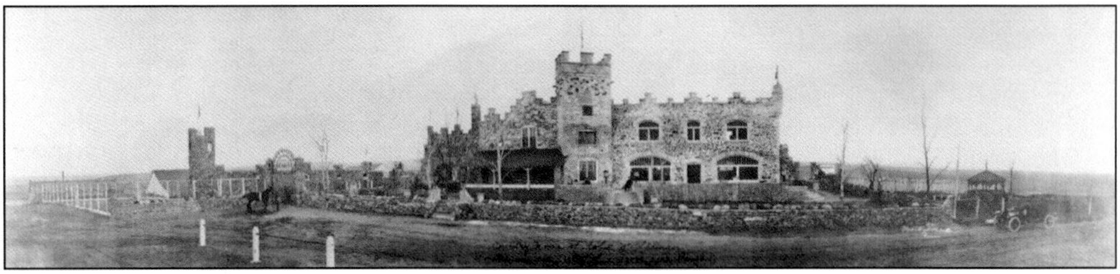

John Springer completed the first major remodel of the original Samuel Long farmhouse. Springer built the mansion to have the feel of a Russian-style castle. A close look shows the front door at this time was not in the entrance tower but in the middle of the living room on the right. At this point, the ranch was called the Springer Cross Country Horse and Cattle Ranch. (Courtesy of Highlands Ranch Metro District.)

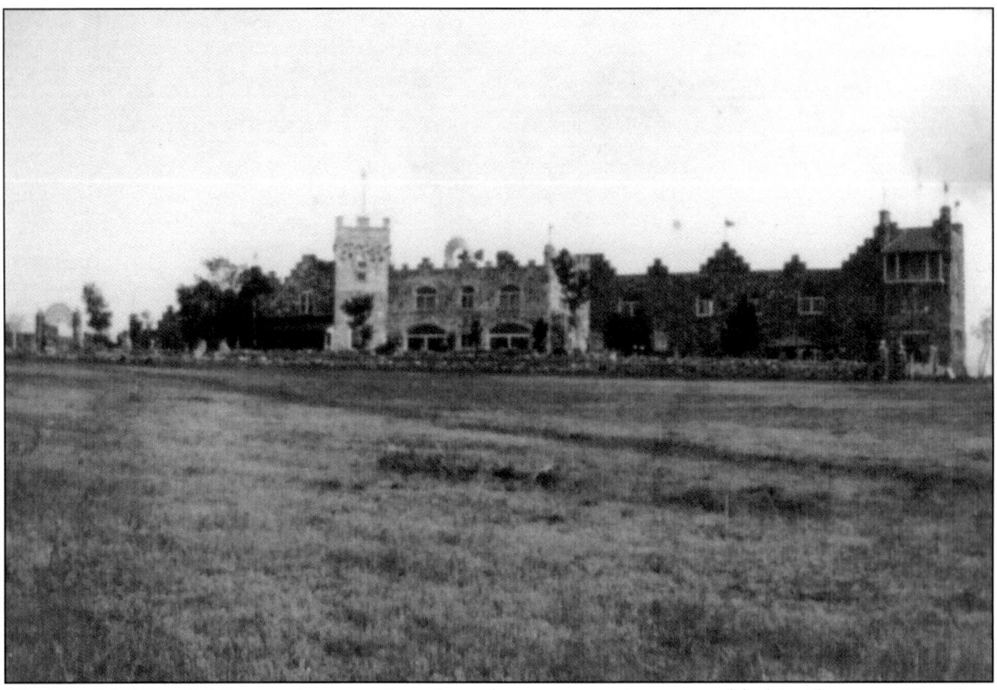

The remodeling of the mansion continued, and a western wing was added in the same Russian-castle style as the previous addition. This photograph shows a third story on the far western end that was later removed for unknown reasons. (Courtesy of Highlands Ranch Metro District.)

With the scandal, John Springer sold the ranch to his first father-in-law, Col. William Hughes. Colonel Hughes was a former Confederate officer, Texas banker, and founder of the Continental Land and Cattle Company with 75,000 head of cattle. Colonel Hughes moved to the property for five years from 1913 to 1918, and he renamed it Sunland Ranch. He was a leading philanthropist in the Denver area. (Courtesy of Highlands Ranch Mansion.)

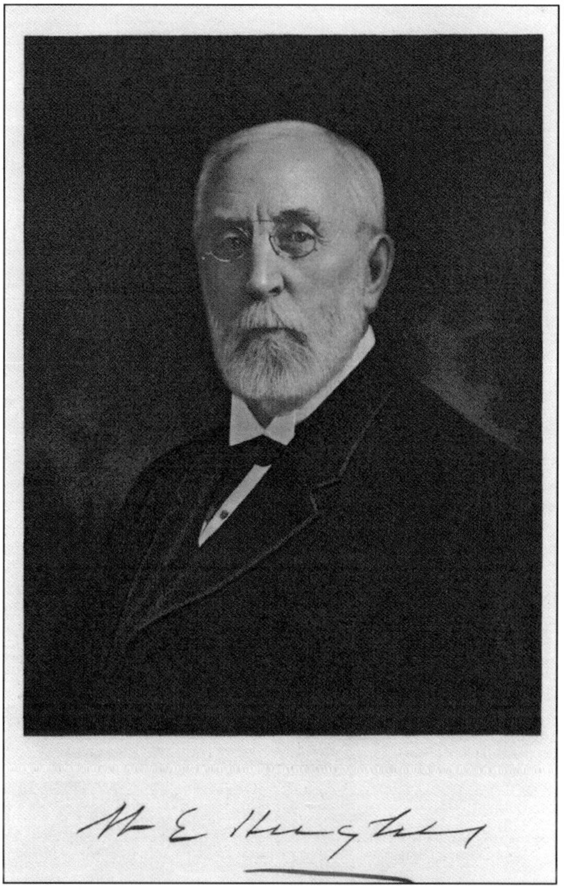

This living room photograph, taken between 1910 and 1918, shows a nice hunting lodge–type interior. The image also gives a look into the history of the renovations of the mansion, as there is a window in the middle of the picture with sunlight indicating the back wall of the mansion. Today, that window is the location of the doorway to the formal dining room. (Courtesy of Highlands Ranch Metro District Collection of Photographs, Douglas County History Research Center, Douglas County Libraries, 2011.008.0007.)

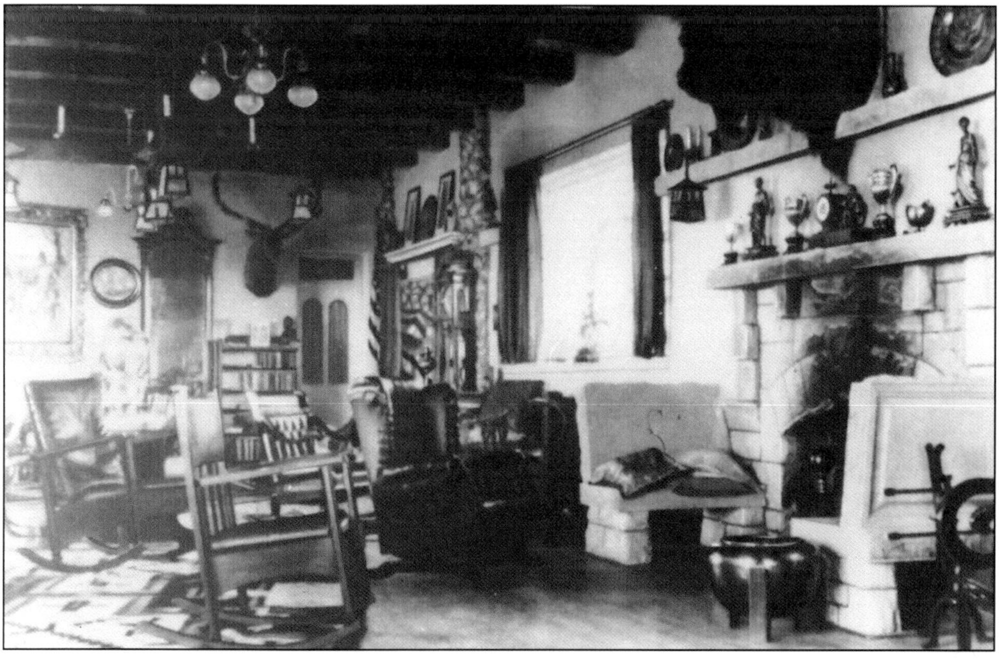

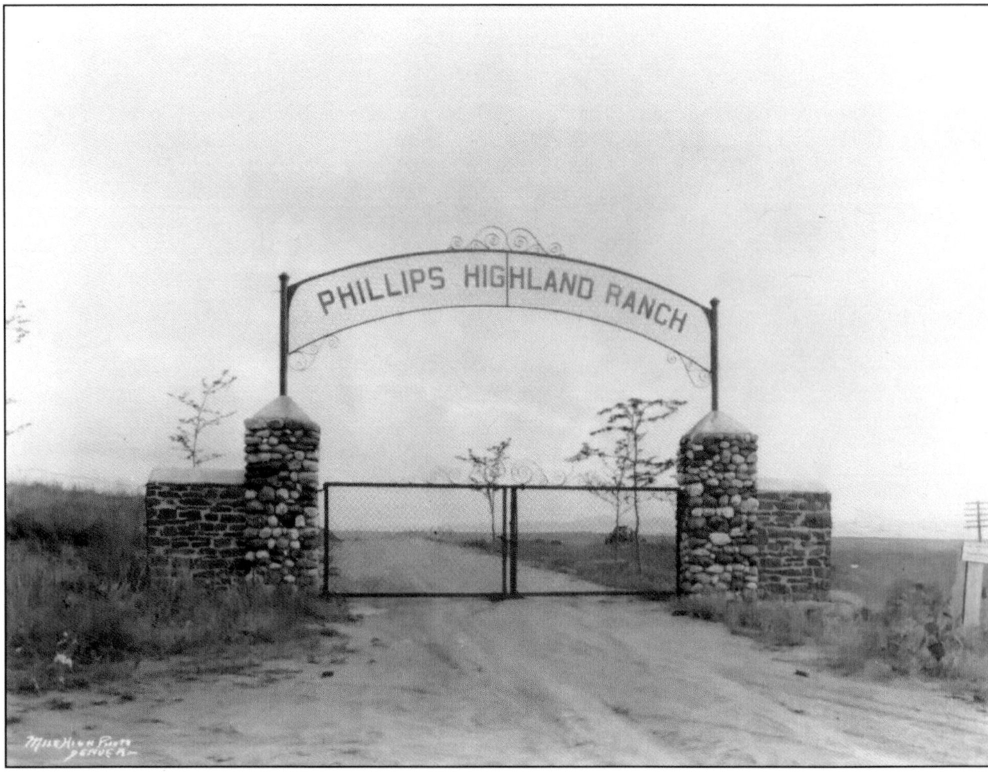

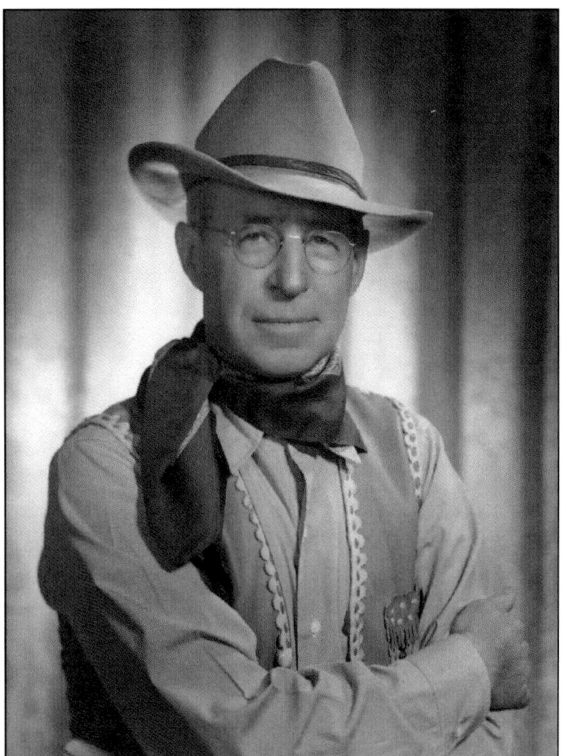

Waite Phillips purchased the ranch in 1920 from Annie Clifton Springer-Hughes, the daughter of John and Eliza Springer and granddaughter of Colonel Hughes. He gave the ranch the first name close to the modern name, Phillips Highland Ranch, which was placed over the entrance gate to the ranch. The name came from the Highland-Hereford cattle that he raised on the ranch. (Courtesy of Highlands Ranch Metro District.)

Waite Phillips was an Oklahoma oilman and brother of the founders of Phillips Petroleum Oil Company. Phillips owned the mansion from 1920 to 1926 along with several other large ranches that stretched from Montana to New Mexico. His Philmont Ranch in northern New Mexico was donated to the Boy Scouts of America and is still an active Scout camp today. (Courtesy of Philbrook Museum.)

Elliot Phillips, Waite Phillips's son, sits on a live pony in the living room. The Phillips Ranch logo is in the center of the fireplace. (Courtesy of Philbrook Museum.)

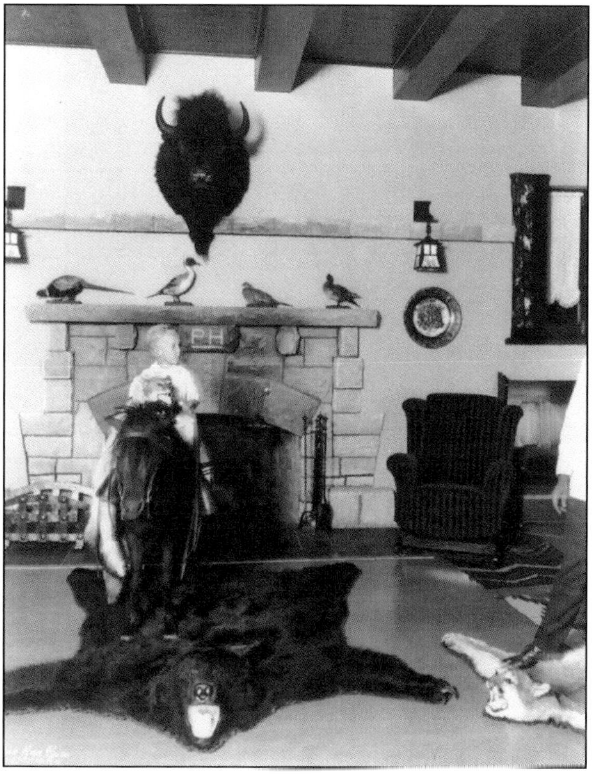

This 1922 photograph shows that the living room continued to have a more rustic feel during the Phillips era. With all of the homes he owned, there is still debate about how much time he actually spent in the mansion. (Courtesy of Philbrook Museum.)

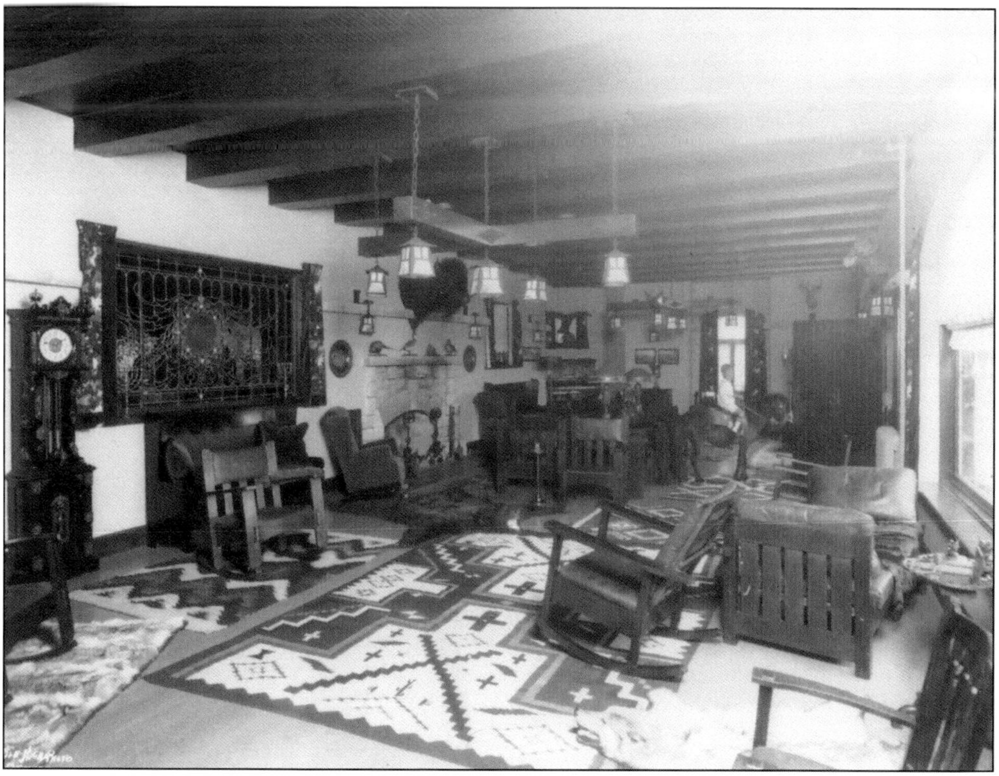

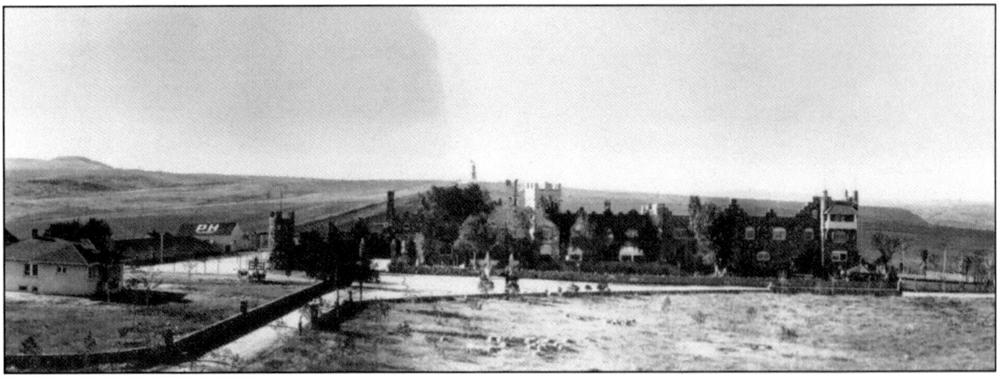

This Phillips-era photograph depicts life on the ranch. People on the property rode horses, and sheep grazed on the grasses of the front yard. (Courtesy of Highland Ranch Metro Districts.)

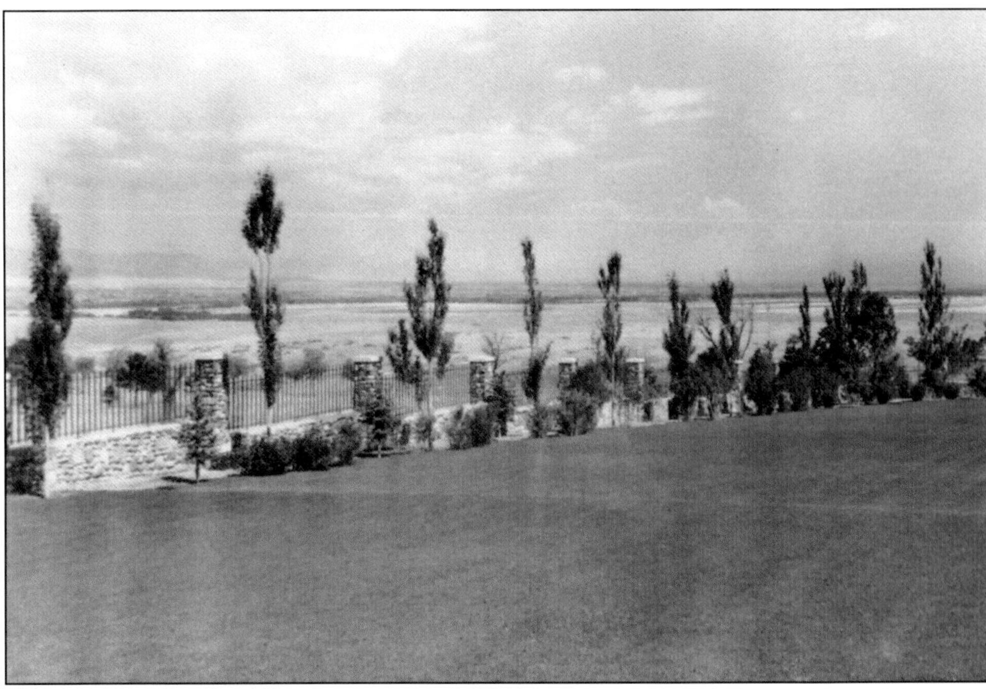

The mansion was located on the native grasslands that make up the eastern plains of Colorado. This picture shows both how isolated the mansion was and the planting of the first trees around the mansion grounds. Over the years, the trees have grown and matured. (Courtesy of Highland Ranch Metro Districts.)

Frank E. Kistler purchased the mansion in 1926 for the price of $425,000 and owned the mansion until 1937. Frank Kistler was a successful entrepreneur in oil and was responsible for the discovery of the largest natural gas field in Texas in the early 1900s. Kistler was also involved in ranching and banking and had business interests with J.D. Rockefeller in New York City and the president of Wolhurst Stock Farms. (Courtesy of Highlands Ranch Mansion.)

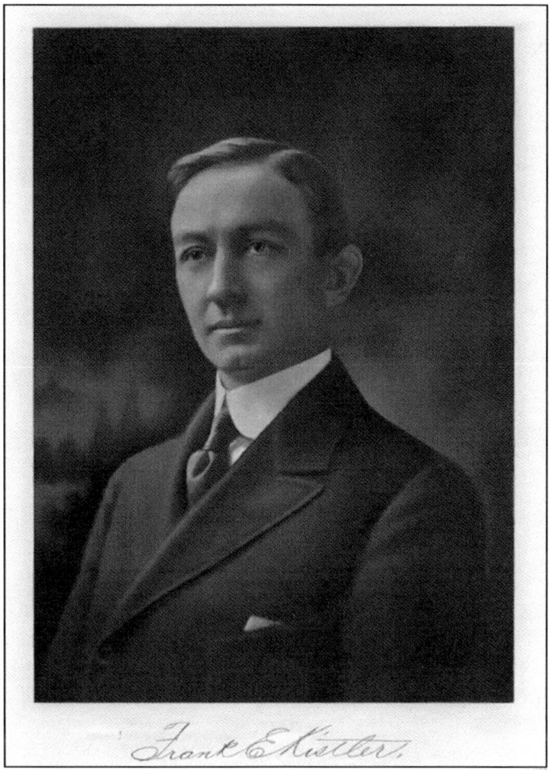

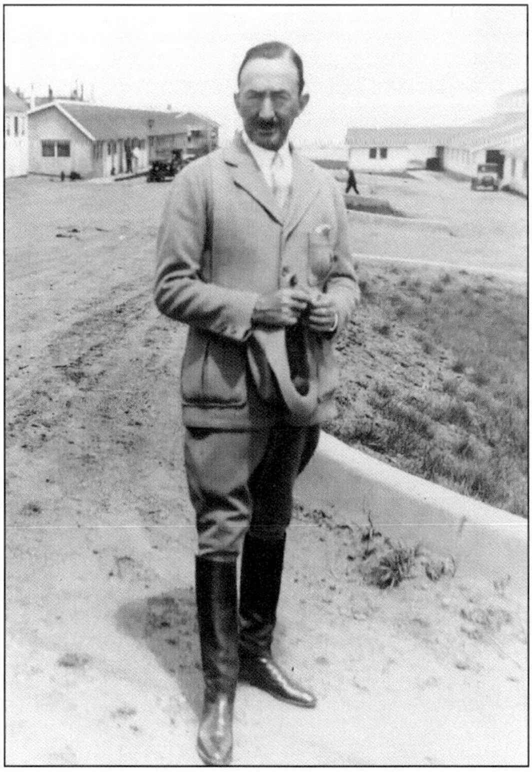

Frank Kistler directed the ranch to focus more on dairy and breeding operations. He renamed the ranch to the Diamond K Ranch. (Courtesy of Highlands Ranch Metro District.)

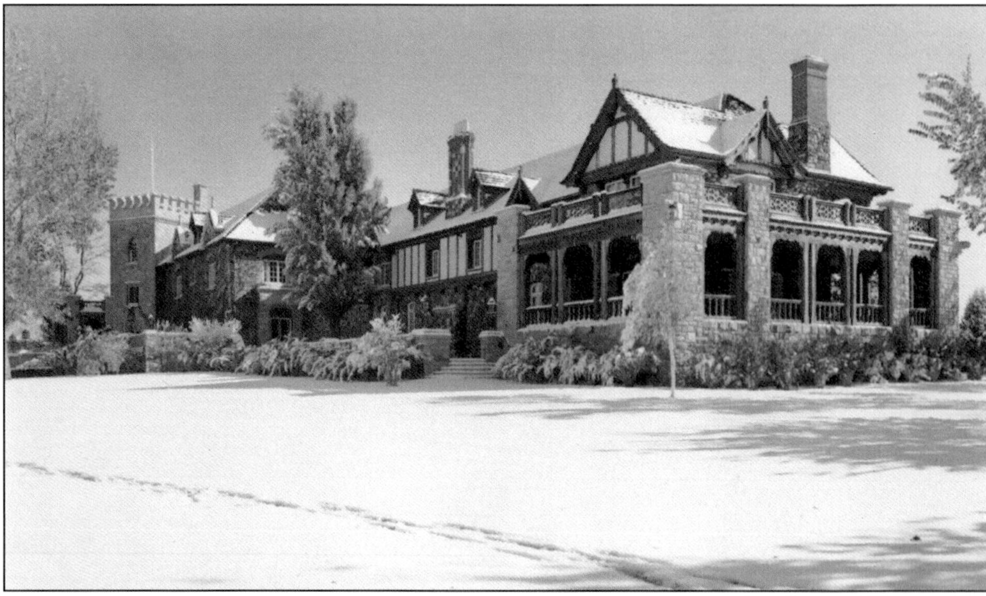

Frank Kistler made the second large renovation and expansion of the mansion, which also changed the style of the exterior of the mansion from a stone castle to an English Tudor manor house. In total, the mansion had 14 bedrooms, 11 bathrooms, and 5 fireplaces all in an area of 22,000 square feet. The upstairs room closest in the photograph is called the west bedroom and has also been called Julia's room after Frank Kistler's oldest daughter. (Courtesy of Highlands Ranch Metro District.)

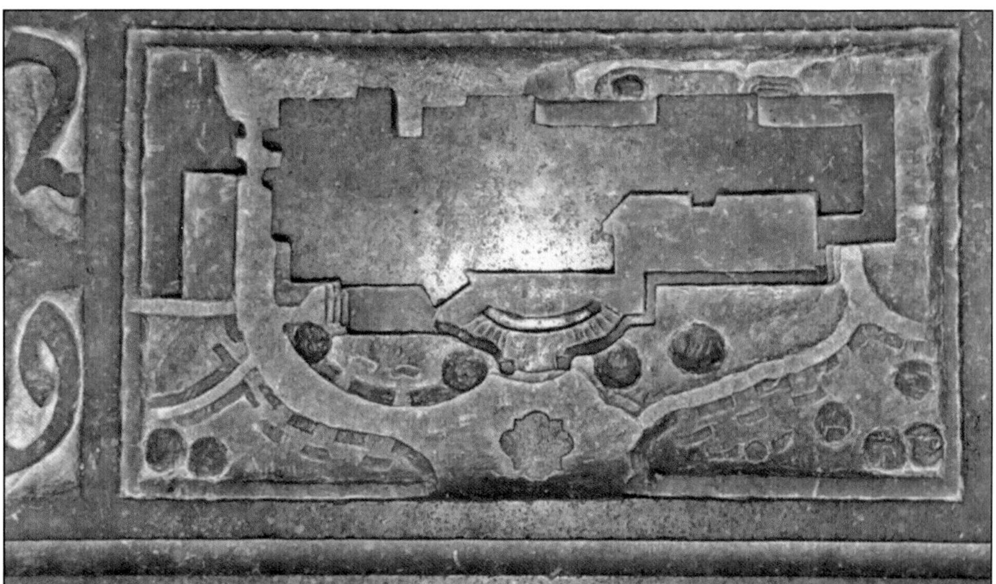

The major renovation of the mansion shows Kistler's attention to detail. In the mansion's fireplace, there are carved reliefs including an overhead view of the renovated mansion. The fireplace also has the Diamond K Ranch logo and the dates of the major renovation in 1929–1930. (Courtesy of Highlands Ranch Mansion Photographic Collection, Douglas County History Research Center, Douglas County Libraries, 2001.064.0009.031A.)

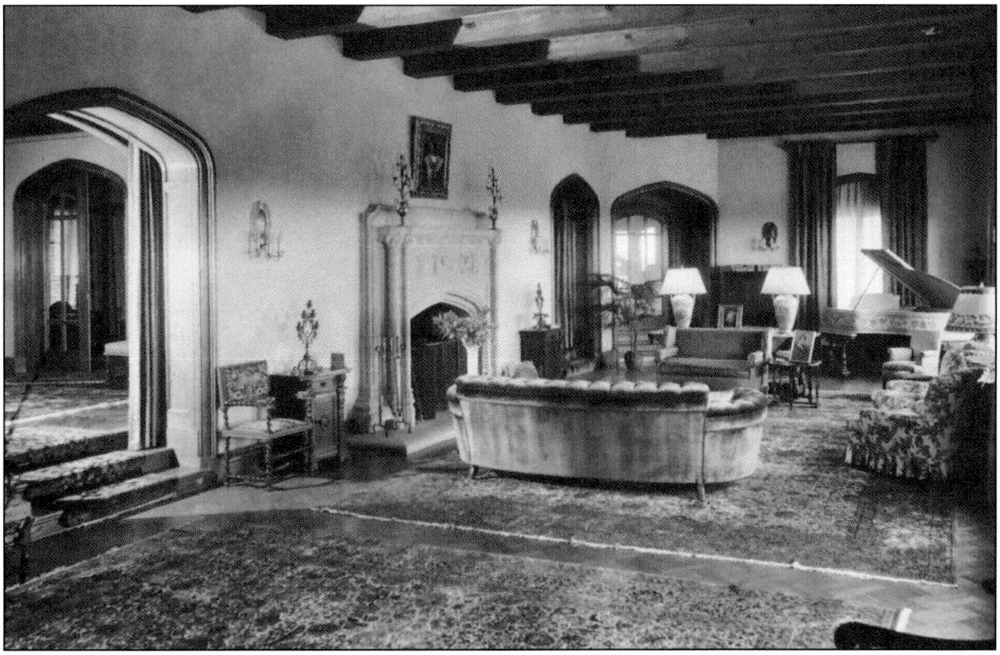

The living room photograph from 1937 during the Kistler era shows that the mansion has changed from a rustic hunting lodge to an upscale society home. The picture also clearly shows the entrance to the dining room on the left and the solarium beyond. (Courtesy of Hunter Antonides Collection, Douglas County History Research Center, Douglas County Libraries, 2011.004.0056.)

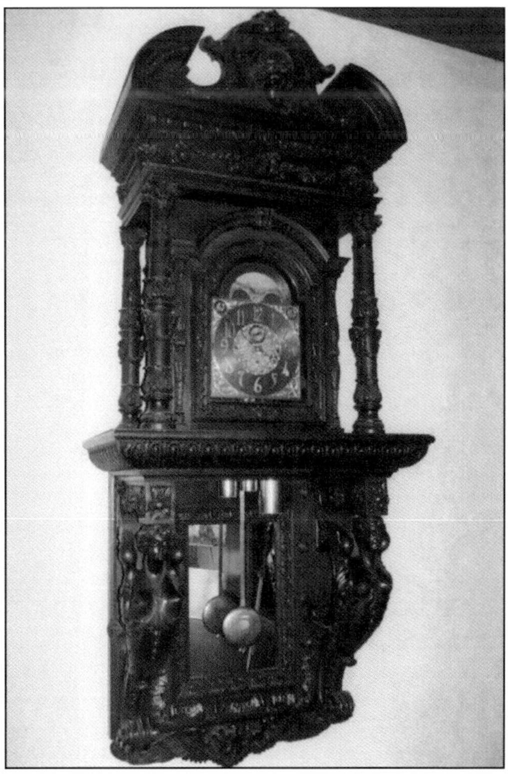

The clock that was installed into the wall also showed the high level of workmanship. The clock has German works. Its woodwork with cherubs is from Italy. The Italian wording translates to "time flies, but man perceives it not," which is from *Dante's Inferno*. (Courtesy of Highlands Ranch Mansion Photographic Collection, Douglas County History Research Center, Douglas County Libraries, 2001.064.0011.036A.)

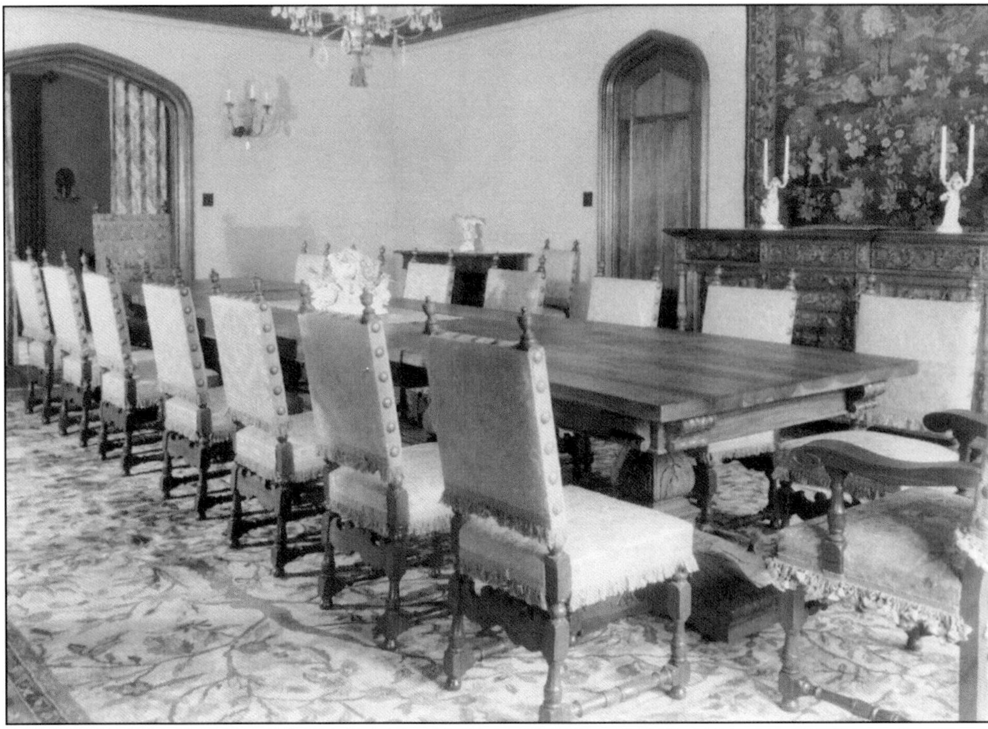

Denver's society class enjoyed meals in the spacious dining room. This photograph shows the dining room table was designed to seat many people. (Courtesy of Highlands Ranch Metro District.)

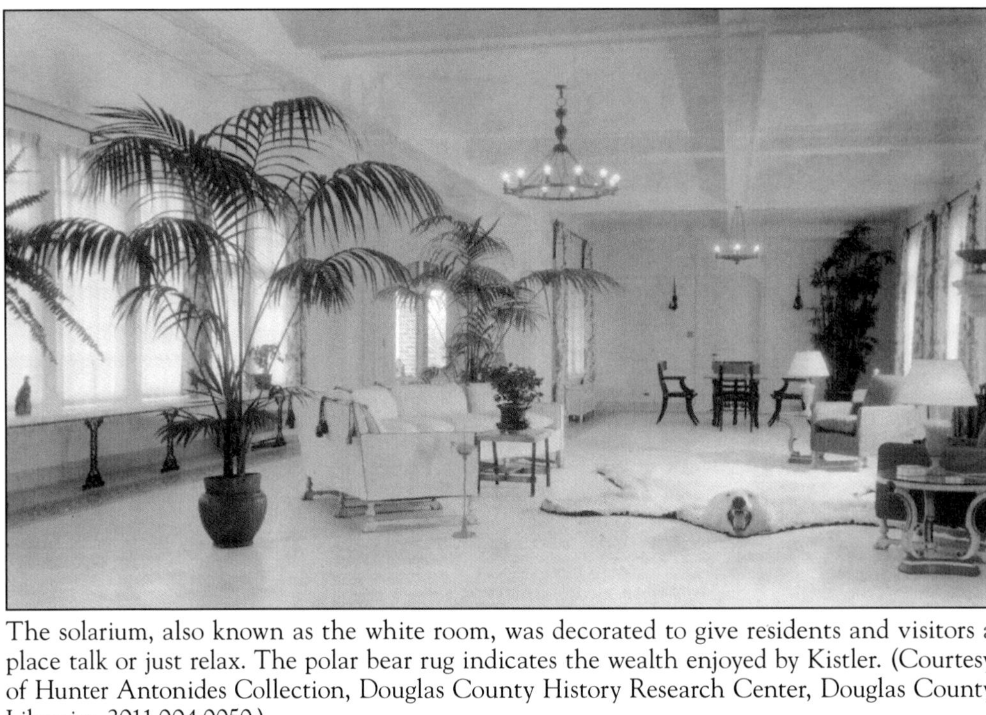

The solarium, also known as the white room, was decorated to give residents and visitors a place talk or just relax. The polar bear rug indicates the wealth enjoyed by Kistler. (Courtesy of Hunter Antonides Collection, Douglas County History Research Center, Douglas County Libraries, 2011.004.0050.)

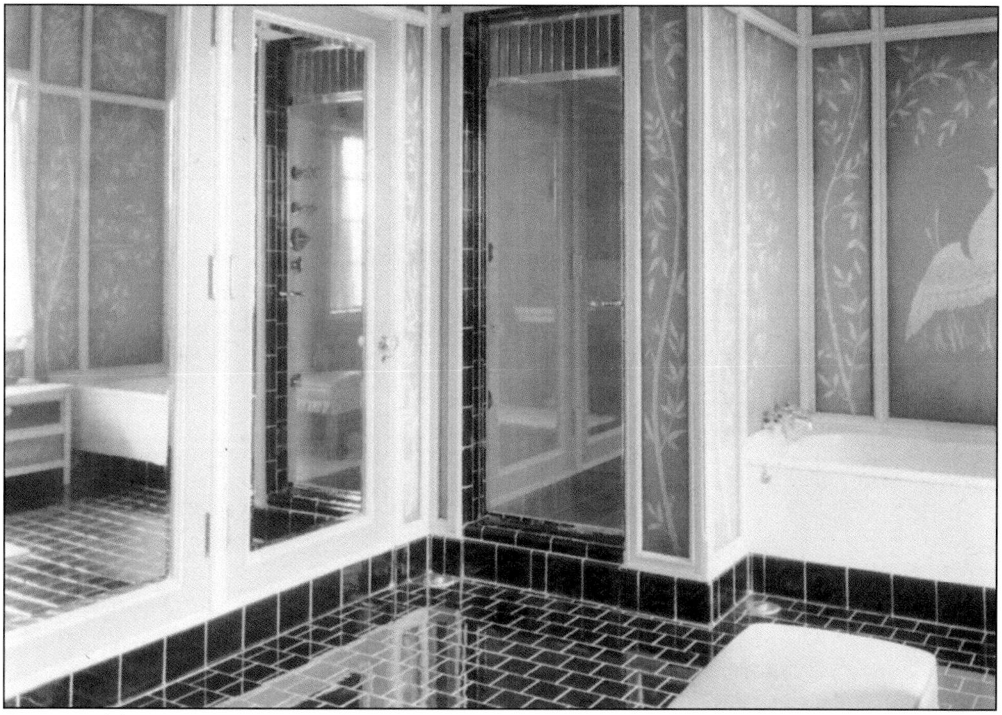

As part of the renovation, a very beautiful bathroom was included adjacent to the west bedroom. Looking at the reflection of the shower closely, one can see that there is not just one overhead showerhead, but several vertically just inside the door. The purpose is to get the dirt and dust of the ranch and roads off faster. (Courtesy of Hunter Antonides Collection, Douglas County History Research Center, Douglas County Libraries, 2011.004.0072.)

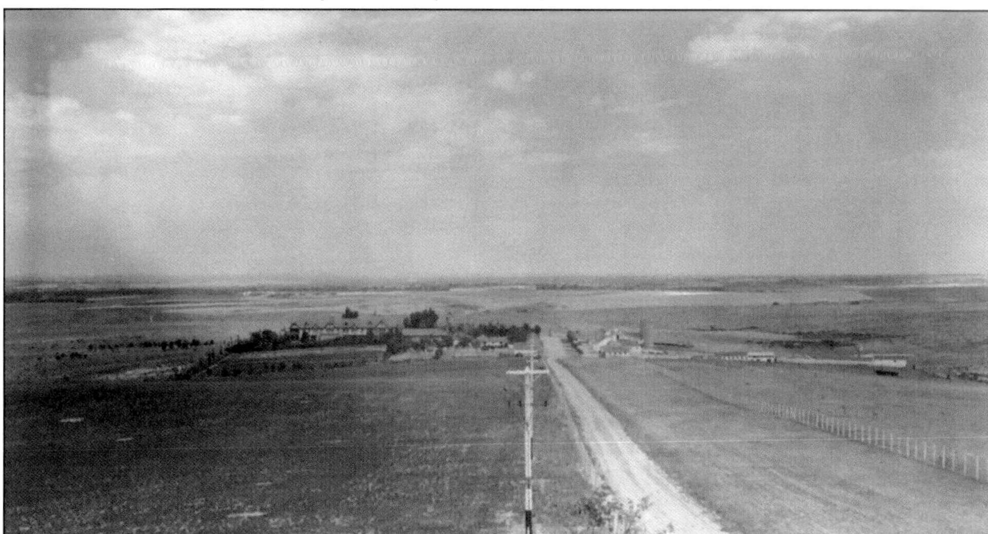

The mansion was still isolated during the time Kistler owned it. This photograph from the hill to the south of the mansion looking north toward Denver shows that nothing was around for miles. (Courtesy of Hunter Antonides Collection, Douglas County History Research Center, Douglas County Libraries, 2011.004.0001.)

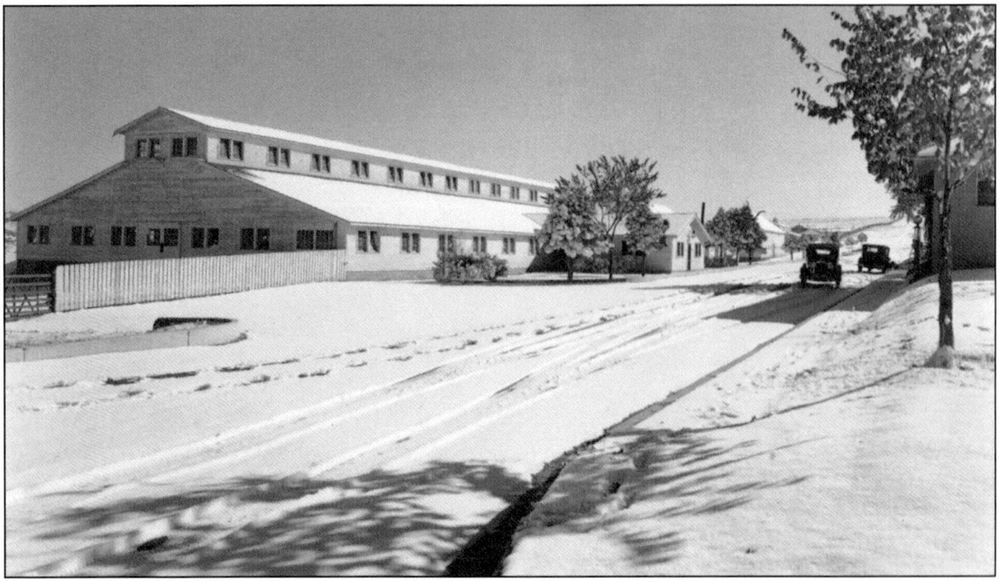

Outside and east of the mansion, ranch life continued on with the barns that are still in use today. Pictured above, cars are driving the snow-covered roads near the barns. Horse training was a regular activity at the ranch. (Above, courtesy of Hunter Antonides Collection, Douglas County History Research Center, Douglas County Libraries, 2011.004.0019; below, courtesy of Highlands Ranch Metro District.)

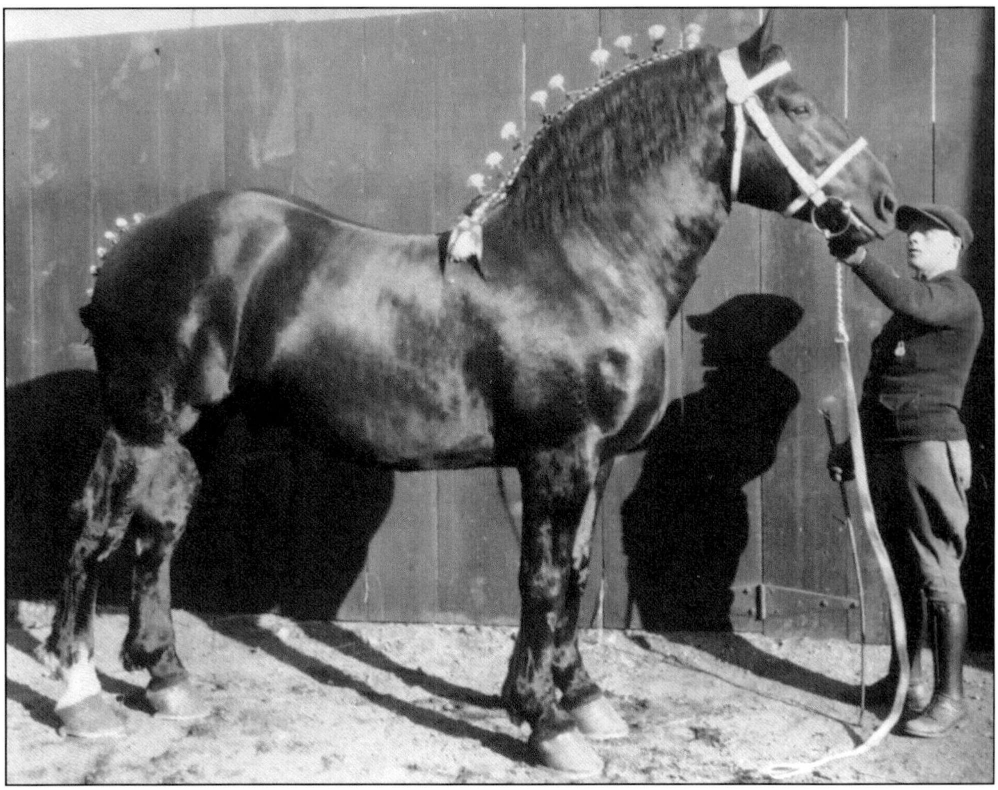

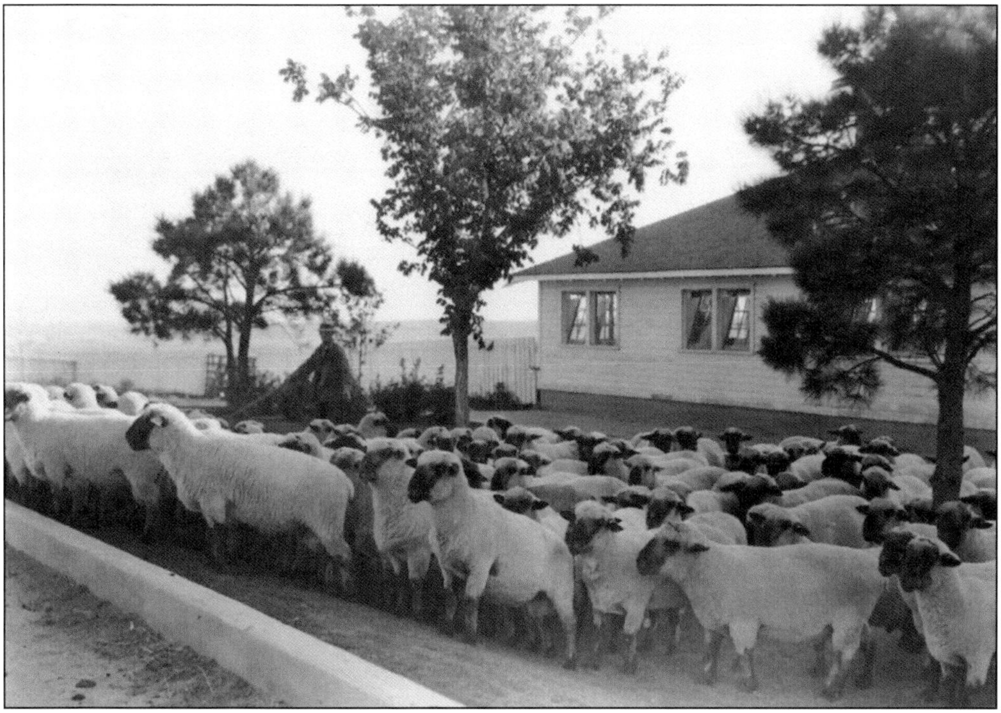

One of the changes around the ranch was the switch to raising purebred sheep, chickens, and hogs. (Courtesy of Highlands Ranch Metro District.)

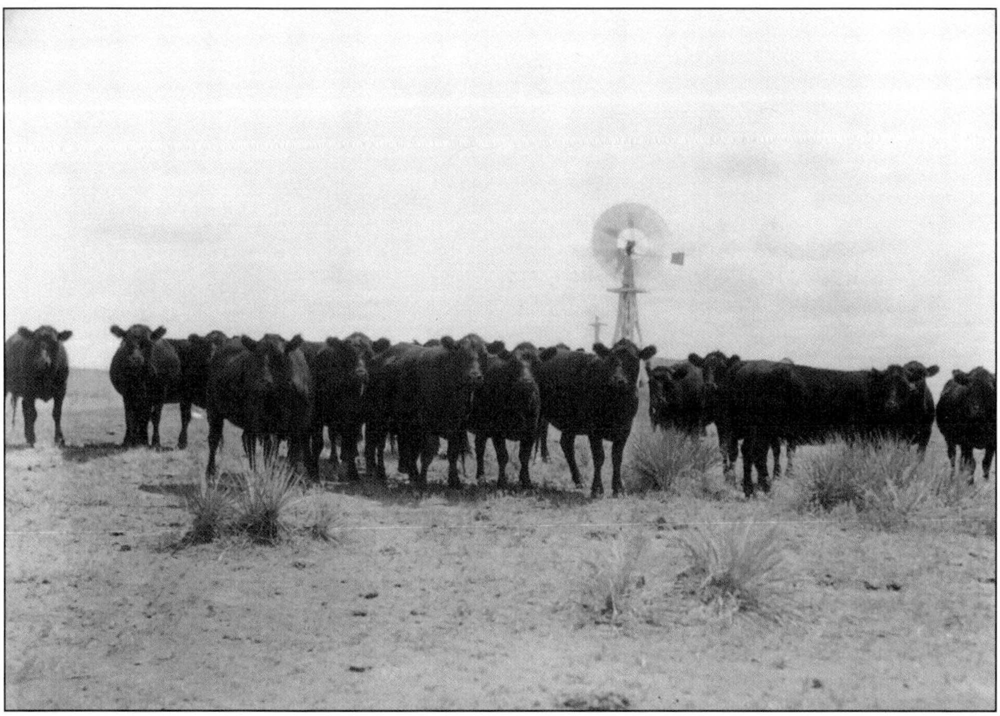

Another change Kistler made was to specialize in dairy and Angus cattle. (Courtesy of Highlands Ranch Metro District.)

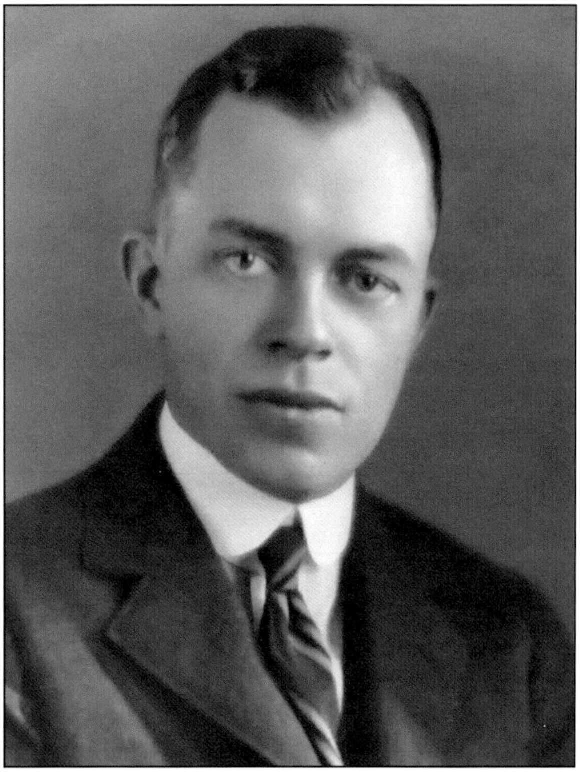

Lawrence Phipps Jr. was the next owner and by far the longest owner of the ranch for the period of 1938 until his death in 1976. Lawrence Phipps Jr. purchased the ranch for $250,000 from his Arapahoe Hunt Club friend Frank Kistler after Kistler had fallen on hard times during the Great Depression. He was the son of the US senator from Colorado (1918–1929) Lawrence C. Phipps, who made his fortune with Carnegie Steel. (Courtesy of Highlands Ranch Mansion.)

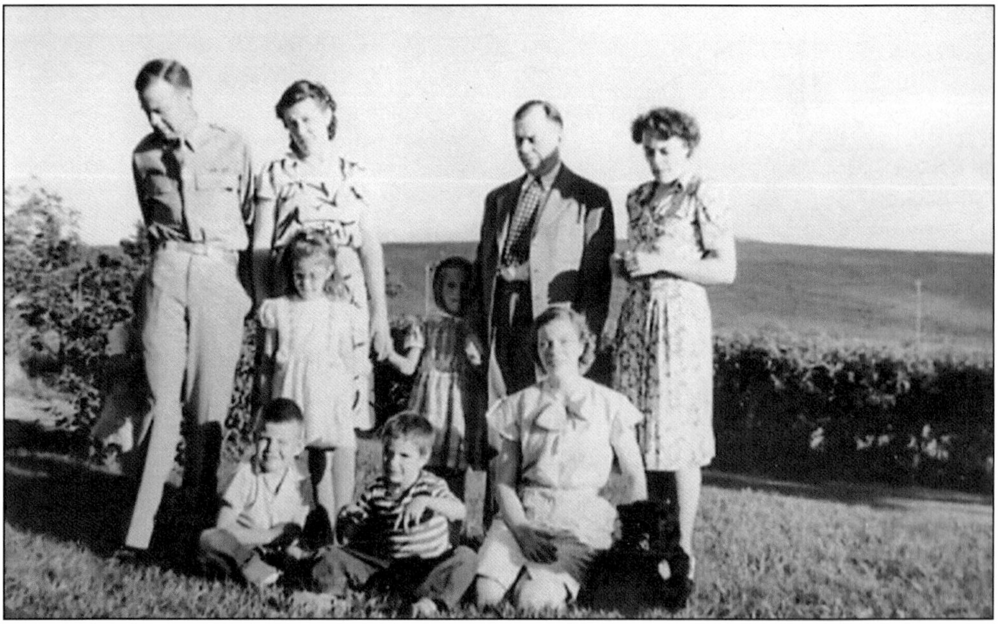

Lawrence Phipps Jr. invested his life living and raising his family in Highlands Ranch. Lawrence also brought back the name Highlands Ranch with the "s" that everyone uses for the name today. He also purchased the Welte ranch on Dry Creek in 1943. In January 1954, Lawrence purchased the Douglas Investment property, continuing to expand the full size of the ranch. (Courtesy of Highlands Ranch Metro District.)

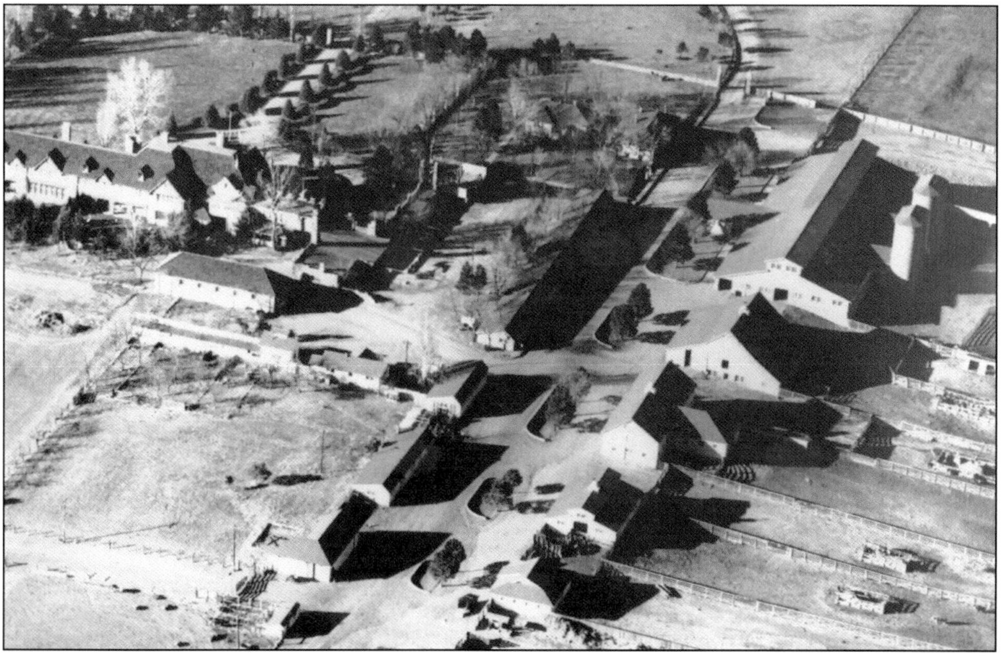

The mansion is visible on the west side or left of the photograph, while the barns and houses for the ranch hands are visible on the east or right side of the photograph. Lawrence Phipps Jr. continued to use all of the buildings on the property. (Courtesy of Highlands Ranch Metro District.)

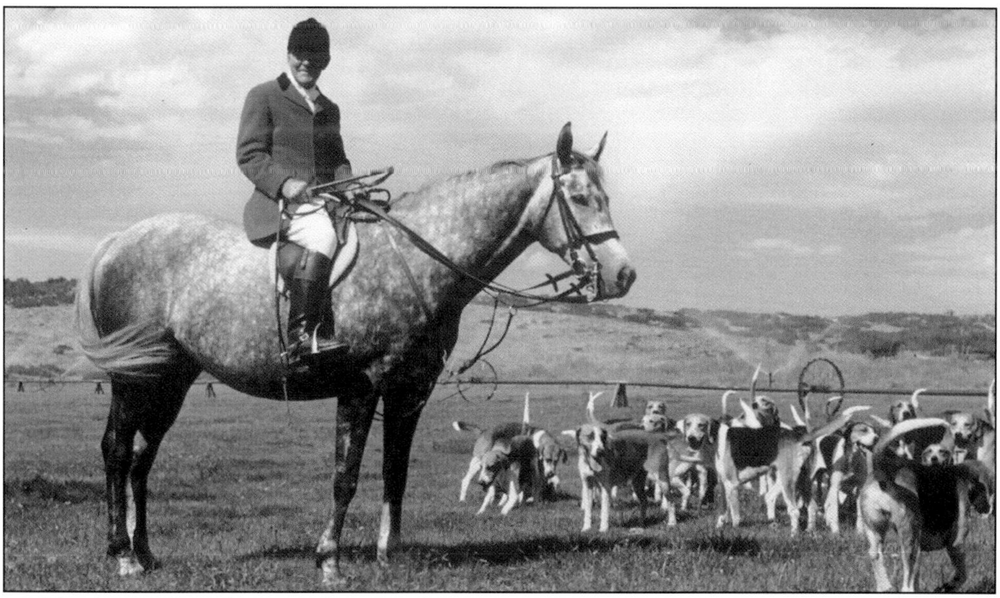

Highlands Ranch was home to the Arapahoe Hunt Club since Lawrence Phillips Jr. asked his friend Frank Kistler to relocate their headquarters from the Denver Country Club to the Diamond K Ranch in 1929. Lawrence Phipps Jr. was active, and even served as joint master, with the Arapahoe Hunt Club from 1929 until his death. The Arapahoe Hunt Club chased coyotes across the ranch. It was always more about the chase than the hunt, so most of the time, the coyote was never caught. Today, the Arapahoe Hunt Club continues, but has moved its home base from Highlands Ranch to the old Lowry bombing range. (Courtesy of Highlands Ranch Metro District.)

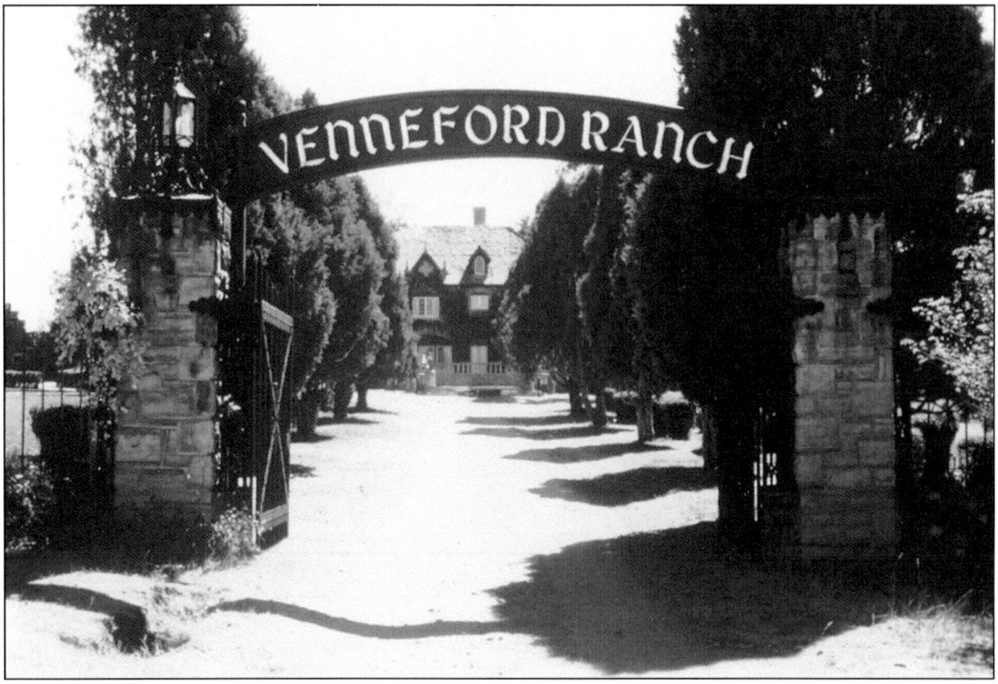

In the late 1970s, Hollywood came to the then vacant mansion to film the TV miniseries *Centennial*. The filming changed the name of the mansion to the Venneford Ranch. Today, there is a Venneford Ranch Road in Highlands Ranch remembering this time in the ranch history. (Courtesy of Highlands Ranch Metro District.)

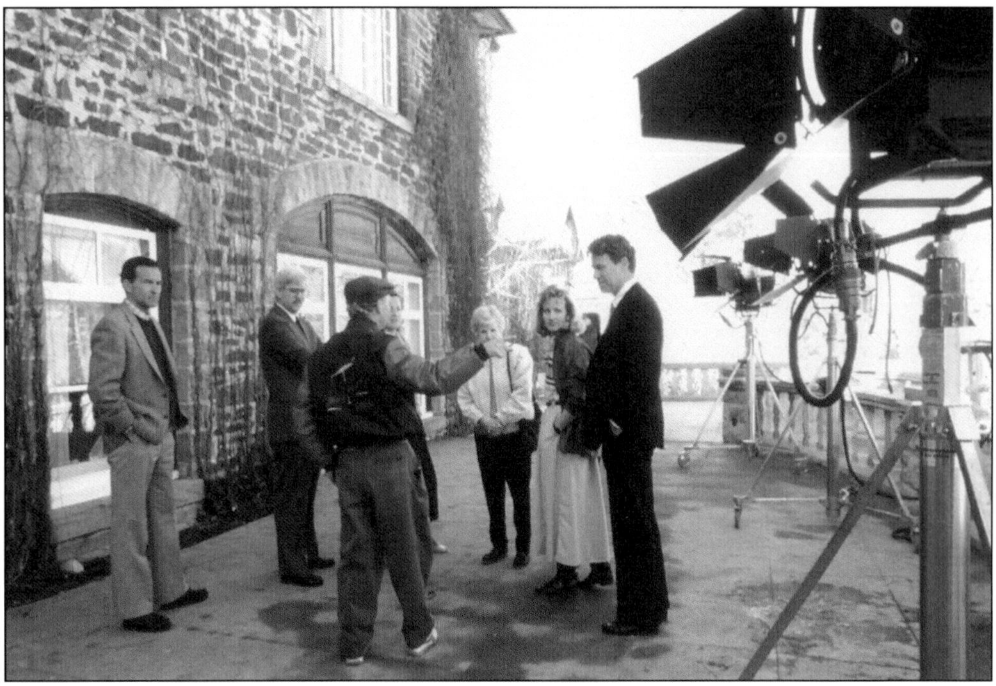

Filming took place throughout the mansion and the grounds. Many of the ranch workers were active in supporting and performing in the series. (Courtesy of Highlands Ranch Metro District.)

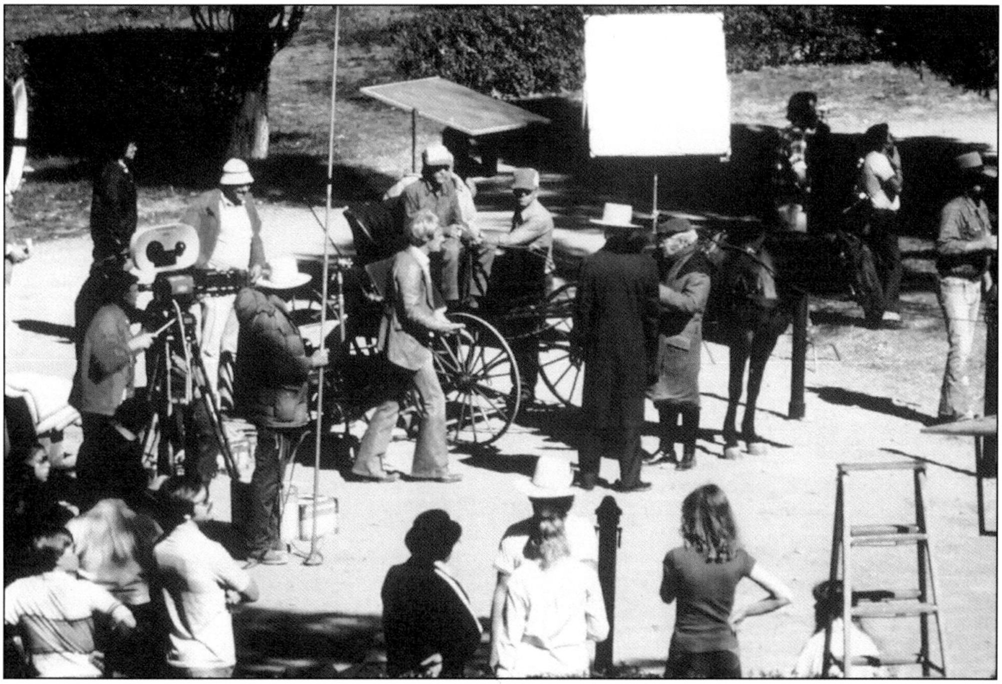

The areas around the mansion also served as locations and sets for the movie. (Courtesy of Highlands Ranch Metro District.)

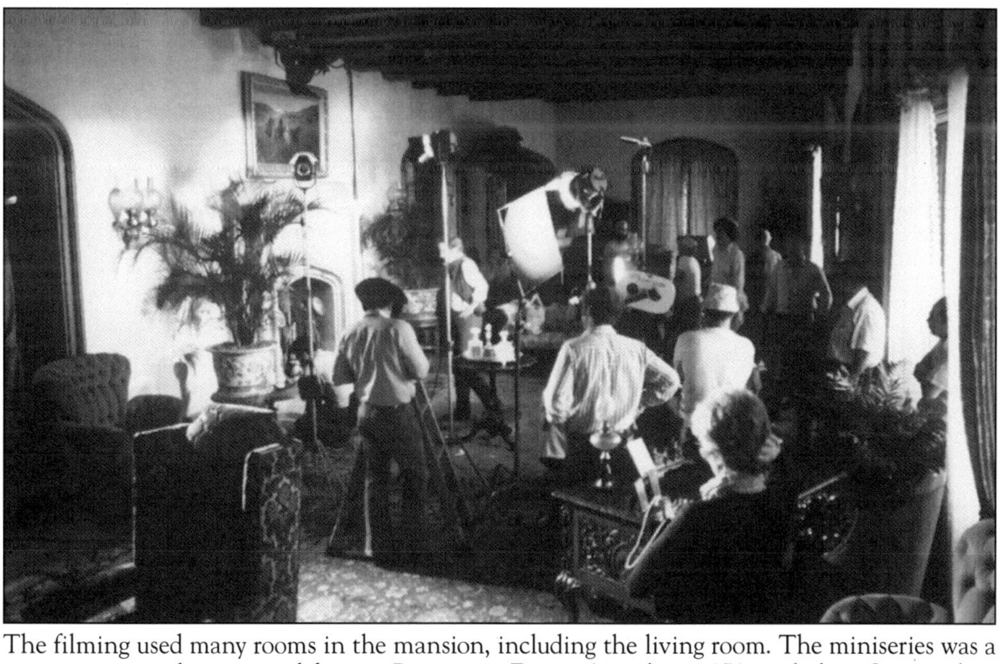

The filming used many rooms in the mansion, including the living room. The miniseries was a great success and nominated for two Primetime Emmy Awards in 1979, including Outstanding Art Direction for a Limited Series Special and Outstanding Film Editing for a Limited Series. The movie also was nominated in 1980 for two Golden Globes for Best TV Series in Drama and Best TV Actor in Drama for star Richard Chamberlain. (Courtesy of Highlands Ranch Metro District.)

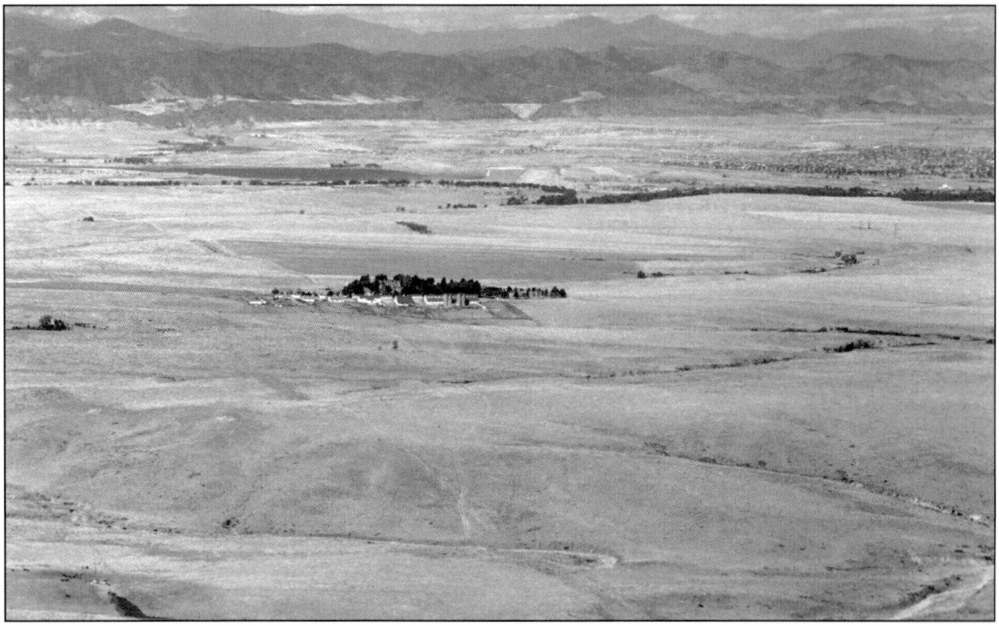

After Lawrence Phipps Jr. passed away in 1976, his family waited another year before selling the ranch in 1977 to Marvin Davis. During this time and the early days of the new development, the mansion and ranch buildings were the only buildings for miles around. The photograph shows the great expanse of plains that made up Highlands Ranch. (Courtesy of Highlands Ranch Metro District.)

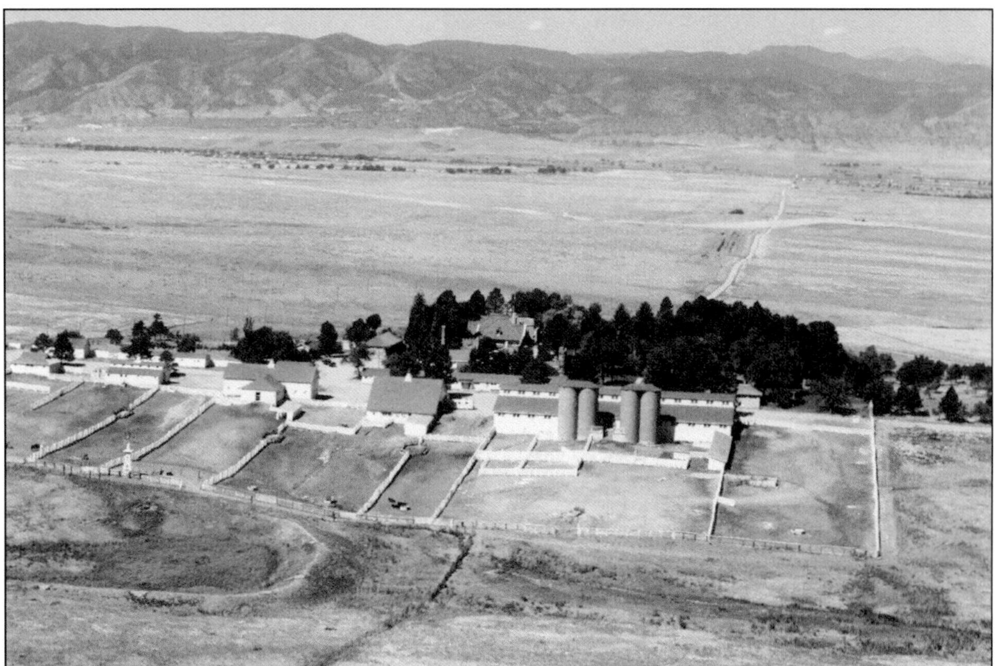

The ranching operations and mansion continued their missions well into the development of Highlands Ranch. Being set so far back, the ranch was surrounded by open space in the area until well into the development of Highlands Ranch. (Courtesy of Highlands Ranch Metro District.)

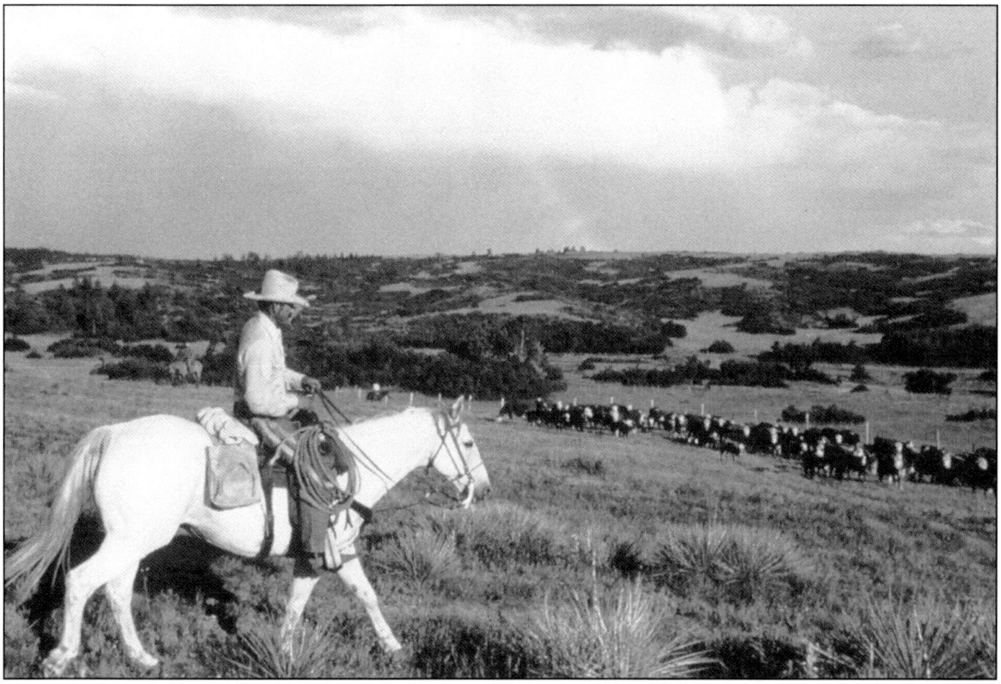

The cattle of Highlands Ranch have played a major role. This 1984 photograph shows a ranch foreman watching over the cattle in the southern part of Highlands Ranch. Today, ranching continues even with Highlands Ranch mostly built out as ranching operations allows Shea Homes to keep the undeveloped portions of land taxed at agricultural rates until the plan calls for their development. (Courtesy of Highlands Ranch Metro District Collection of Photographs, Douglas County History Research Center, Douglas County Libraries, 2011.008.0006.)

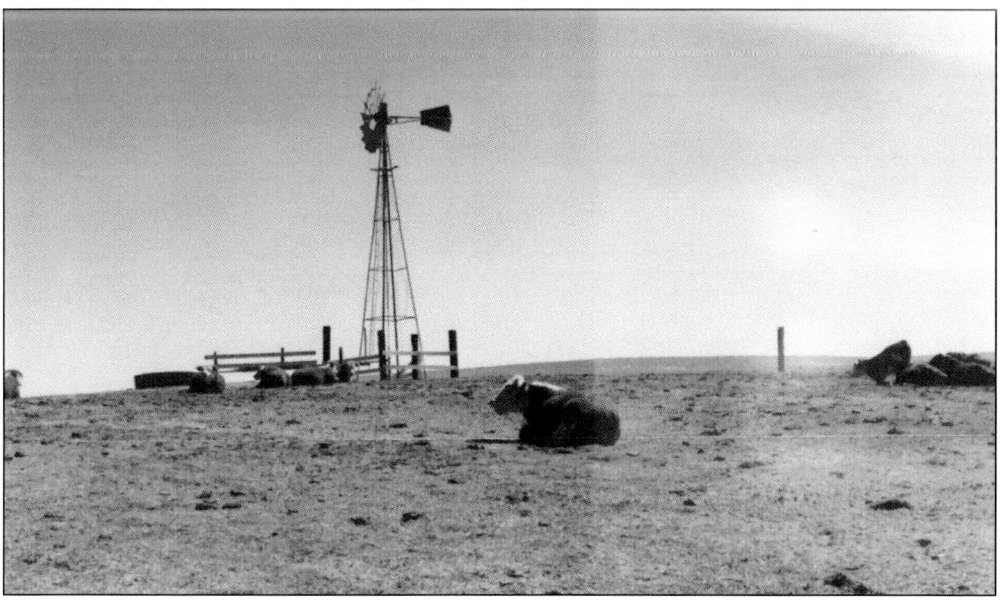

At least 12 other windmill sites were located around Highlands Ranch. Well site No. 6, seen above, provided much needed water to the cattle living on the plains of Highlands Ranch. (Courtesy of Highlands Ranch Metro District.)

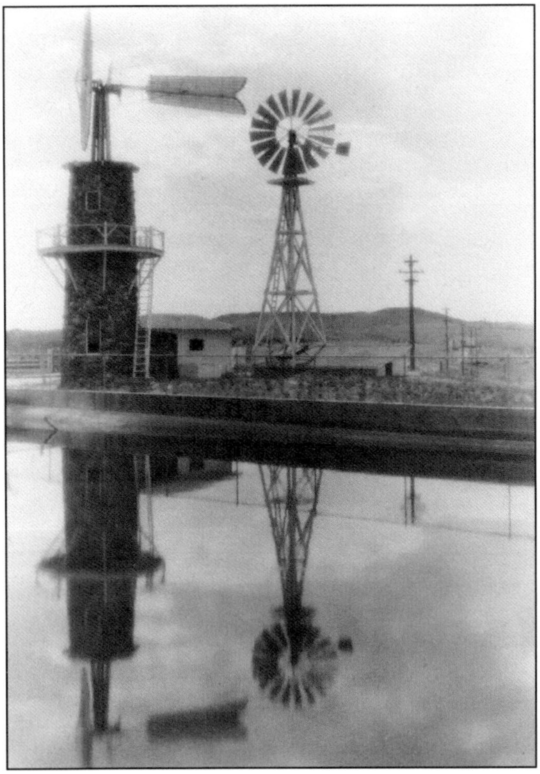

The mansion owners thought water was so important that they historically maintained two windmills and a reservoir on the hill above the mansion. (Courtesy of Kistler Family Photos, Douglas County History Research Center, Douglas County Libraries, 2011.004.0034.)

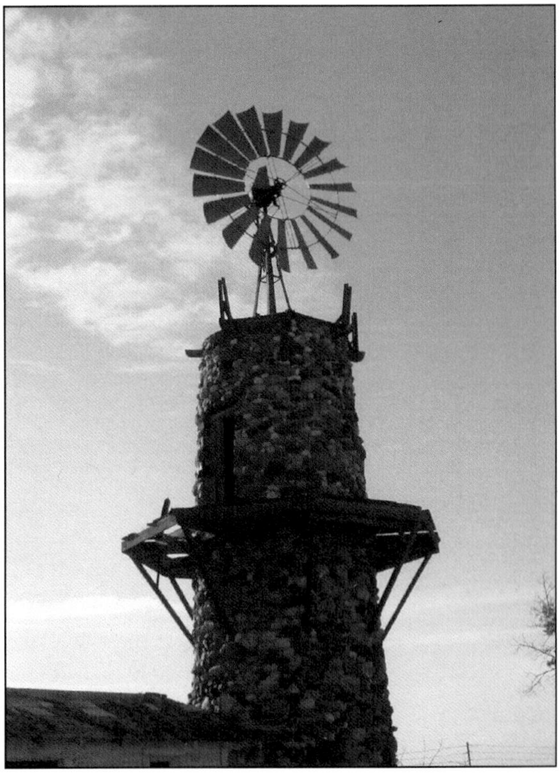

For the last century, this windmill has remained an image of not only the mansion, but Highlands Ranch in general. At the time of this book, the windmill is still a prominent feature on the hill behind the mansion and can be seen from many locations across Highlands Ranch. The windmill is expected to play a dominant role in the future Highlands Ranch Historic Park. (Courtesy of Highlands Ranch Metro District.)

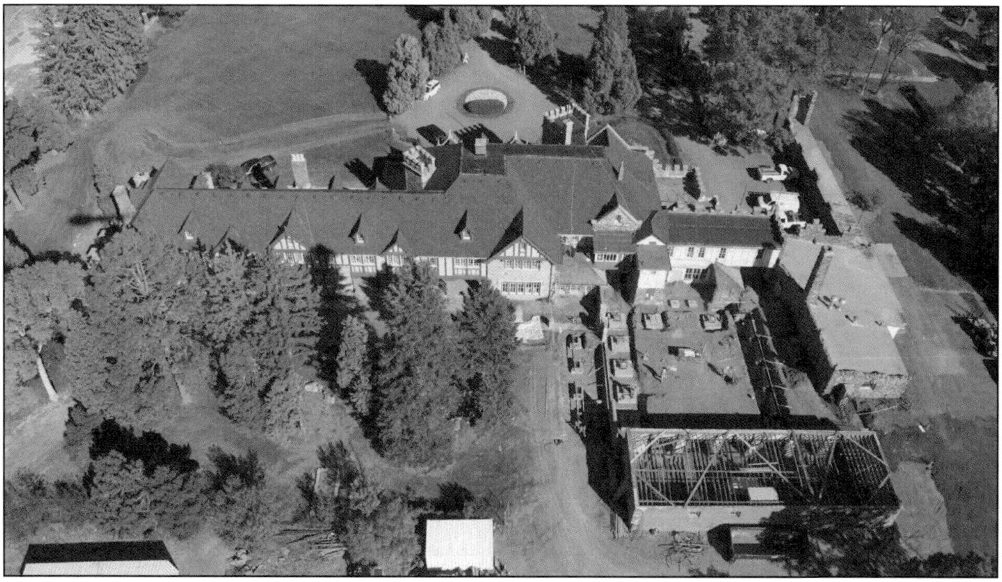

The last major renovation and expansion of the mansion occurred between late 2010 and May 2012 when the Highlands Ranch Metro District took ownership of the mansion. The $6 million renovation was done with a gift from Shea Homes and includes the addition of the 5,000-square-foot great hall. This new addition connected the back of the mansion to the carriage house behind the mansion. (Courtesy of Highlands Ranch Metro District.)

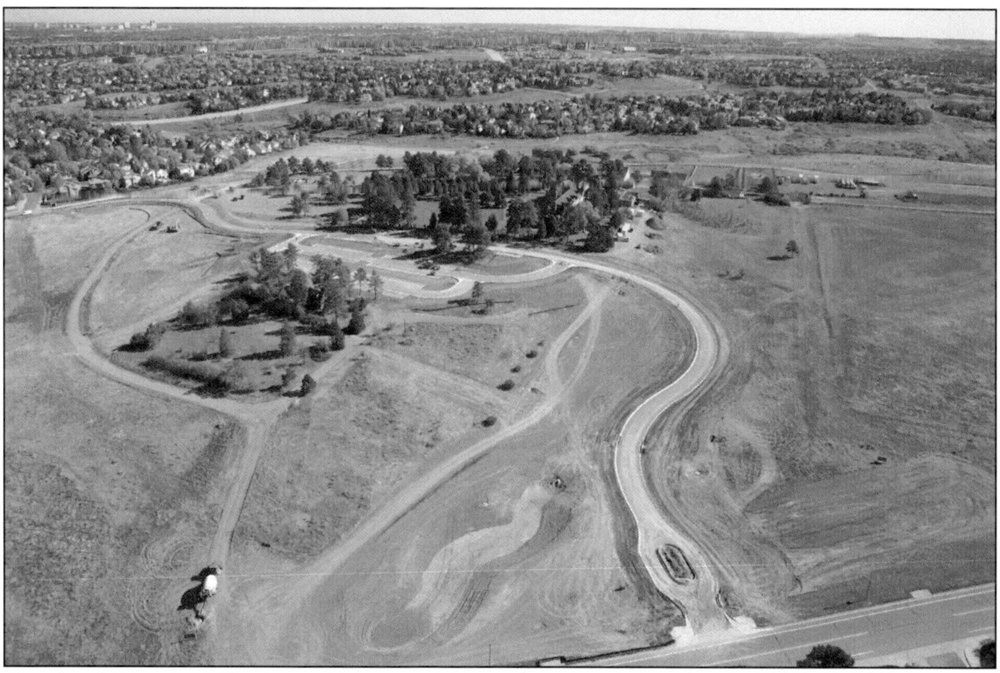

Another big part of the renovation was moving the primary entrance to the mansion from the north side on Ranch Road to the east side off Gateway Drive. The change in location reduced traffic through the neighborhood and allowed easier access to the parking lots at Mountain Vista High School that can be used for parking and shuttle buses during big events like Highlands Ranch Days. (Courtesy of Highlands Ranch Metro District.)

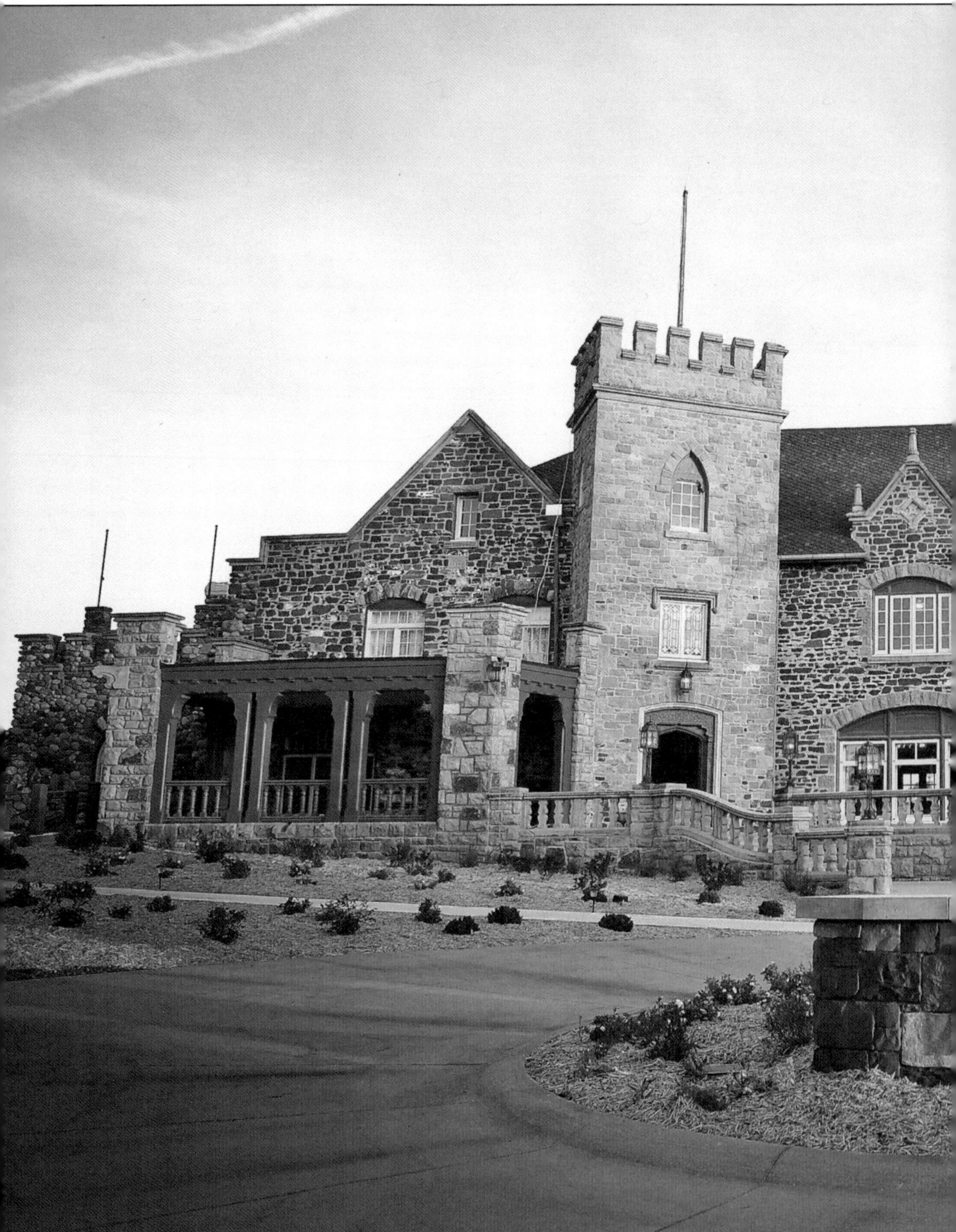

The mansion continues to be the soul of Highlands Ranch and a centerpiece of its history and identity. The mansion is regularly open to the public a couple days a week. It has also become a

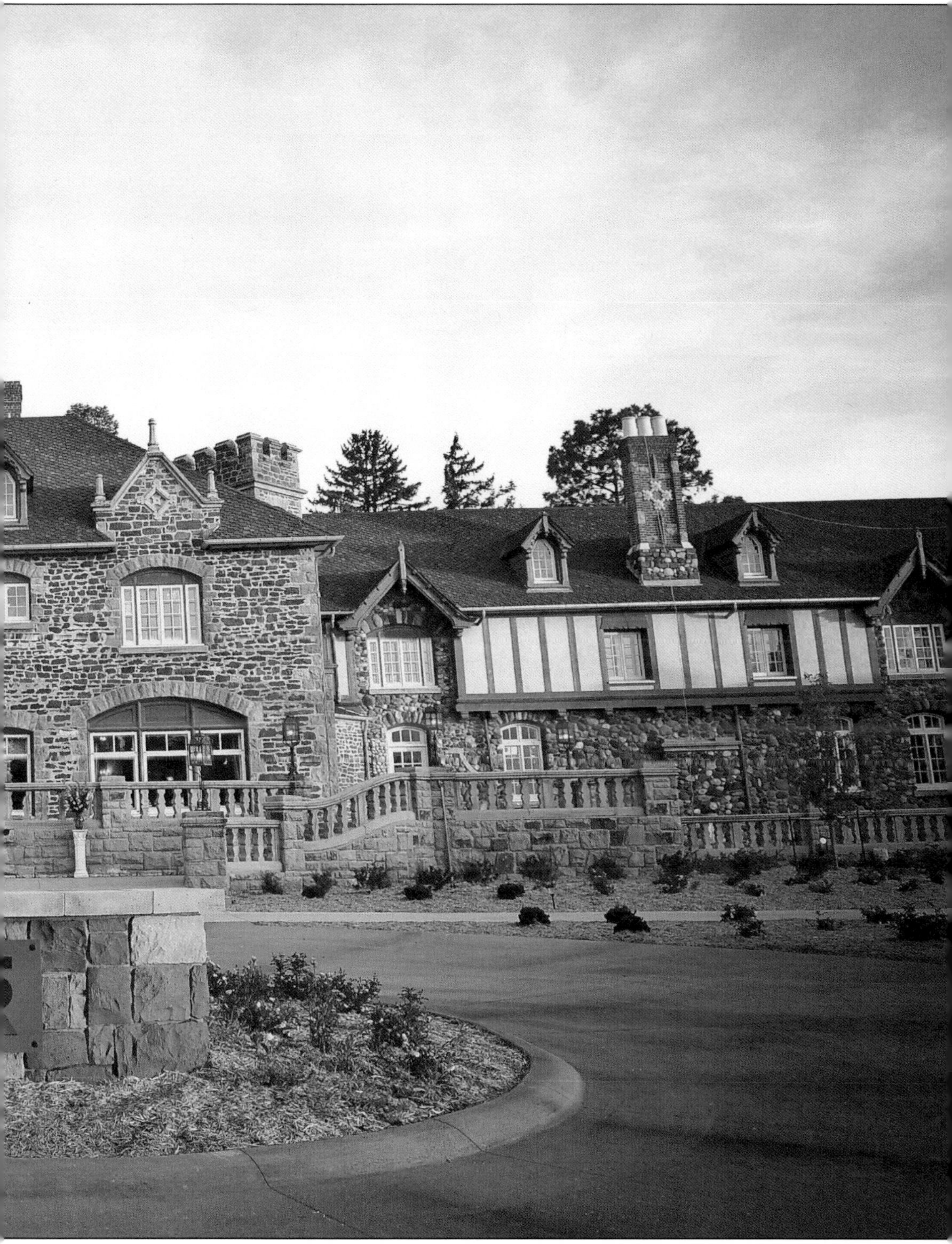

great wedding and event venue. The fee charged to rent the mansion covers the operating costs so it can operate free of taxpayer funding. (Courtesy of Highlands Ranch Mansion.)

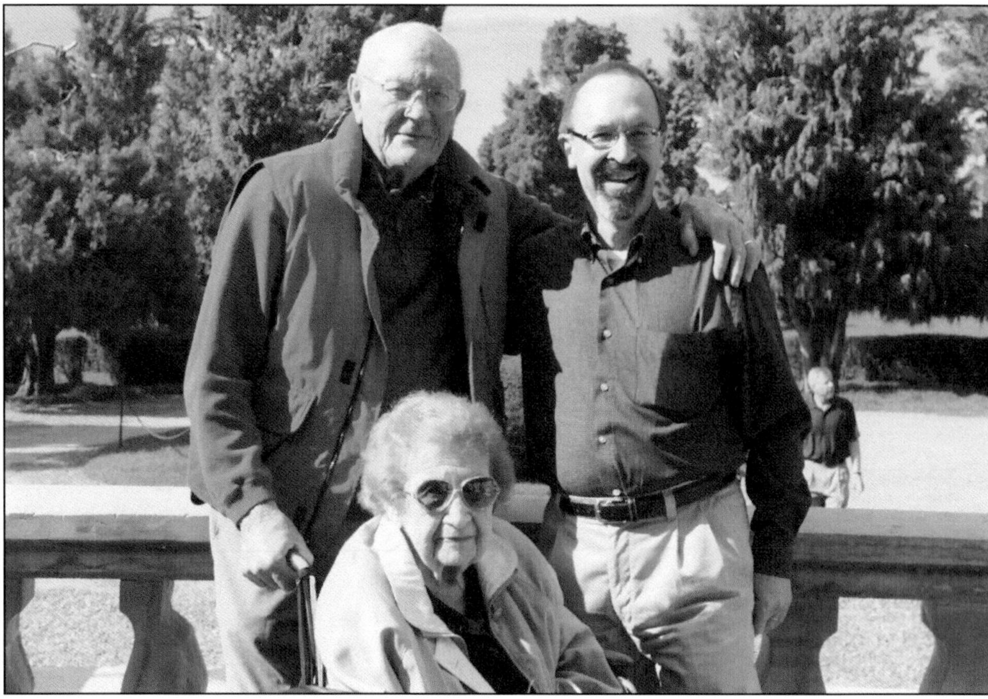

Marian Morgan was the last resident to live on the mansion grounds. Jim Toepfer was essential in planning the future of the Highlands Ranch. The Highlands Ranch Metro District director of public works, Jeff Case (right), was responsible for the mansion's renovation and many of the public works around Highlands Ranch. (Courtesy of Highlands Ranch Metro District.)

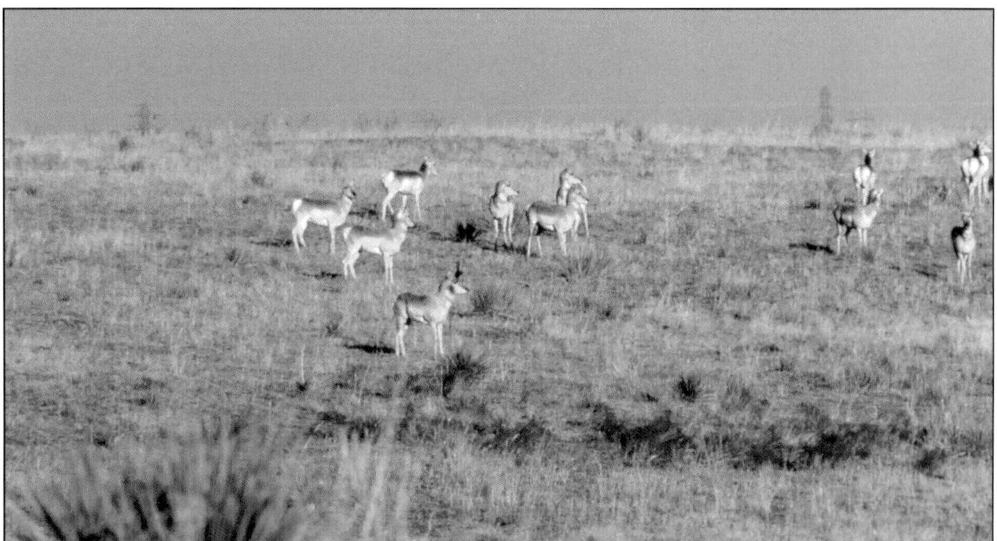

For many years, the ranch continued to be a home on the range where the antelope did play. The antelope have spent many years in Highlands Ranch, but as the power tower in the distance indicates, development would follow. The antelope for the most part have moved east farther into the plains of Colorado. (Courtesy of Highlands Ranch Metro District.)

Three

DEVELOPING A PLANNED COMMUNITY

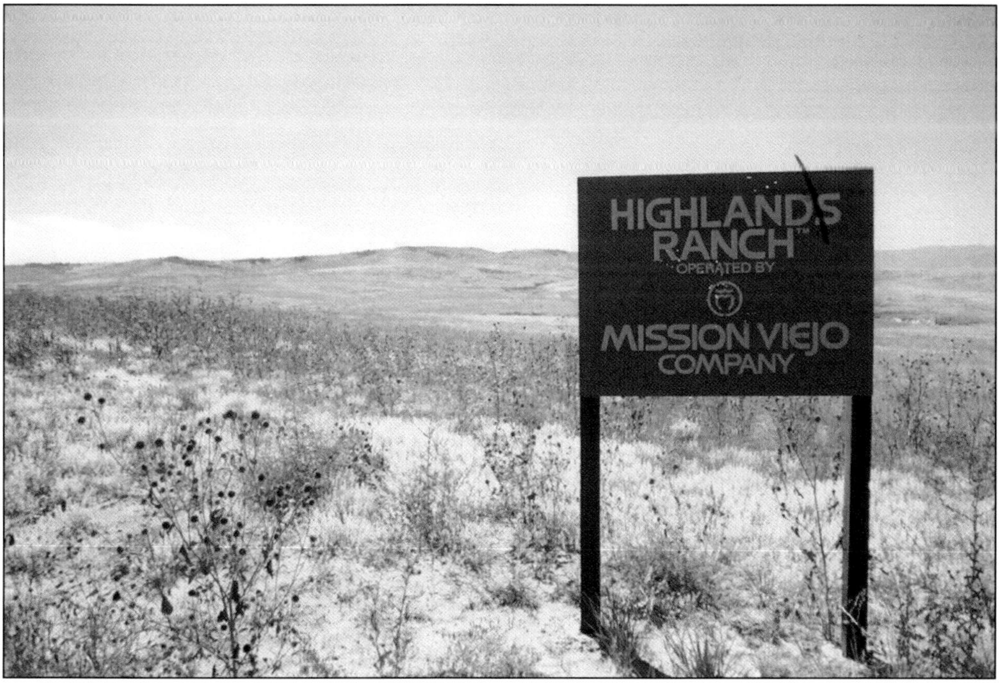

Marvin Davis purchased the ranch in 1977 from the family of Lawrence Phipps Jr. The Mission Viejo Company acquired the option to purchase Highlands Ranch from Marvin Davis in January 1978, which it exercised in January 1980. Mission Viejo Company had experience developing master-planned communities in California. (Courtesy of Highlands Ranch Metro District.)

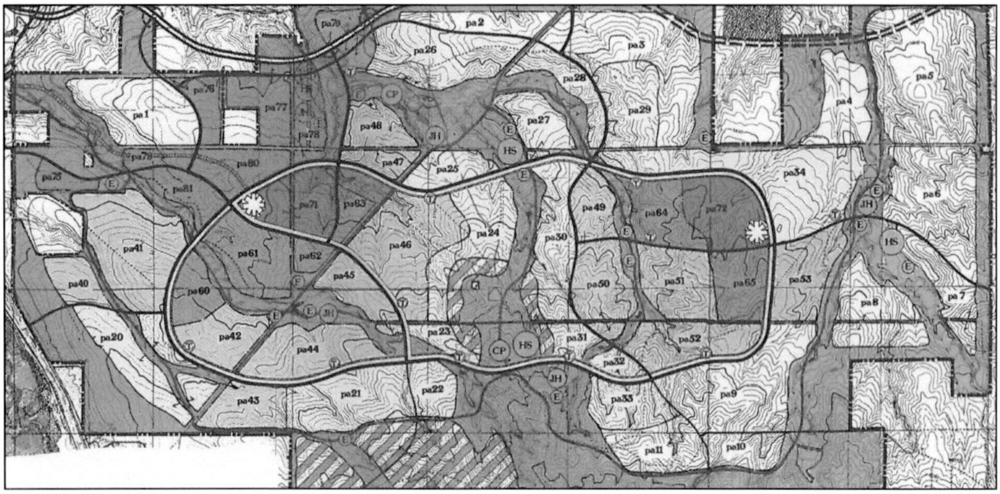

Highlands Ranch is one of the first and the largest master-planned communities in the United States. Being a "master-planned community" means that Highlands Ranch was not built in the traditional way of one small area at a time, but development was planned four to five decades ahead. The community development today is still largely following the original development master plan from 1979. (Courtesy of Highlands Ranch Metro District.)

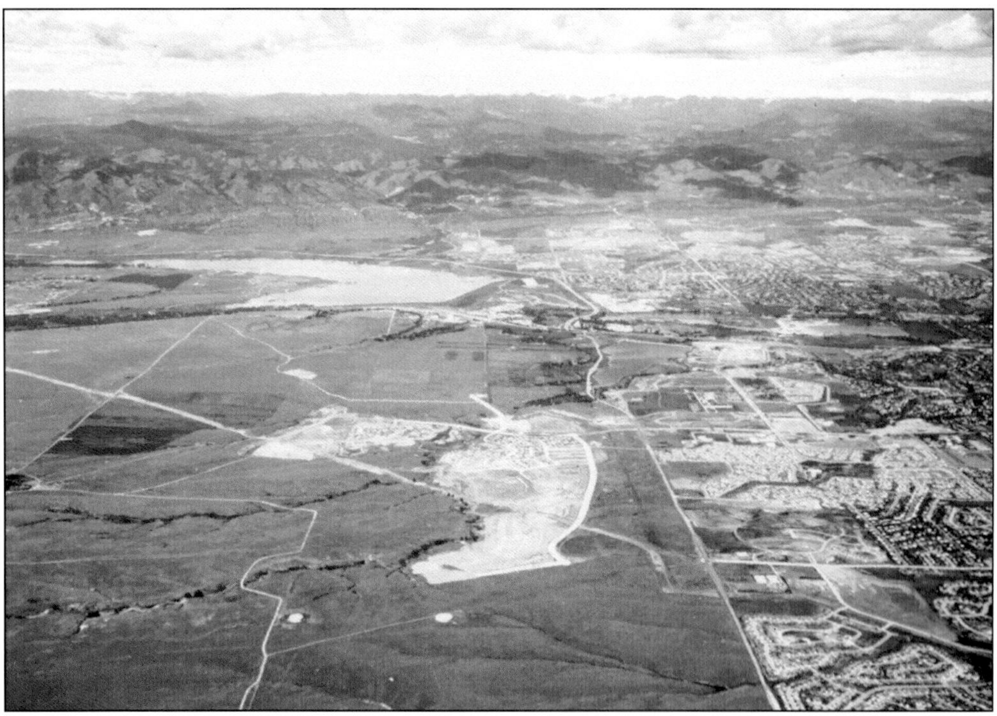

The open plains of northern Douglas County south of County Line Road provided the perfect empty area to develop a full community. The image shows the first land disruptions during the initial development of Highlands Ranch. (Courtesy of Highlands Ranch Metro District.)

Phil Reilly was the chief executive officer of Mission Viejo and therefore the primary overseer of all its projects across the country. Highlands Ranch was very important to the company, as was demonstrated by his many trips to Colorado to check on the operation. (Courtesy of Highlands Ranch Metro District.)

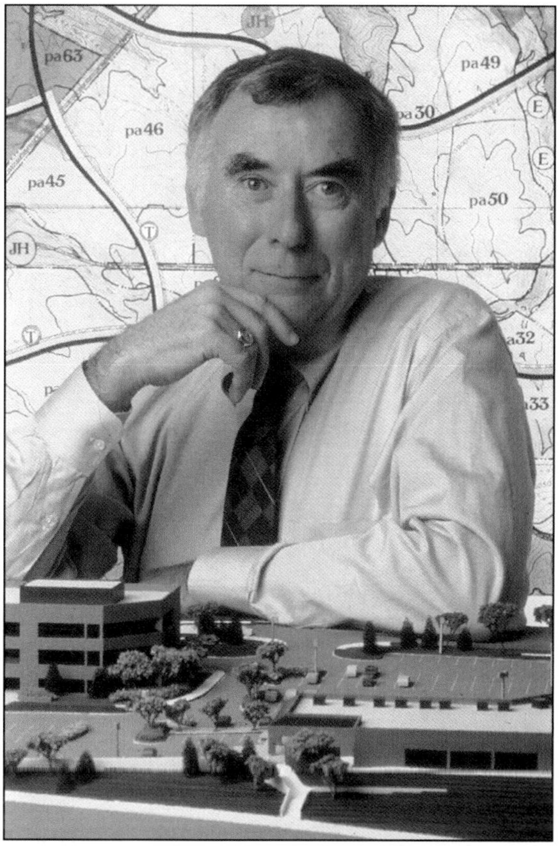

Jim Toepfer was put in charge of Mission Viejo's Colorado operations, and the largest of which was the development of the Highlands Ranch community. Toepfer became known as the "Father of Highlands Ranch." (Courtesy of Highlands Ranch Metro District.)

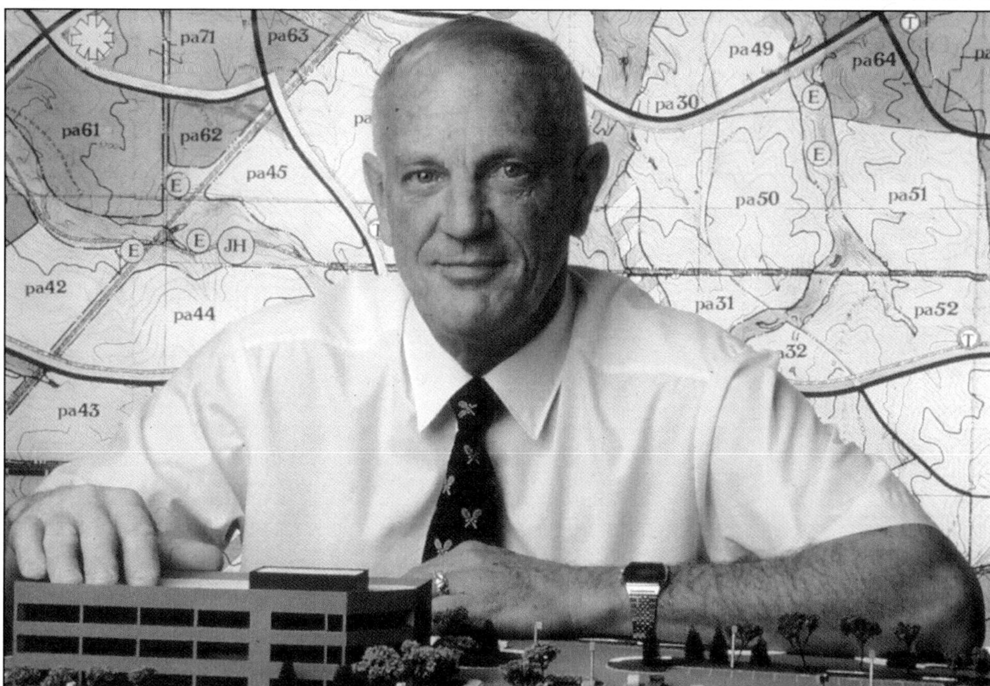

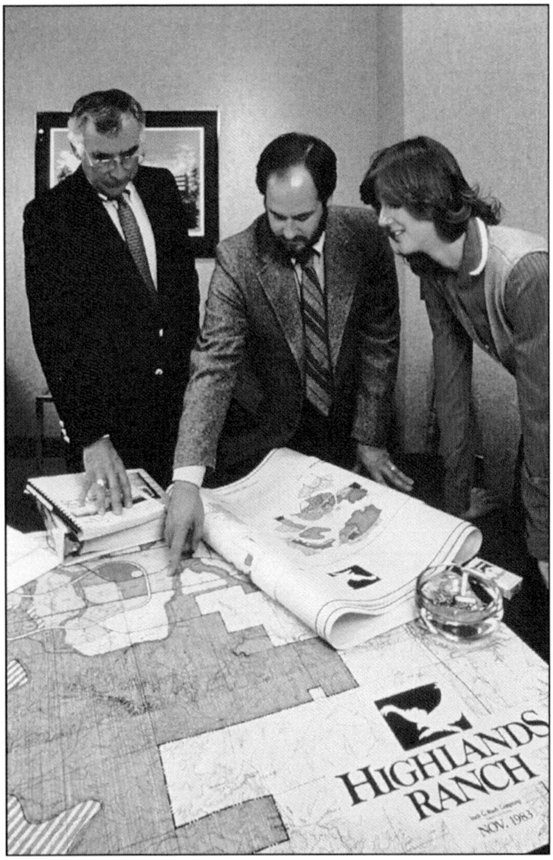

Steve Ormiston, center, was in charge of planning the Highlands Ranch community. Steve is showing the plan to Mission Viejo chief executive officer Phil Reilly and a representative from the public sector. (Courtesy of Highlands Ranch Metro District.)

The master plan required feedback and acceptance from the current Douglas County community. Here, Jim Toepfer presents the plans for Highlands Ranch to the Douglas County Planning Commission during a meeting at the Highlands Ranch Mansion. (Courtesy of Highlands Ranch Metro District.)

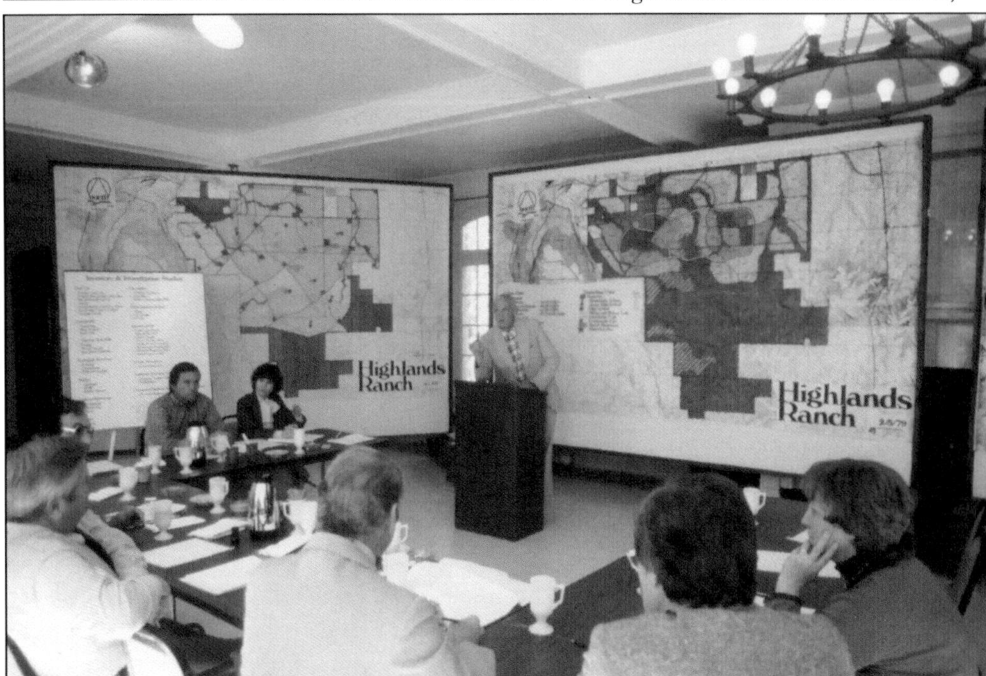

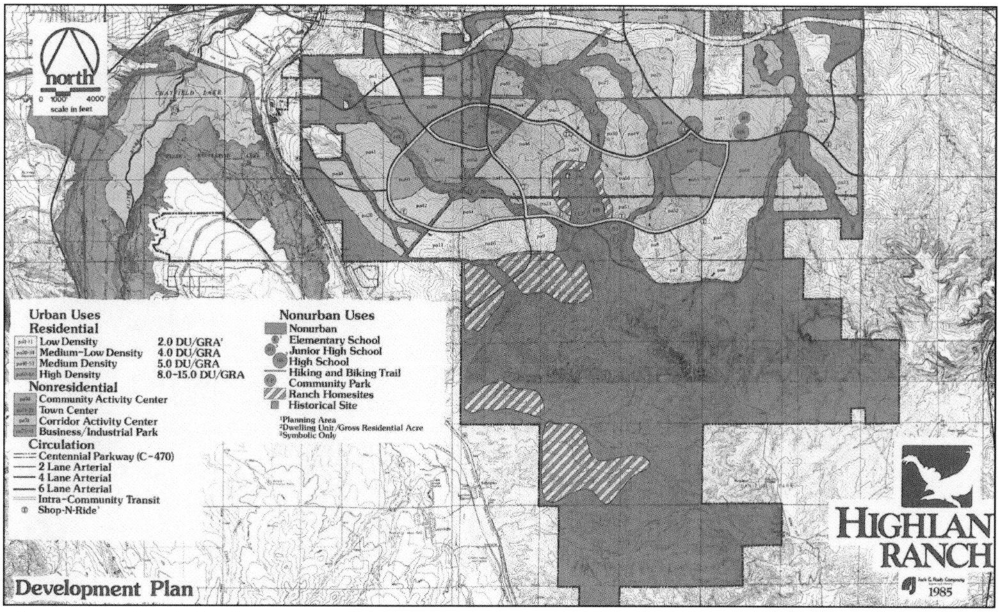

The master plan helped map out one of main environmental and recreational features of Highlands Ranch, a series of open spaces. These open spaces follow the drainage patterns, directing runoff and helping with flood control. They also provide wildlife corridors with water and are full of natural, sheltered areas. Because they are interconnected, this creates a large network of trails for recreation and travel through many of these beautiful, natural areas. The master plan also shows the large backcountry area, which was set aside in the south to keep the surrounding cities separated. (Courtesy of Highlands Ranch Metro District.)

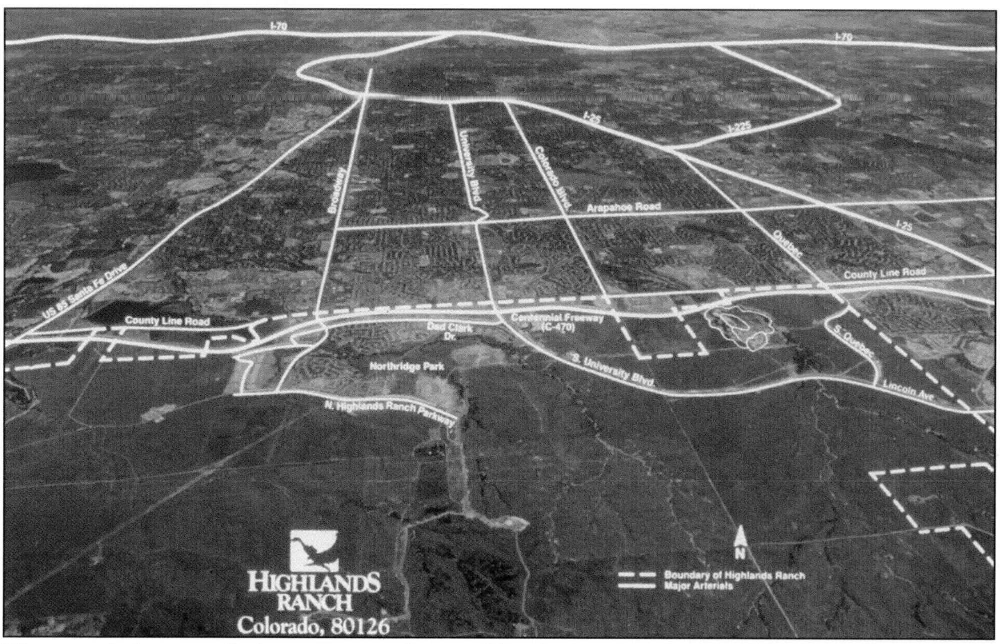

This aerial photograph demonstrates that Highlands Ranch was not a stand-alone community, but a major player in shaping the southern side of metro Denver. As such, this tie into the major roadways was a concern for many in the area. (Courtesy of Highlands Ranch Metro District.)

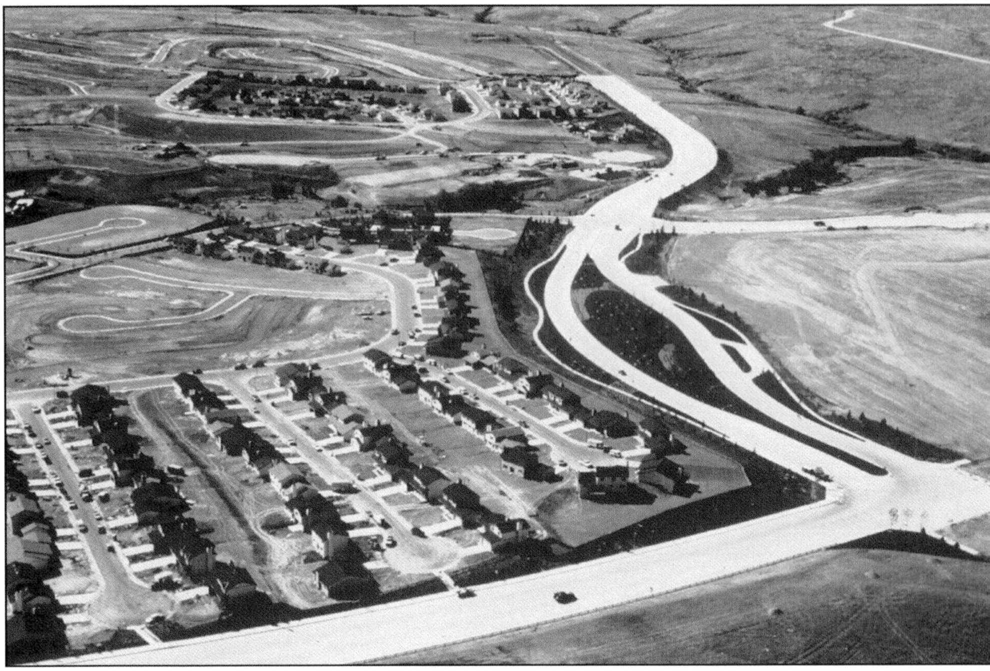

In September 1981, the first homes of Highlands Ranch were sold near South Broadway. Soon, the development of Highlands Ranch was underway. Street upon street of homes were built, quickly transforming the countryside into a community. (Courtesy of Highlands Ranch Metro District.)

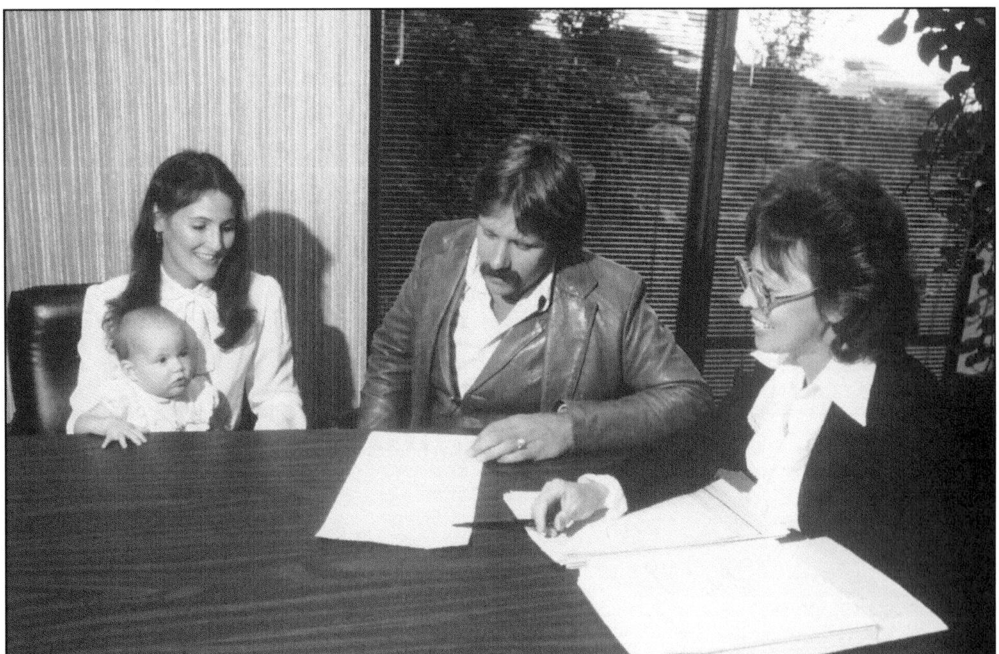

Phil Scott and family are officially credited with the first purchase of a home in Highlands Ranch. This photograph records the historic occasion of him signing the paperwork (Courtesy of Highlands Ranch Metro District.)

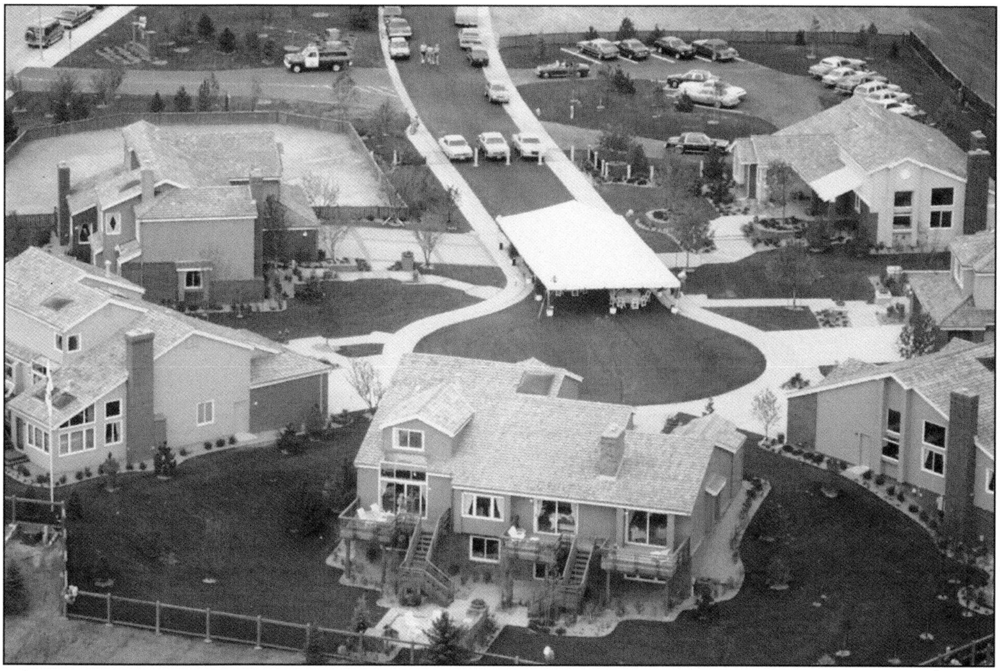

These early model homes in Stratton Ridge near C-470 and University Boulevard illustrate the types of homes that were typical in the early days of Highlands Ranch. (Courtesy of Highlands Ranch Metro District.)

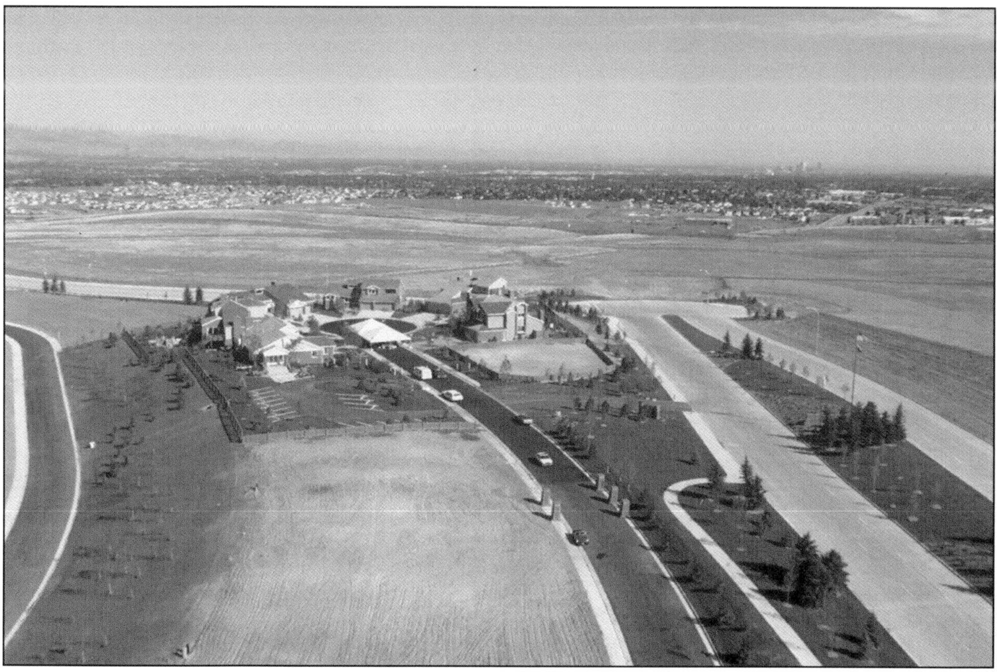

These early homes near University Boulevard show that major roadways had already been put in place and landscaped prior to home construction. The photograph also shows just how remote the first homes still were. (Courtesy of Highlands Ranch Metro District.)

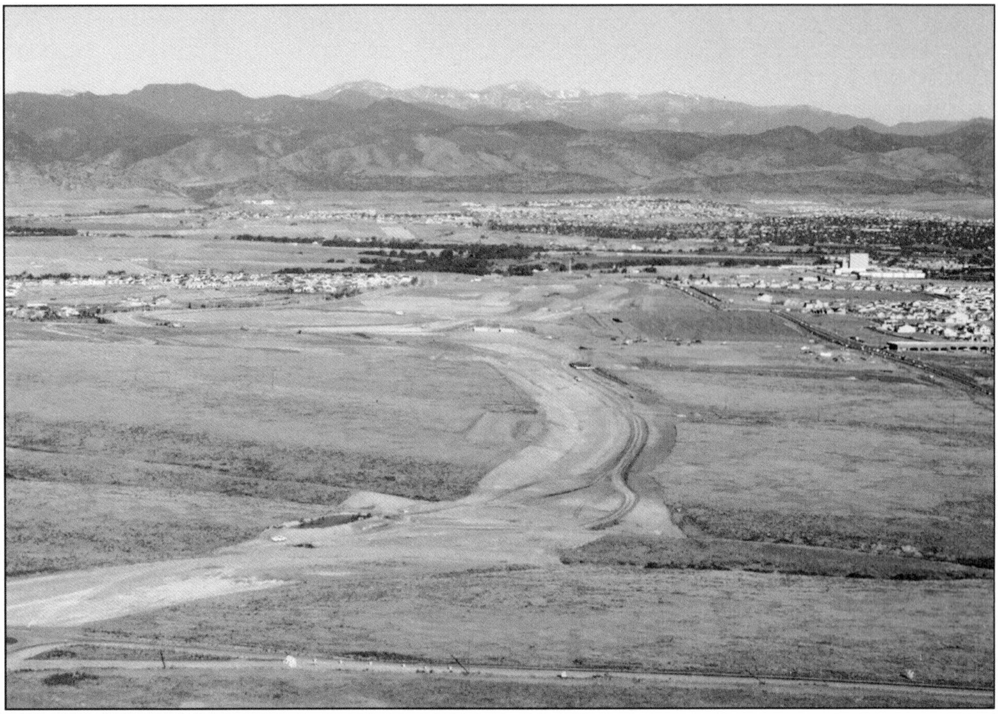

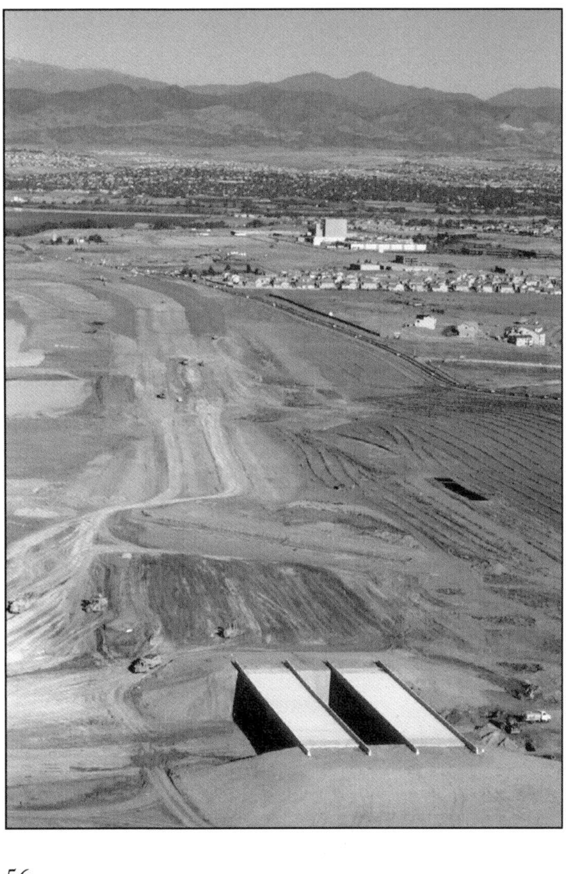

Colorado has a long history of being transformed by its trails and roads. C-470 did more to transform both northern Douglas County and south metro Denver than any other single building project. The first grading shows the path C-470 will take through the grasses of Highlands Ranch. (Courtesy of Highlands Ranch Metro District.)

C-470, like most major highways, also required good interchanges. The interchange at University Boulevard is shown under construction here with the initial bridges being put in place and the grading of the general roadway for C-470 continuing. (Courtesy of Highlands Ranch Metro District.)

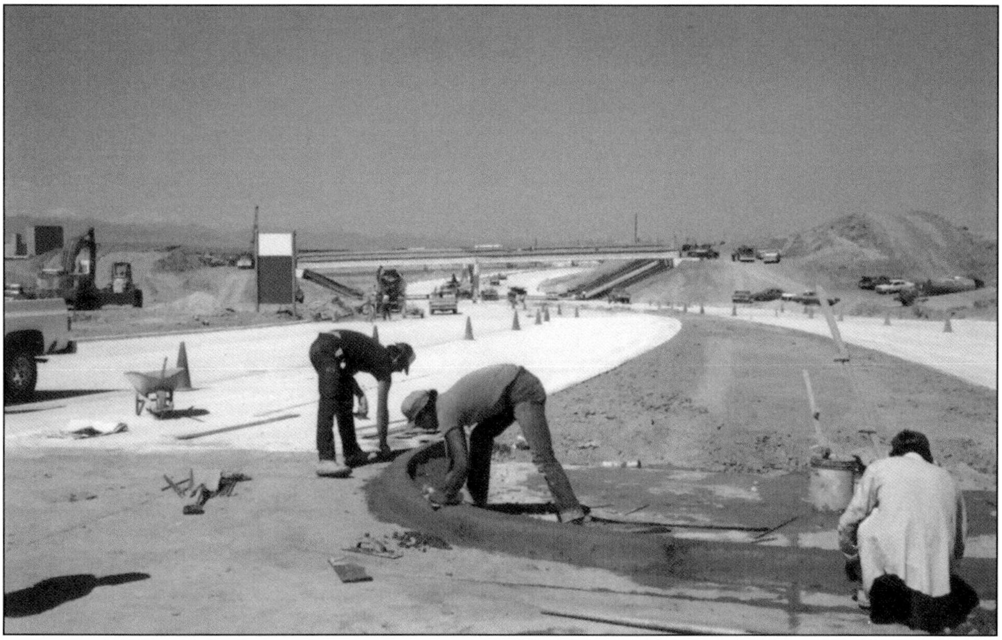

Construction workers are shown building the Broadway entrance to Highlands Ranch under the future C-470 highway in 1983. Today, from the north, one can reach Highlands Ranch from the historic Santa Fe Drive, Broadway, University Boulevard, Quebec Street, Colorado Boulevard, or the newest entrance at Lucent Boulevard. (Courtesy of Highlands Ranch Metro District.)

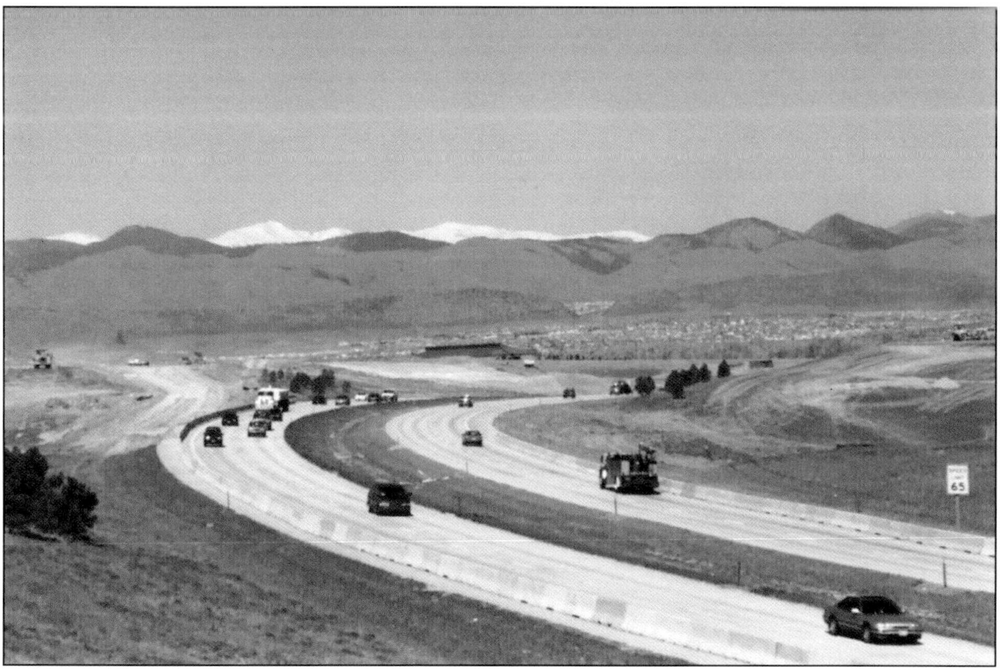

C-470 opened and provided easy east-west passage across northern Douglas County. The volume of traffic continued to grow over the next three decades with the continuing development of Highlands Ranch and the addition of more homes to the west. Plans are being finalized for the next expansion of C-470. (Courtesy of Highlands Ranch Metro District.)

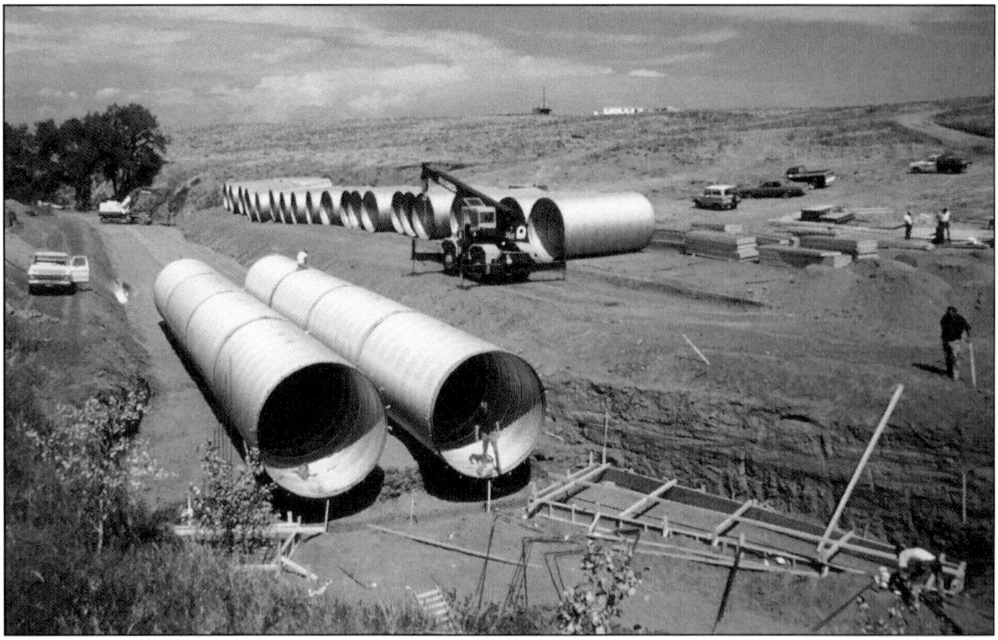

Water in all its forms is critical to life and development. Here, workers are shown installing a culvert to control the flow of water across Broadway, south of Plaza Drive. Metal culverts are normally used for the flow of water underneath the roadways of Highlands Ranch, ensuring they do not wash out even during the heaviest of rains. (Courtesy of Highlands Ranch Metro District.)

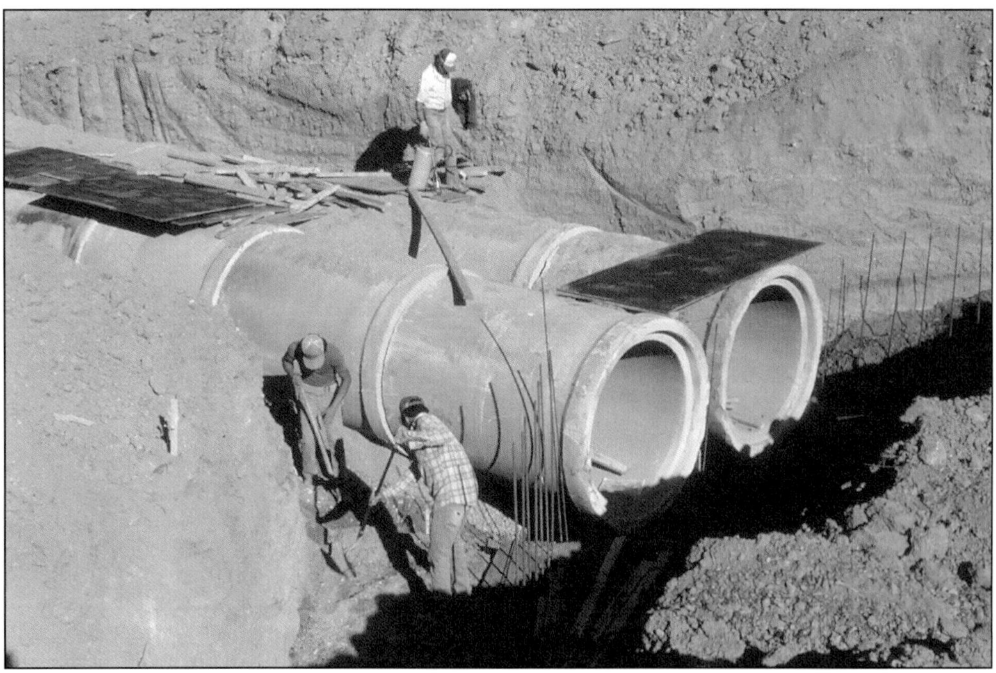

Concrete storm drains were used in the areas where homes would be built in the future. The workers here are putting the storm drains in place that will protect homes. (Courtesy of Highlands Ranch Metro District.)

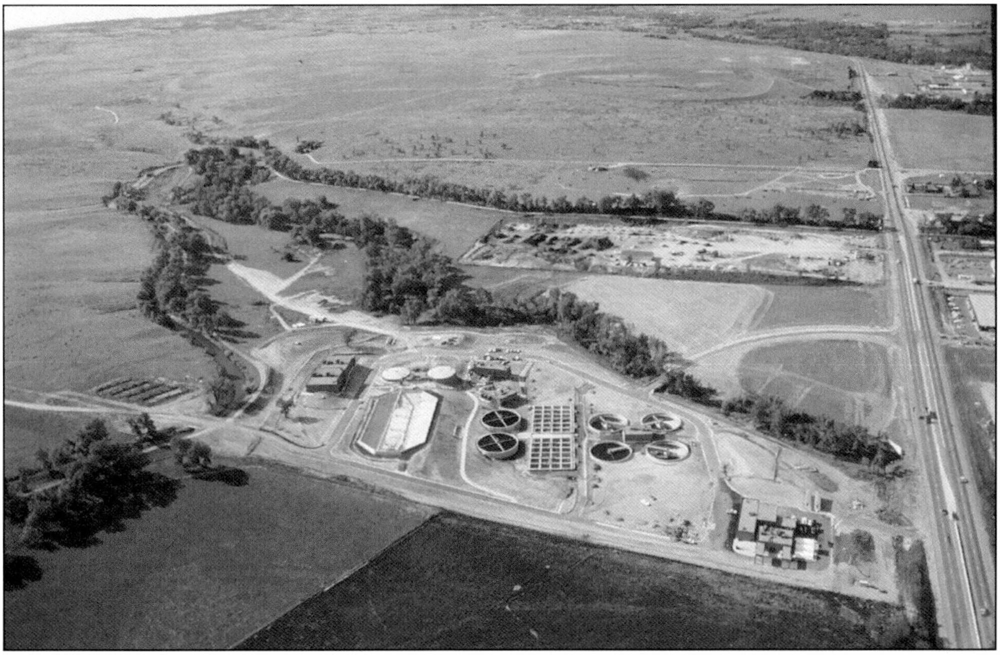

For a large community to responsibly use its water, treatment care of used water is essential. The water treatment plant located between the Highline Canal and Santa Fe Drive manages this. This state-of-the-art facility was named after Joseph B. Blake in recognition of his efforts. (Courtesy of Highlands Ranch Metro District.)

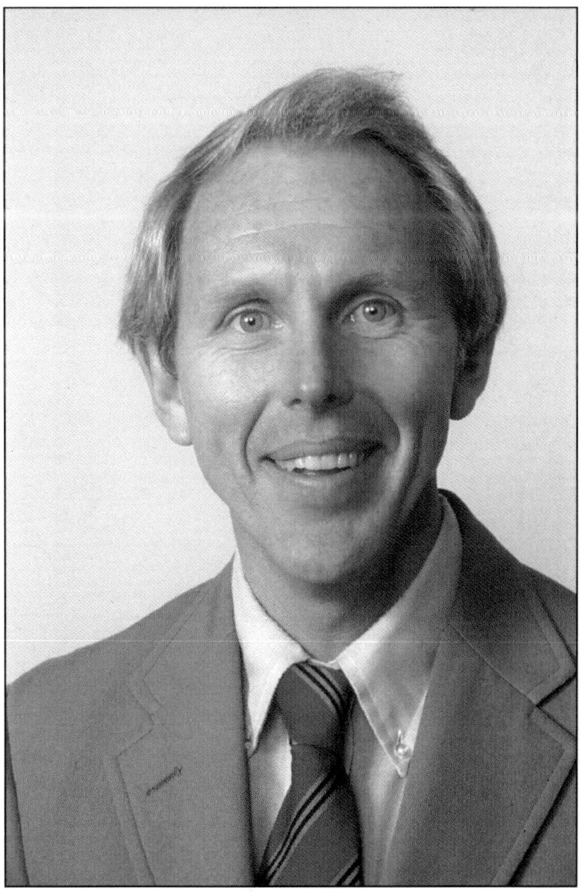

Joe Blake was important to Centennial Water, setting up various partnerships that would help ensure that the residents of Highlands Ranch would have water for years to come and the county commissioners would be satisfied with the planning and the water outlook well into the future. (Courtesy of Highlands Ranch Metro District.)

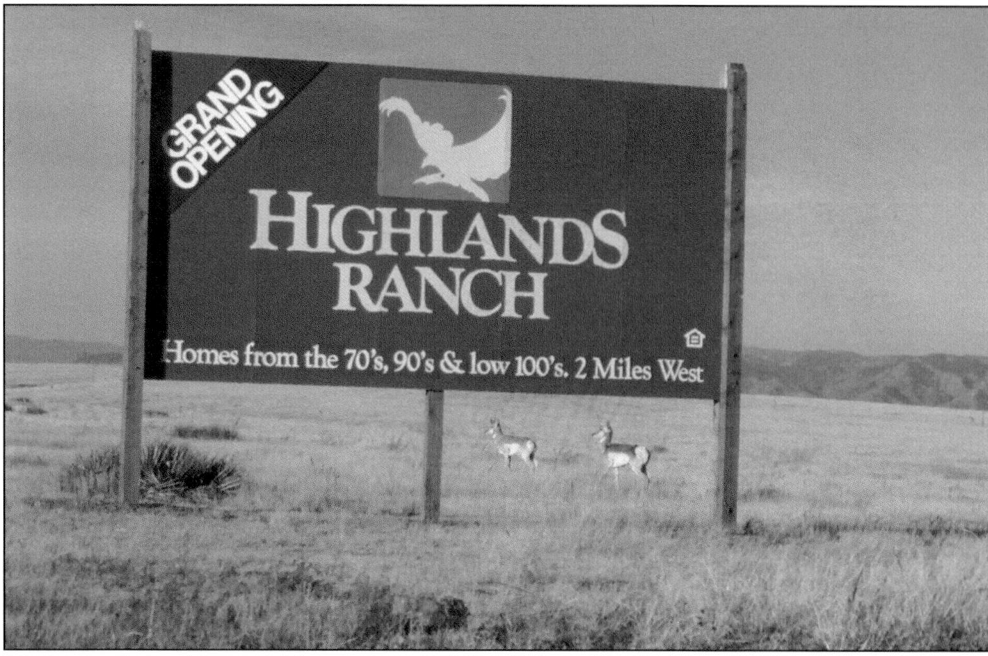

The 1980s brought many changes to Highlands Ranch. As the community developed, the antelope that called Highlands Ranch home needed to find a new home. Many moved out to the east of Highlands Ranch and then farther out into the plains. (Courtesy of Highlands Ranch Metro District.)

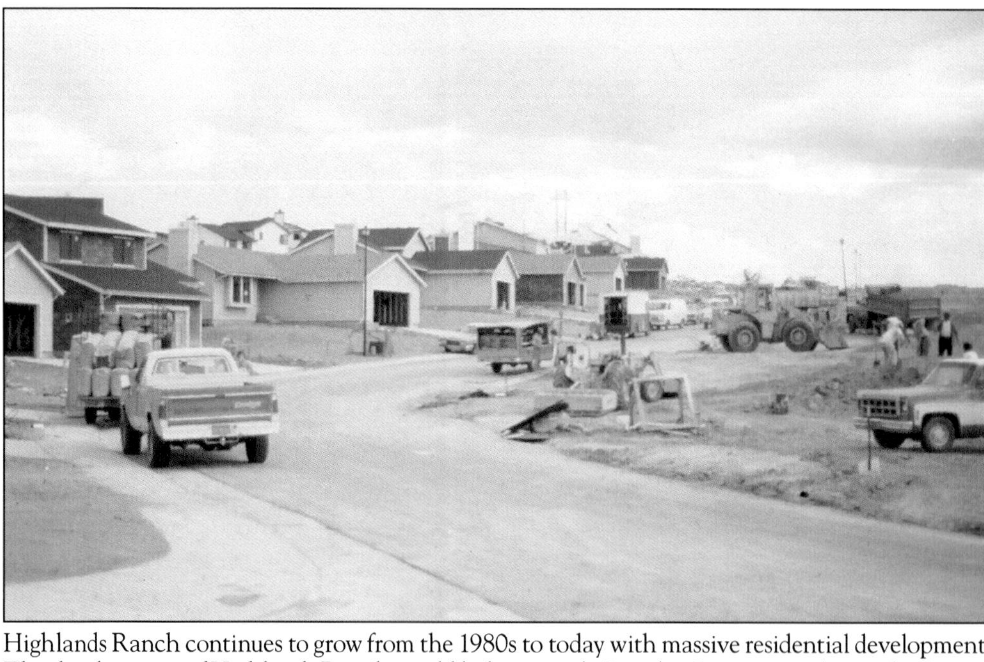

Highlands Ranch continues to grow from the 1980s to today with massive residential development. The development of Highlands Ranch would help catapult Douglas County into being the fastest-growing county in the entire nation. Home development went quickly, thanks to multiple builders all developing different areas of Highlands Ranch at the same time. (Courtesy of Highlands Ranch Metro District.)

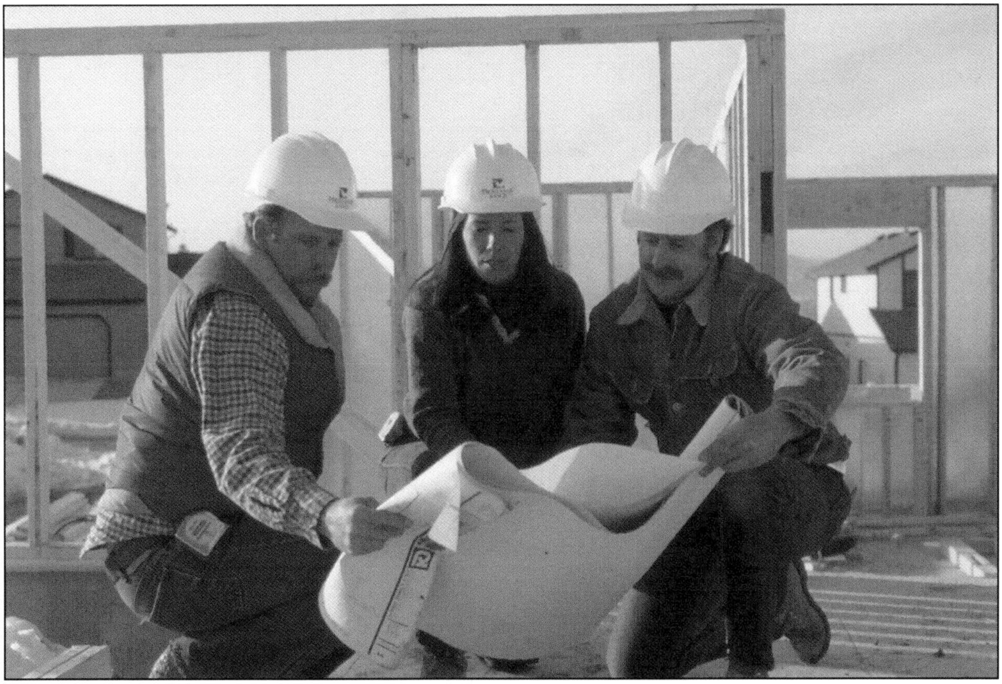

The development of Highlands Ranch brought many construction jobs to the area as homes were continually being built. (Courtesy of Highlands Ranch Metro District.)

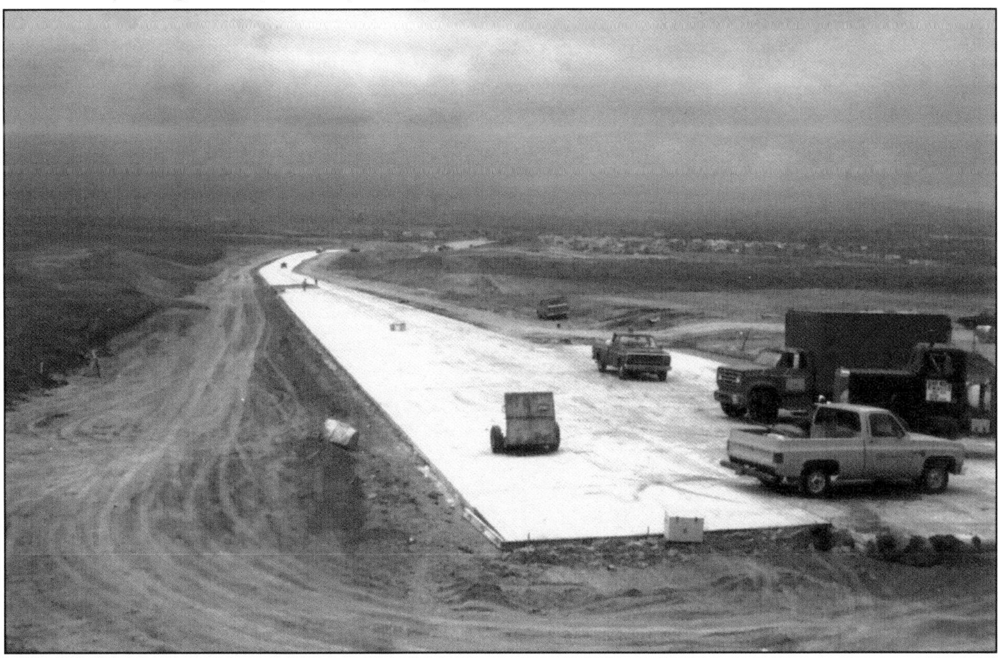

An early decision was made when developing Highlands Ranch that the main roadways should be built out well before many of the homes. While this required more up-front investment, it allowed the roads to be in place and usable when the early residents moved in. The roads also provided a vision in concrete of the planned future growth. (Courtesy of Highlands Ranch Metro District.)

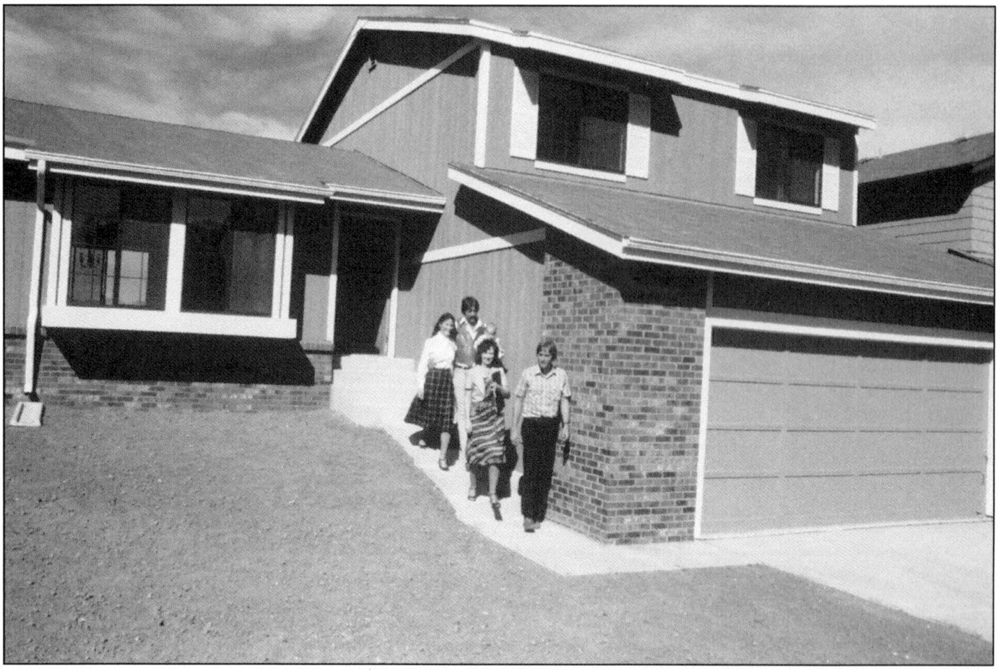

One sign of the community coming to life is the early home-buyers looking for a place to live. Typically, many homes were originally shown and sold before the landscaping was completed, leaving that as one of the early requirements for the homeowner to complete. (Courtesy of Highlands Ranch Metro District.)

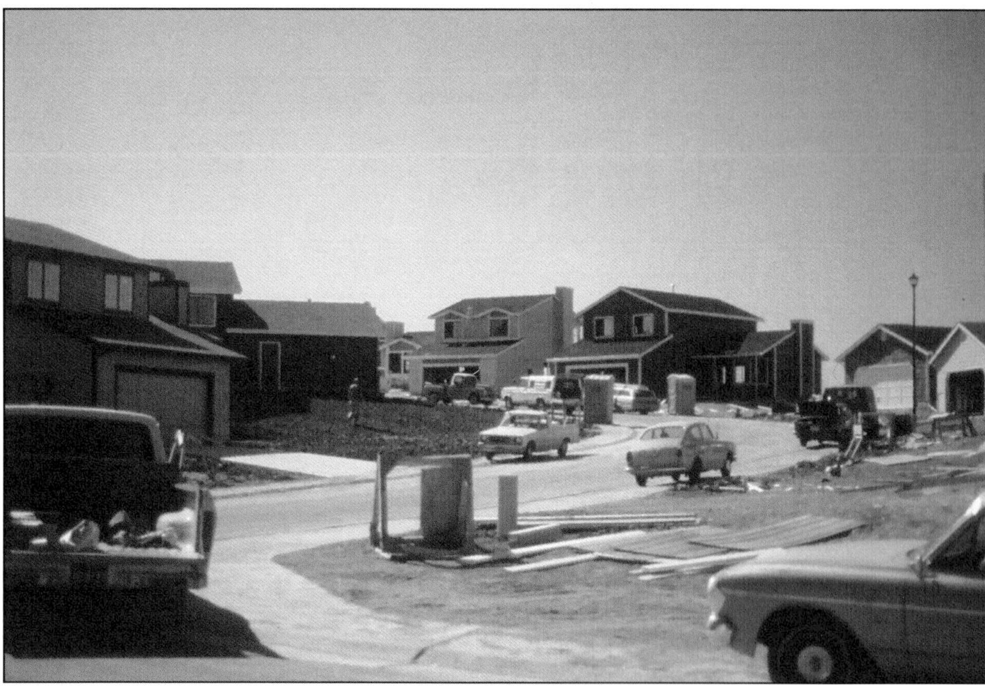

Construction activity around Highlands Ranch was a near constant for years as the homes were constructed. (Courtesy of Highlands Ranch Metro District.)

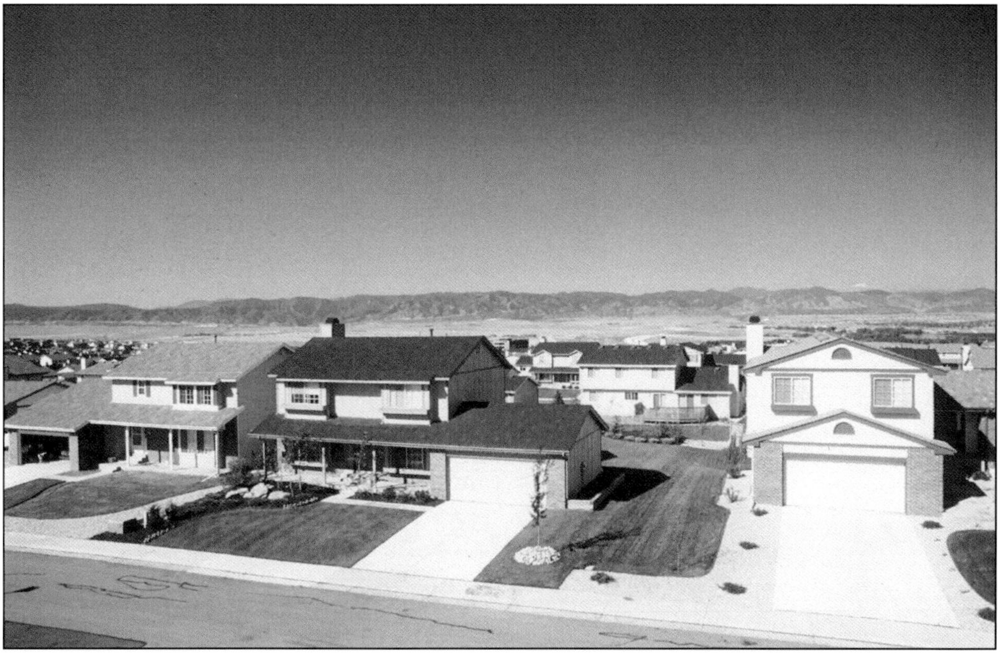

Soon, a community was completed, and life evolved into the quiet of suburbia. Houses with their newly landscaped yards are shown here in a typical new neighborhood. Several years are needed for the trees to start maturing and take their true place in the landscape. (Courtesy of Highlands Ranch Metro District.)

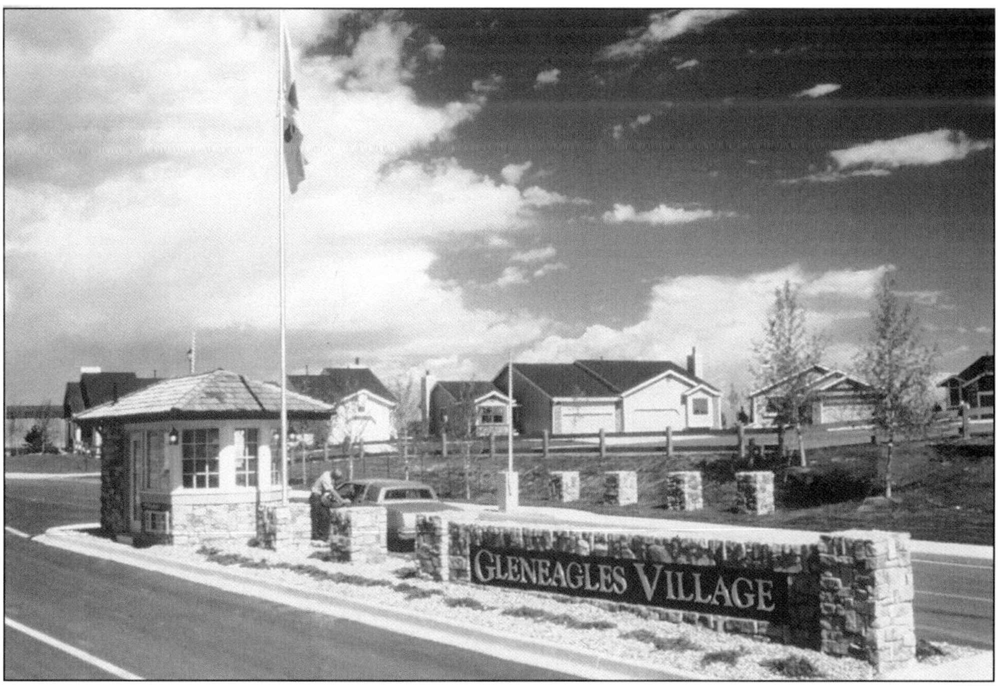

Gleneagles Village is located on the east side of Highlands Ranch near the historic Welte Cheese Ranch. The homes at Gleneagles Village are mostly surrounded by the Links at Highlands Ranch Golf Course. (Courtesy of Highlands Ranch Metro District.)

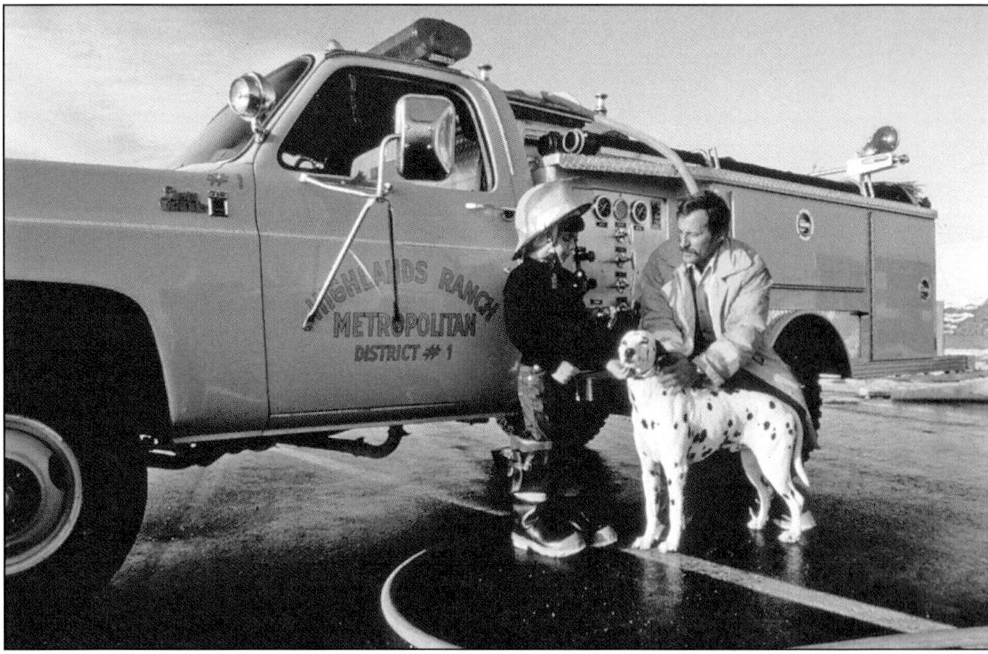

Right from the start, Highlands Ranch needed basic fire services. The first fire truck is an important symbol that draws kids and spotted dogs. This first fire truck was primarily focused on fighting a possible wildfire. However, the first time it was called upon, the responders found that the water had frozen up in the fire truck. (Courtesy of Highlands Ranch Metro District.)

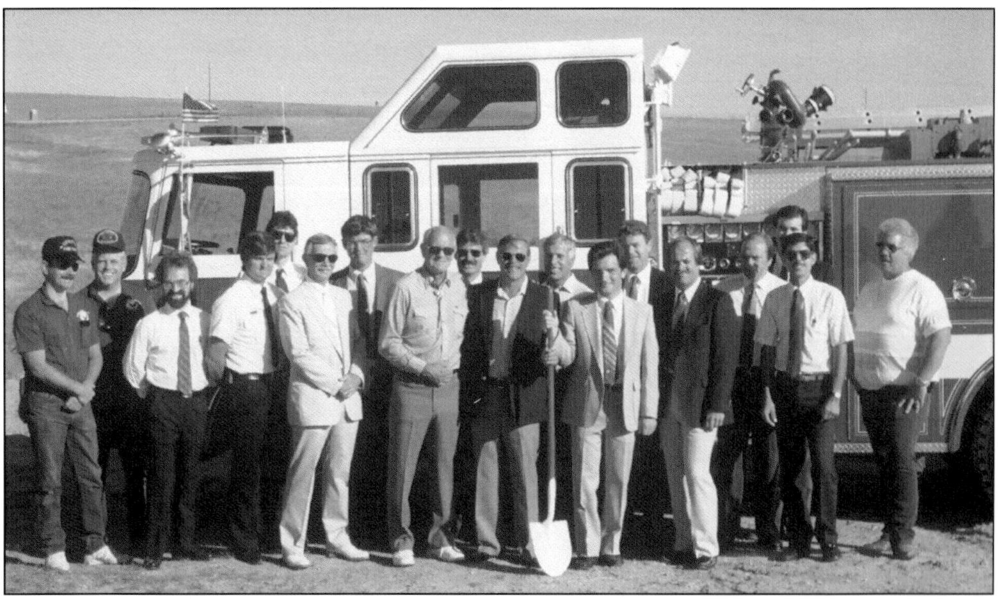

Highlands Ranch Metro District determined it needed to work with a larger fire district to provide the services that the residents on the new and growing suburb were going to need. Metro district signed an agreement with the Littleton Fire Department to provide those services. Here, members of Highlands Ranch Metro District and Littleton Fire Department perform the groundbreaking ceremony for Station No. 17, which is still in use today. (Courtesy of Highlands Ranch Metro District.)

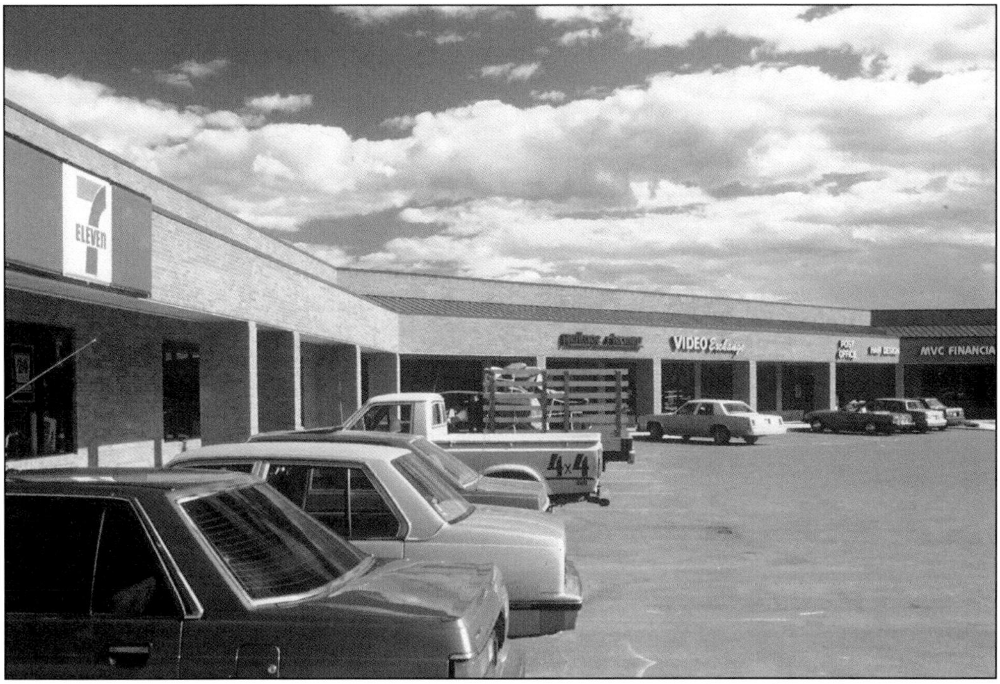

A small and growing community needed a convenience store for the early residents to get the essentials. The shopping center located at South Broadway and West Springer Drive provided the location for the early shops. (Courtesy of Highlands Ranch Metro District.)

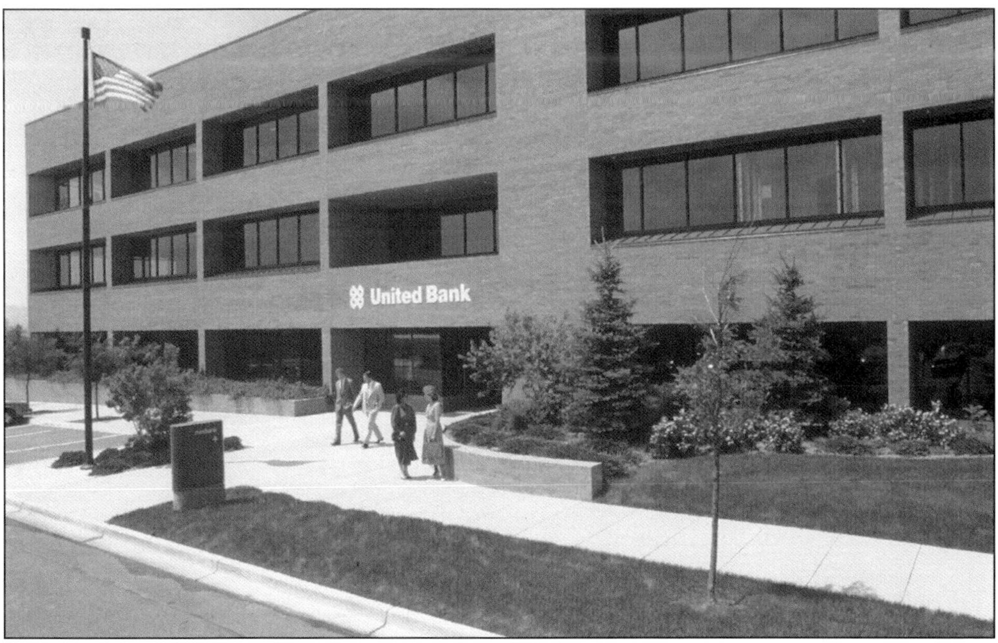

Banking is also important to a community, and the first large bank in Highlands Ranch was the United Bank. Today, the building is a Wells Fargo Bank. (Courtesy of Highlands Ranch Metro District.)

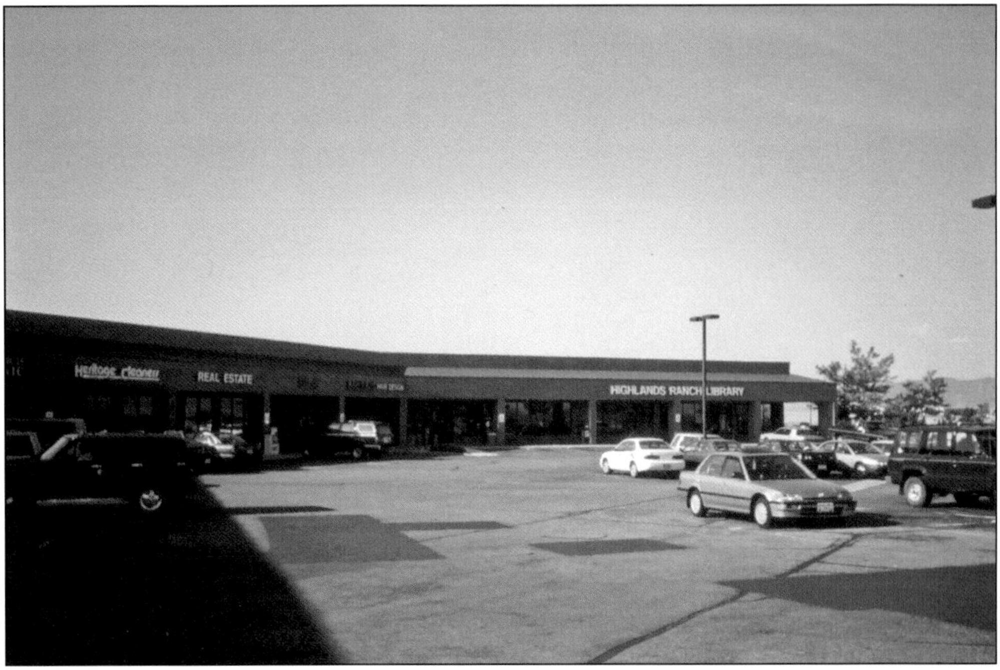

The community also needed a library, so the Douglas County Libraries placed the first Highlands Ranch Library at the end of the first strip mall in Highlands Ranch. This library served the community well. (Courtesy of Highlands Ranch Metro District.)

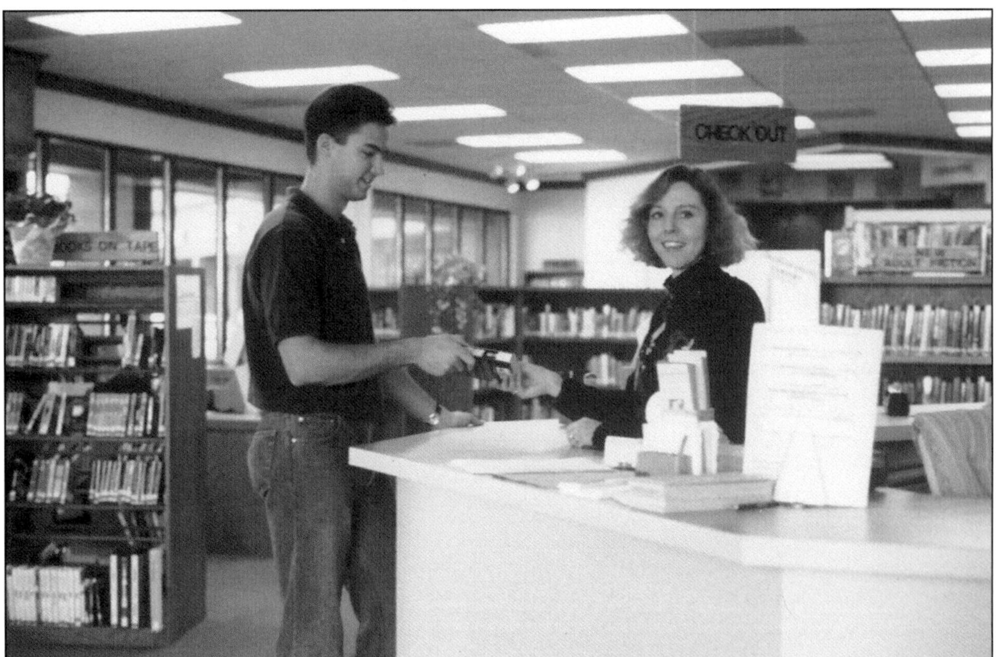

Andriette Pieron, seen here helping a guest, was a librarian at the Highlands Ranch Library. The library provided easy access to many books for the residents of Highlands Ranch. (Courtesy of Highlands Ranch Metro District.)

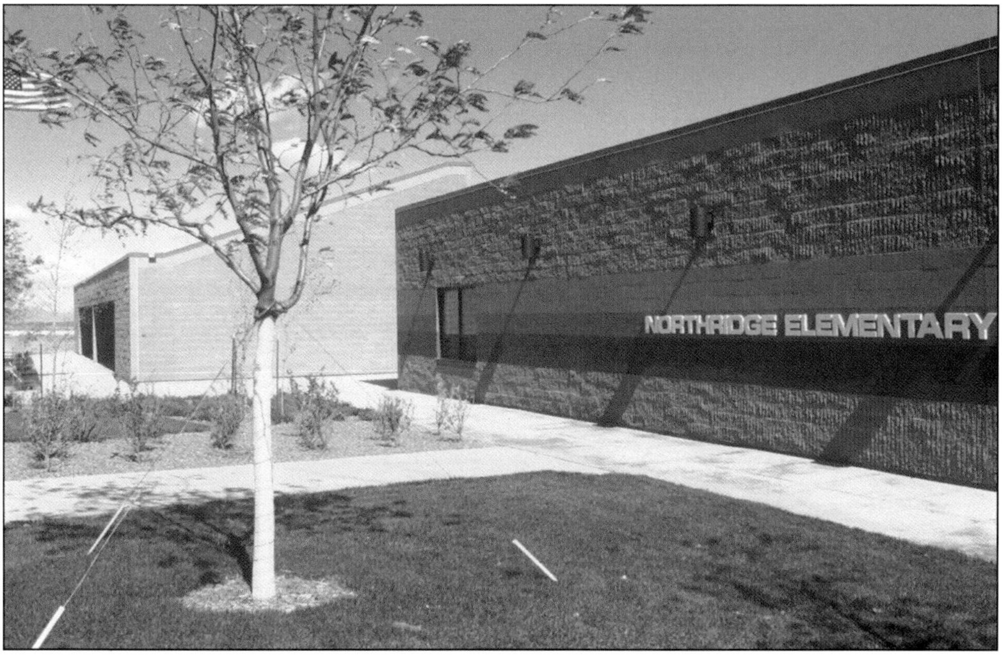

Schools were also essential to ensuring the growth of the community. Every parent feels it is very important to raise and educate his or her kids in good schools, and most prefer local schools to long commutes in the morning and afternoon. Northridge Elementary was the first elementary school in Highlands Ranch. (Courtesy of Highlands Ranch Metro District.)

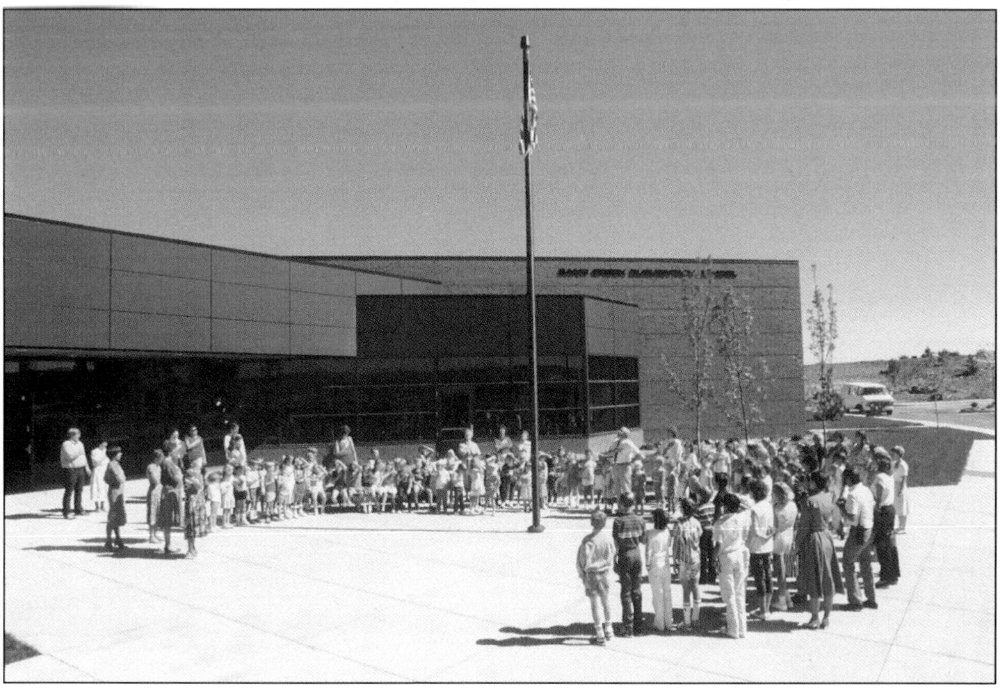

With the growth of Highlands Ranch, the number of elementary schools also continued to grow. Students at Sand Creek Elementary are seen here saying the Pledge of Allegiance around the flag in front of the school. (Courtesy of Highlands Ranch Metro District.)

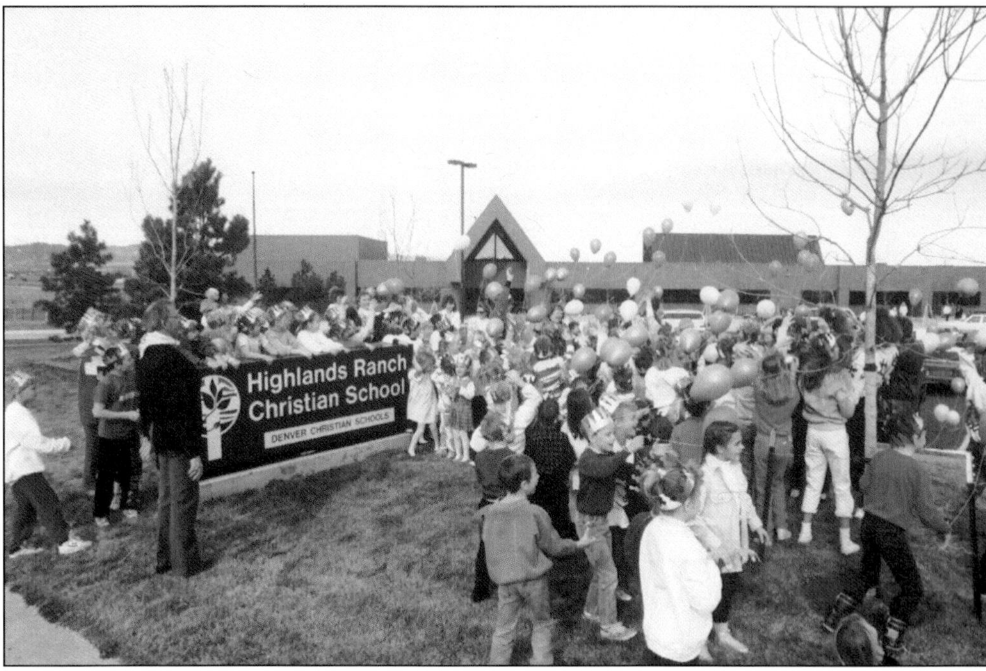

Some parents of Highlands Ranch also opted to send their children to private schools, like the Highlands Ranch Christian School. (Courtesy of Highlands Ranch Metro District.)

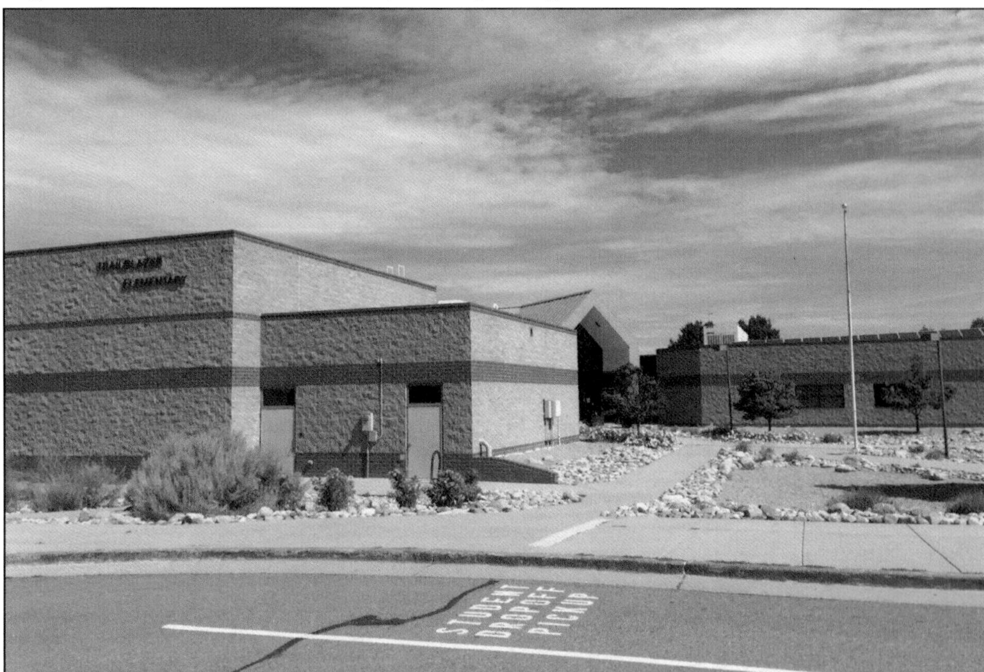

By the late 1990s, many schools, like Trailblazer Elementary, were being built with a common floor plan so that the same or similar plans could be used for other schools. The common floor plan also allowed for easier design of upgrades. In 2015, there were 15 traditional elementary schools serving Highlands Ranch.

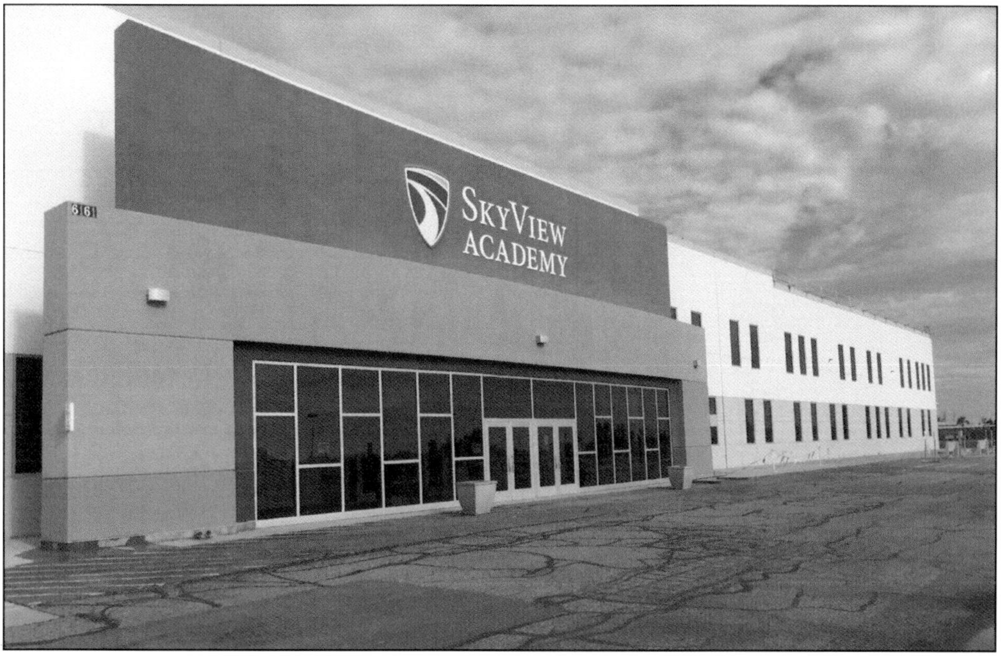

The 2000s brought a new concept in public schools with the introduction of charter schools. Charter schools incorporate some of the uniqueness and involvement of private schools but are still available to the general public. In 2015, Highlands Ranch had four charter schools; one of the four, Sky View Academy, is seen here.

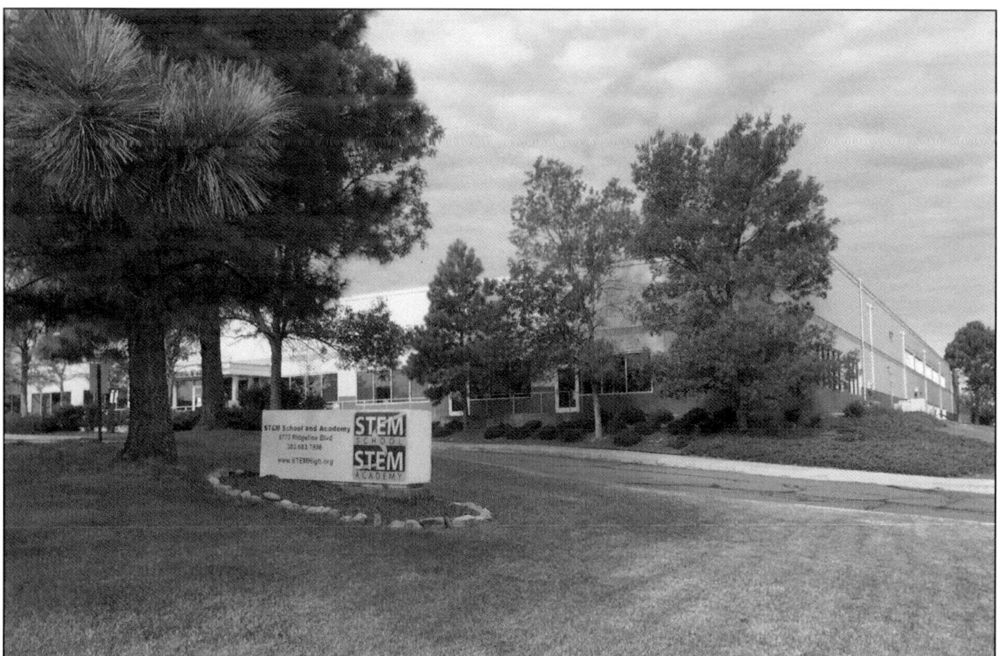

Another charter school serving upper elementary through high school was the STEM School. STEM focuses on educating students who are interested in science, technology, engineering, and math.

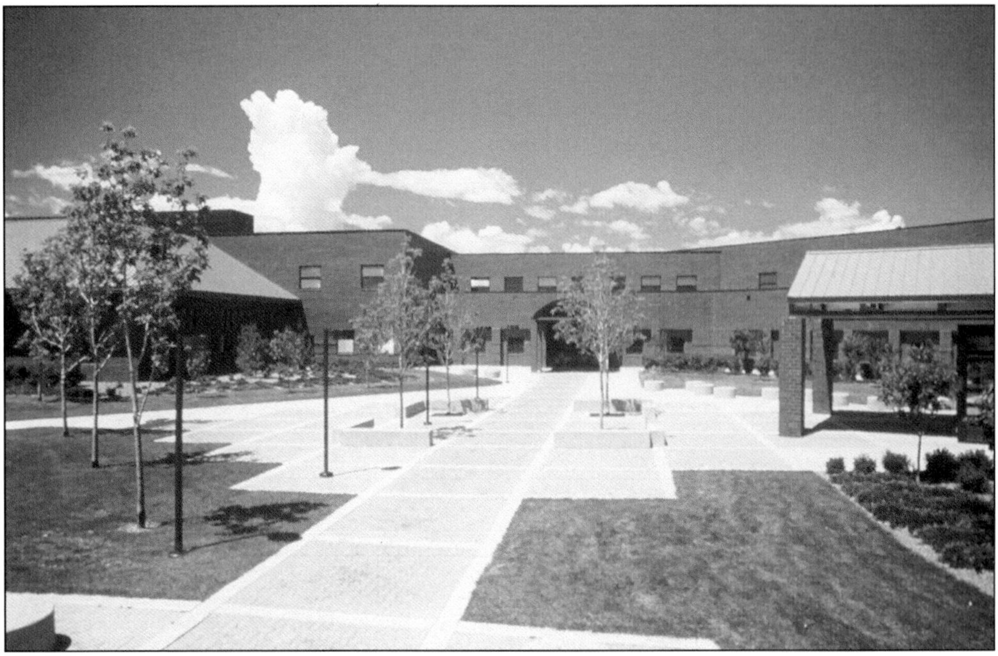

The first public high school in Highlands Ranch was Highlands Ranch High School in 1987. The high school serves ninth- through twelfth-grade students while the accompanying Cresthill Middle School serves seventh and eighth graders. (Courtesy of Highlands Ranch Metro District.)

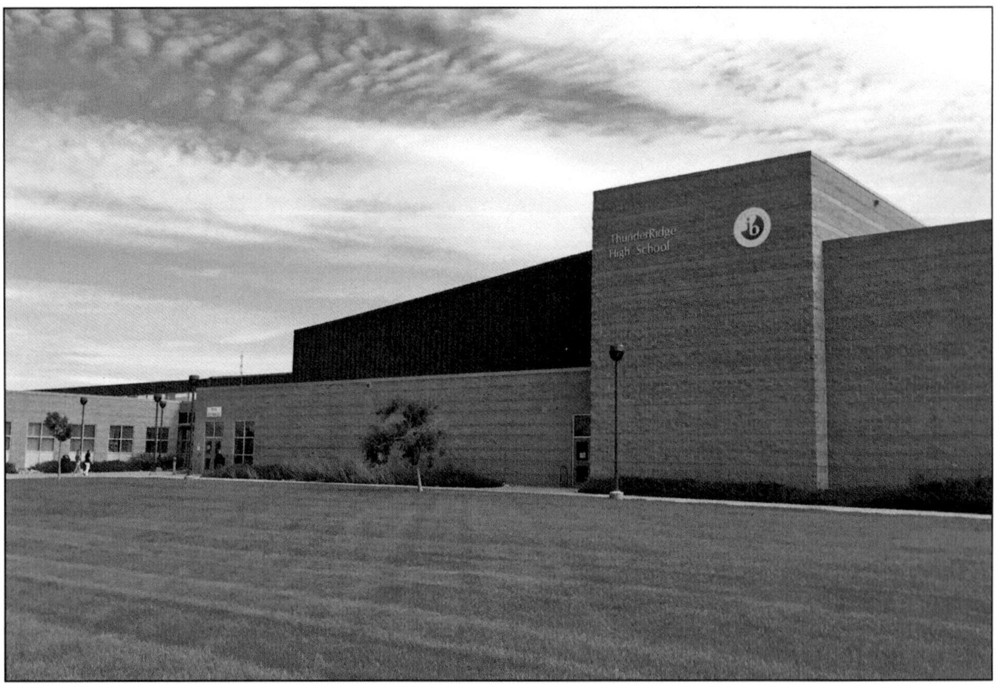

The second public high school in Highlands Ranch was Thunder Ridge High School in 1996. The high school serves the west side of Highlands Ranch, including five surrounding elementary schools and one from Roxborough. The Ranch View Middle School is also located just to the southeast.

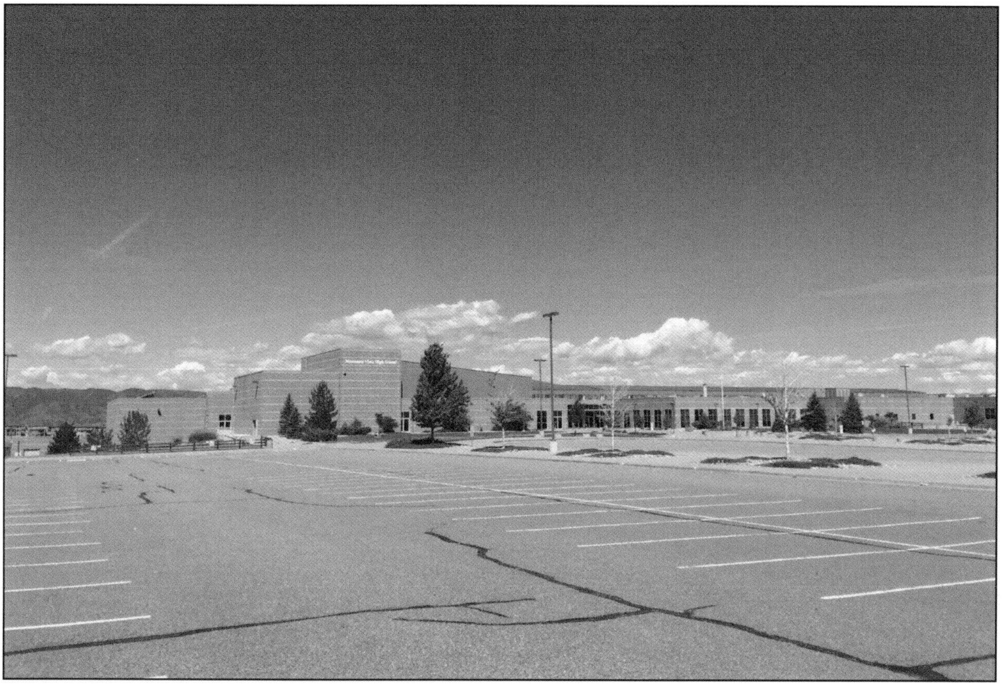

In 2001, continued growth brought about the addition of a third high school called Mountain Vista High School. The size of the school pictured here was common of all the high schools in Highlands Ranch. Mountain Ridge Middle School is located to the east of the high school.

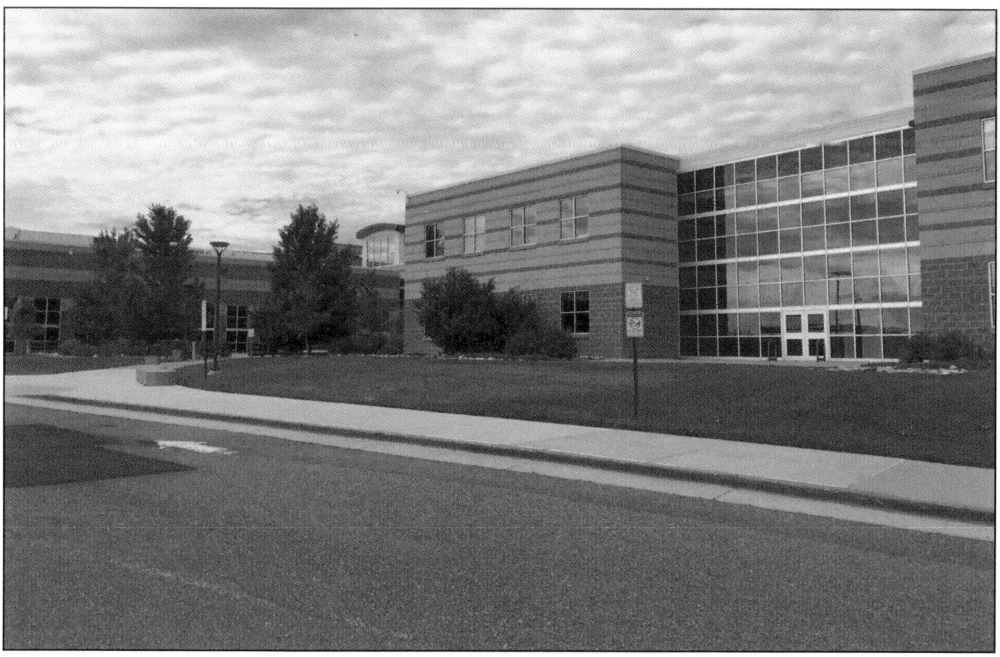

A fourth high school, Rock Canyon High School, was added in 2003. Rock Canyon High School serves some of Highlands Ranch, but many of the students come from Castle Pines and communities to the immediate east. Rocky Heights Middle School is situated directly to the south of the high school.

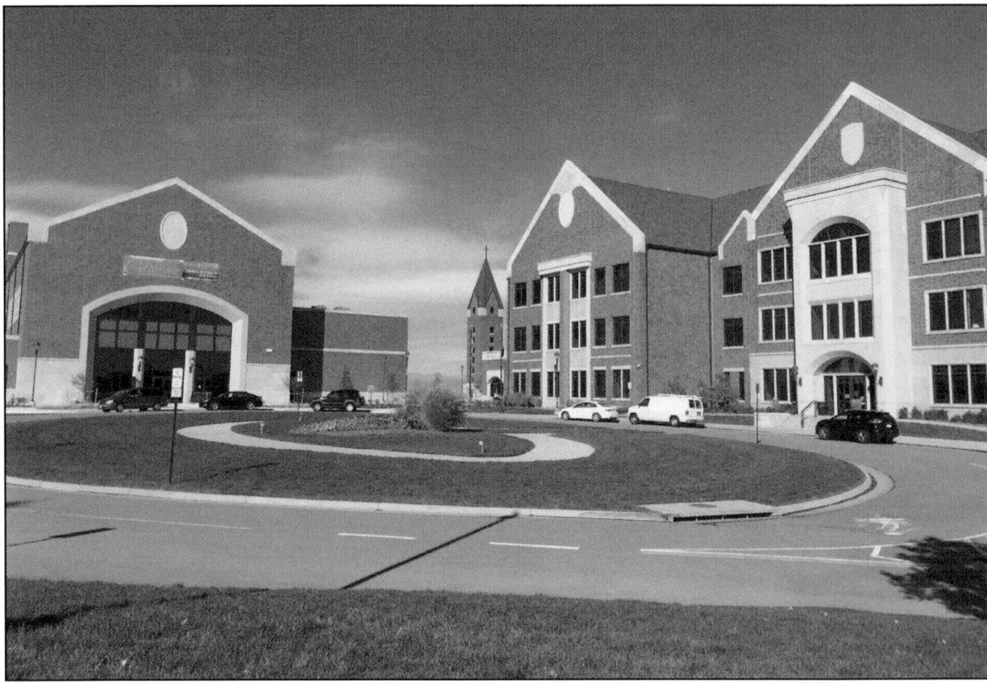

In 2007, the private Valor Christian High School opened in the center of Highlands Ranch. The school quickly gained a reputation for high-quality education and state champion-level sports teams.

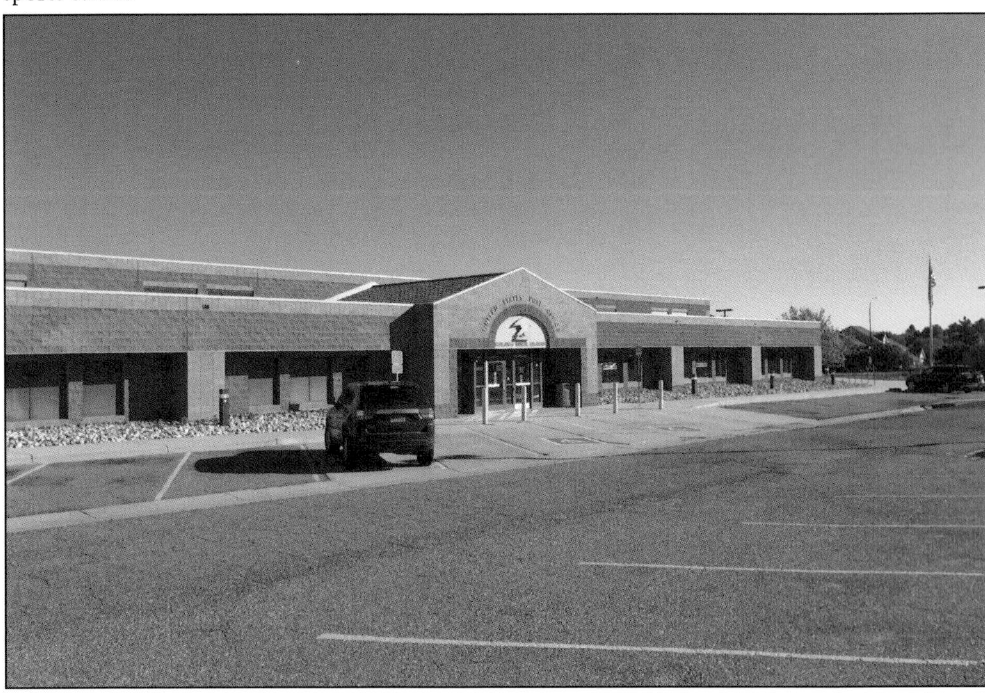

Another key development was the addition of a major post office on the east side of Highlands Ranch in 1992. With a large post office, Highlands Ranch, which has yet to become a city, became a mailing address. Residents could now put Highlands Ranch instead of Littleton on their mail.

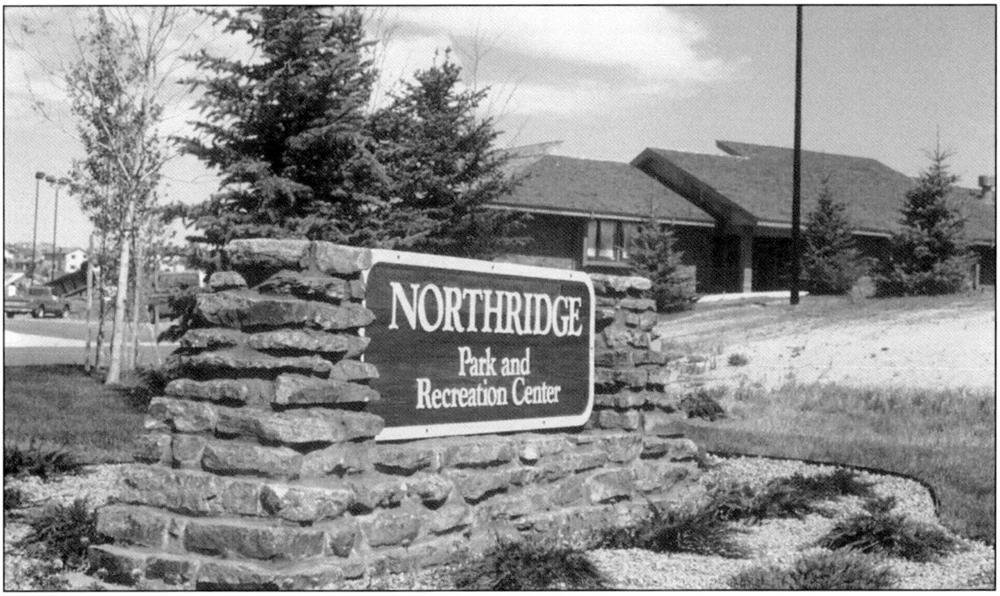

A new important feature of the community was the creation of a strong Highlands Ranch Community Association. The community association focuses on improving the lives of those who live in Highlands Ranch. The recreation center has continued to be improved, and today, it serves as one of four recreation centers, with the others being Eastridge, Westridge, and Southridge. The four recreation centers combined have over 329,000 square feet of facilities. (Courtesy of Highlands Ranch Metro District.)

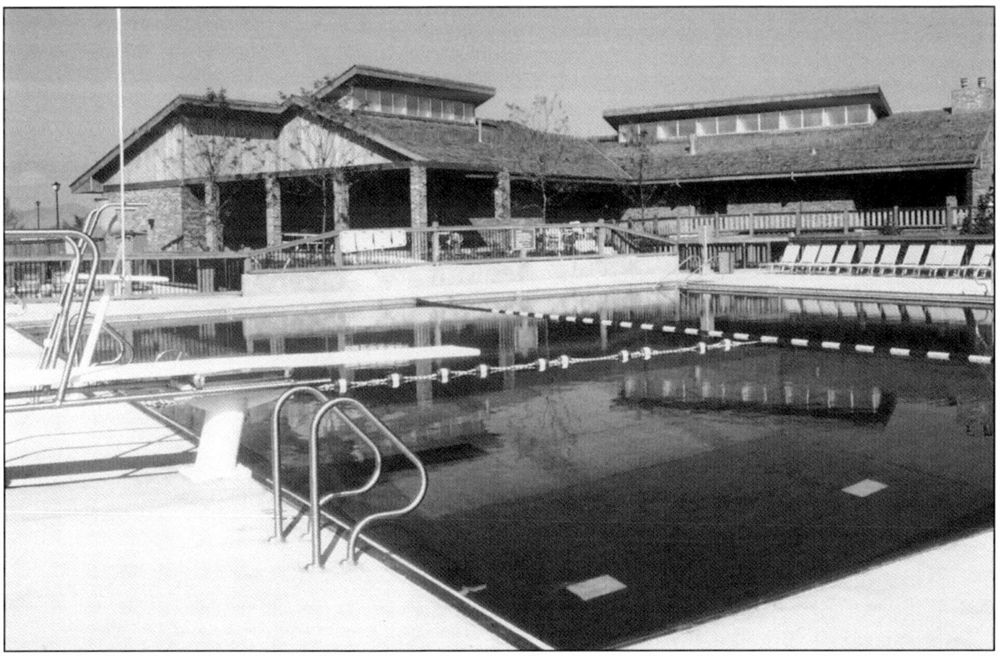

Northridge recreation center offered pools that would become central features in all four recreation centers. The pools are a great way to socialize with friends, family, and the community. The easy access to pools has also allowed Highlands Ranch to maintain competitive swim teams. (Courtesy of Highlands Ranch Metro District.)

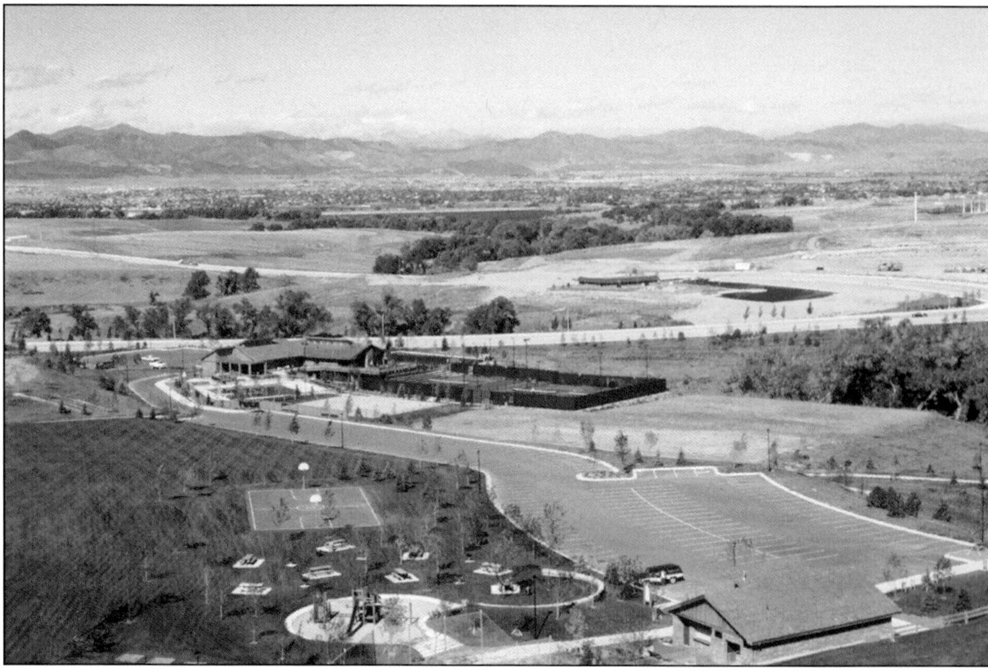

In this photograph, one can see the original Northridge Recreation Center and Northridge Park. When Northridge was built in 1982, like many places in Highlands Ranch, most of the trees were still small and needed time to grow. (Courtesy of Highlands Ranch Metro District.)

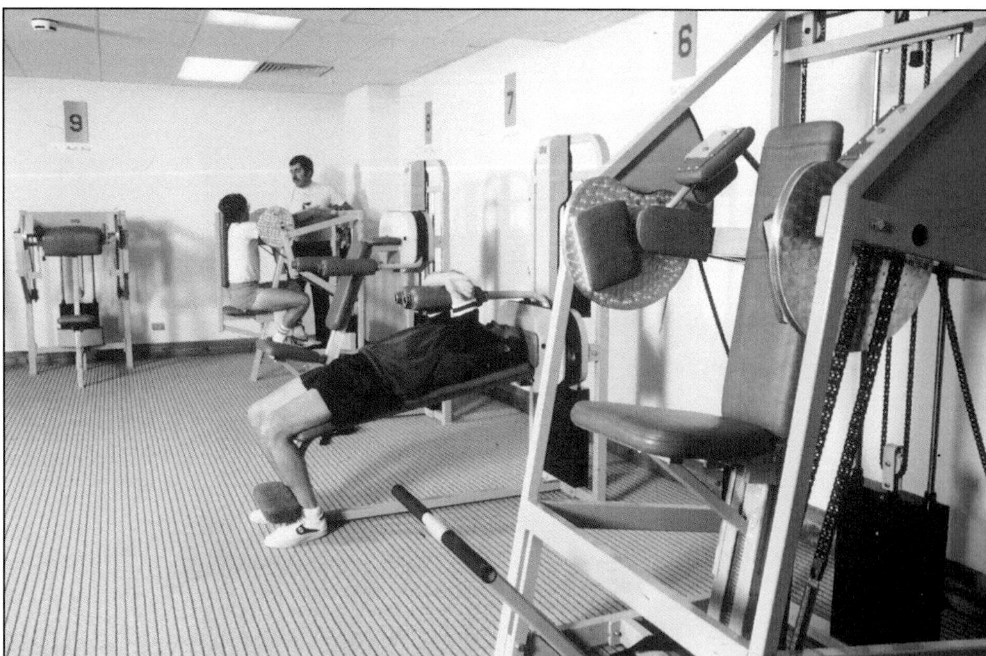

Staying fit and active are important to the people of Highlands Ranch as well as many in Colorado. All four of the recreation centers have state-of-the-art exercise equipment. (Courtesy of Highlands Ranch Metro District.)

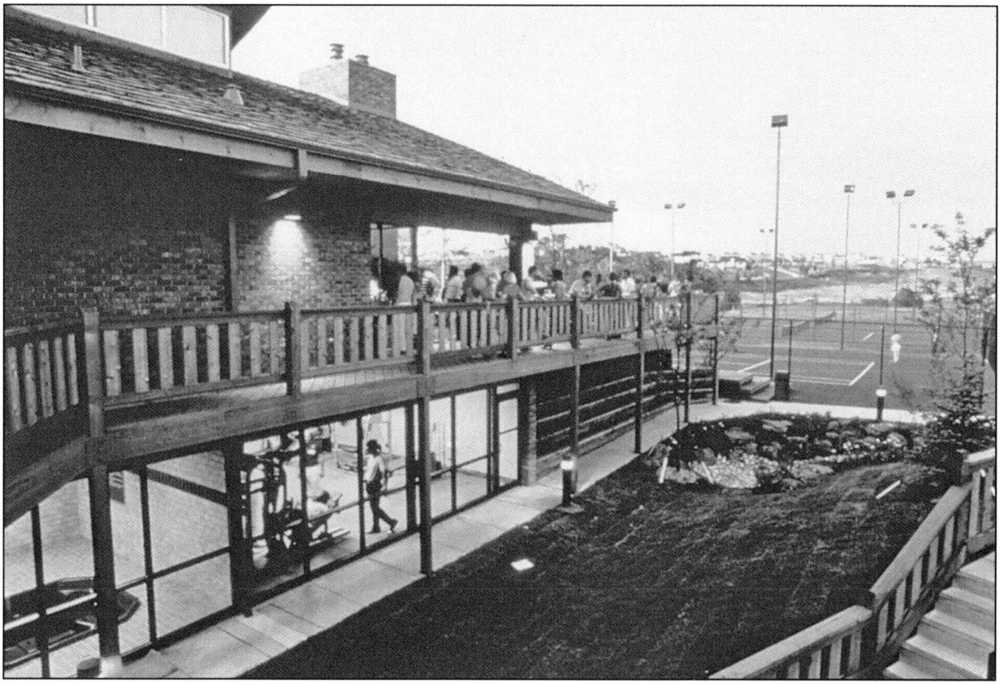

Northridge Recreation Center served not only as a recreation center, but also as an early community gathering location. This photograph shows many of the tennis courts and workout facilities. (Courtesy of Highlands Ranch Metro District.)

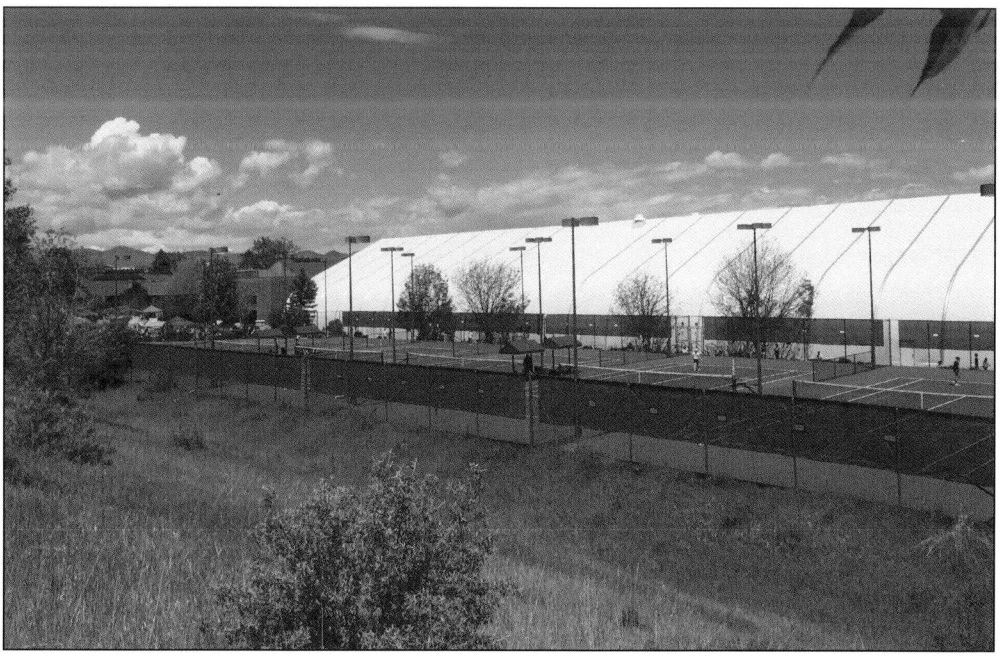

Northridge Recreation Center continued to grow, and today, it offers the addition of tennis courts in a year-round dome. Northridge also continues to have pools, a diving well, workout facilities, basketball, racquetball courts, a running track, saunas, and more. In 2015, Northridge hosted a national racquetball tournament.

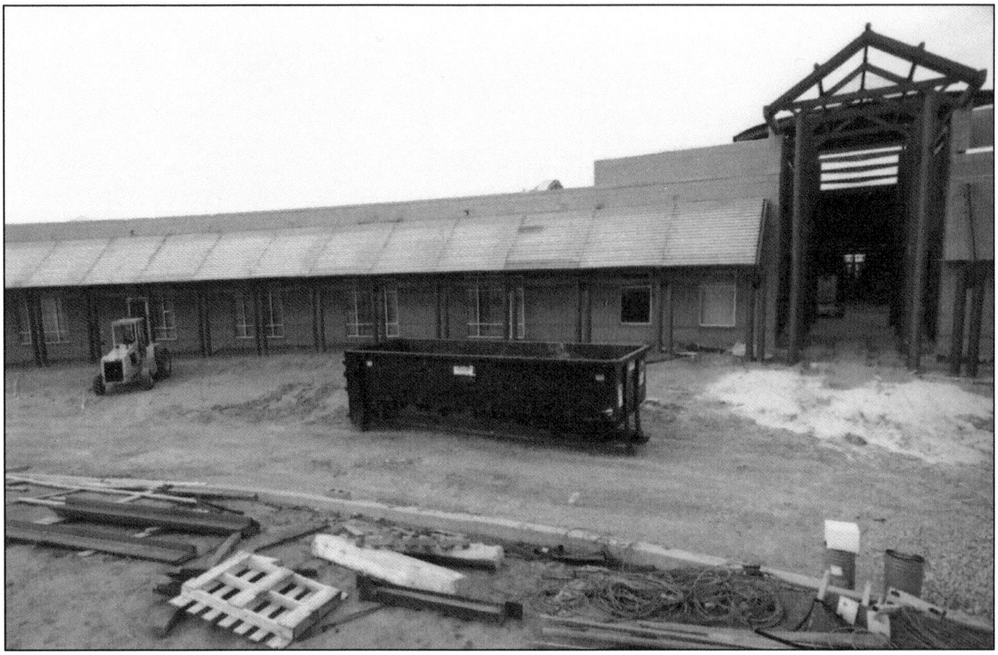

As the community grew, so did the need for recreation centers. The second recreation center was Eastridge, built in 1997. This facility was designed with an easy pull-up and drop-off area, and parking was moved around to the back of the facility. (Courtesy of Highlands Ranch Metro District.)

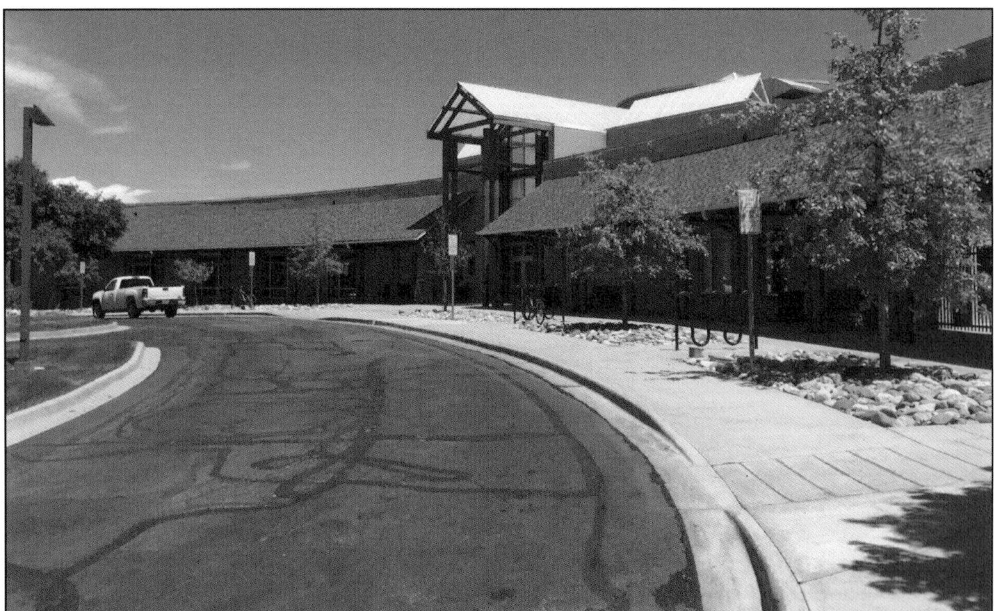

Upon completion of the Eastridge Recreation Center in 1998, many of the offices of the Highlands Ranch Community Association were moved into the facility. This facility has pools, basketball courts, a track, workout facilities, a dance studio, a rock climbing wall, meeting rooms, a whole wing for preschool, and outdoor sand volleyball courts. Eastridge also has a steam room and a hot tub for relaxing and recovering.

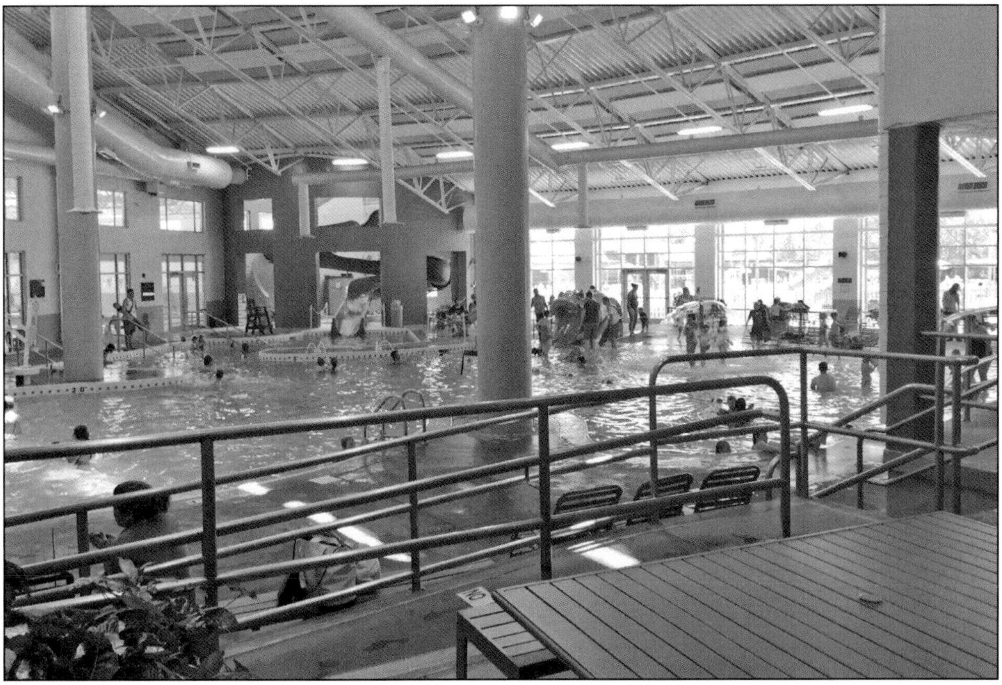

Eastridge contains the most-used kids' recreation pool. Many refer to it as "the frog pool" due to the kids' frog slide. The water depth ranges from zero to three feet, making it good for most kids. There is also a large water slide for the older kids.

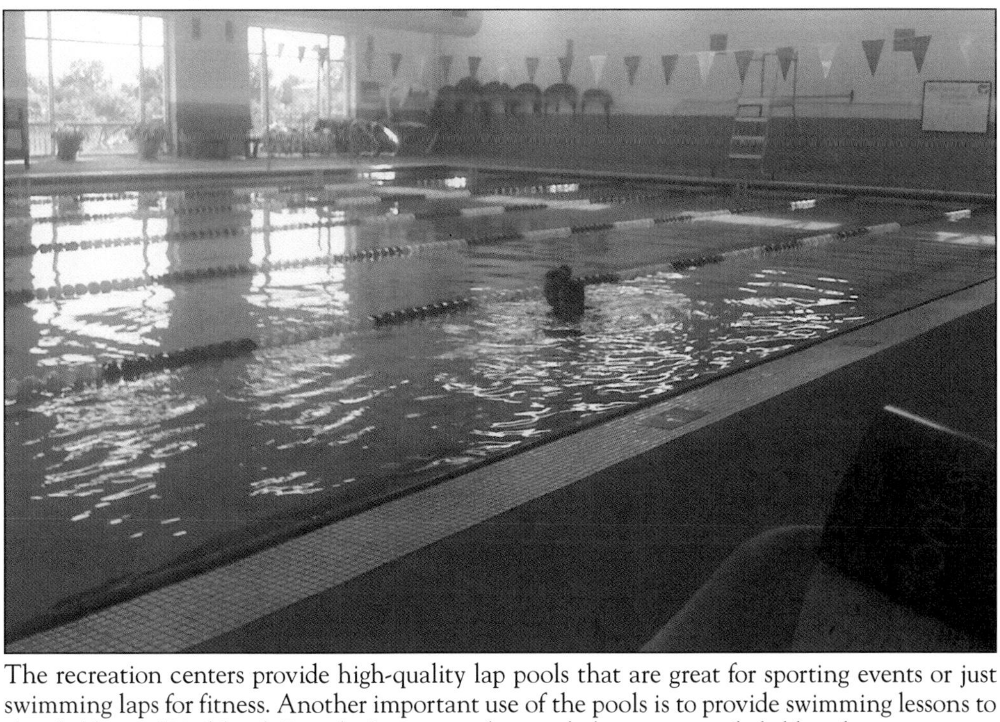

The recreation centers provide high-quality lap pools that are great for sporting events or just swimming laps for fitness. Another important use of the pools is to provide swimming lessons to the children of Highlands Ranch. Swimming lessons help parents and children learn, practice, and get comfortable with water safety.

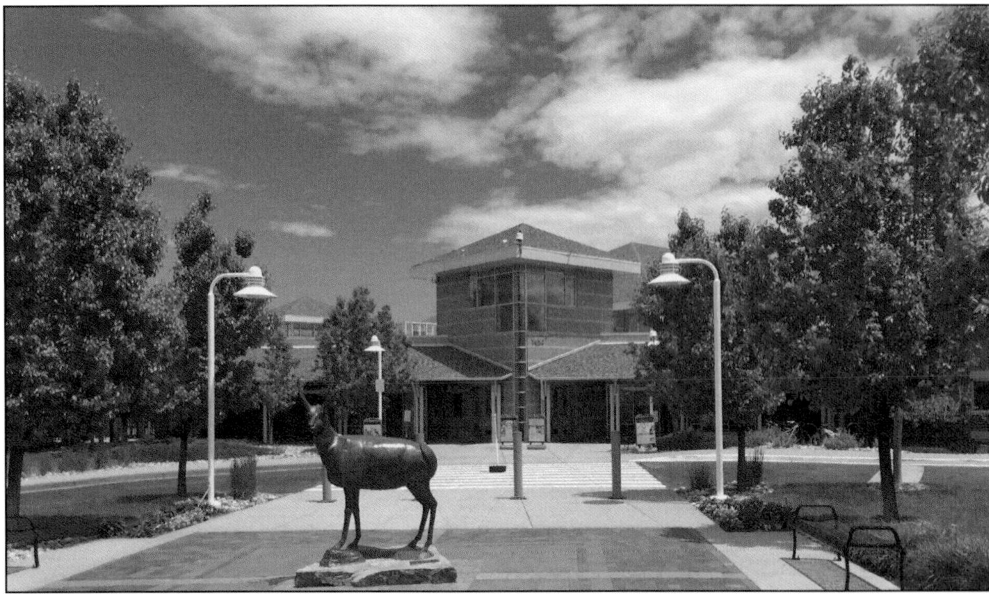

In 2001, Westridge was built to serve the residents in the western side of Highlands Ranch more conveniently. The Westridge facility includes an indoor turf field used as a multisport field for soccer, lacrosse, football, field hockey, and training camps. The Westridge facility also has a running track, a deeper lap pool (up to nine feet), hot tub, tennis courts, batting cages, a pitching structure, a bike spinning studio, and a studio for dance and martial arts. Westridge also provides a preschool wing for the local residents.

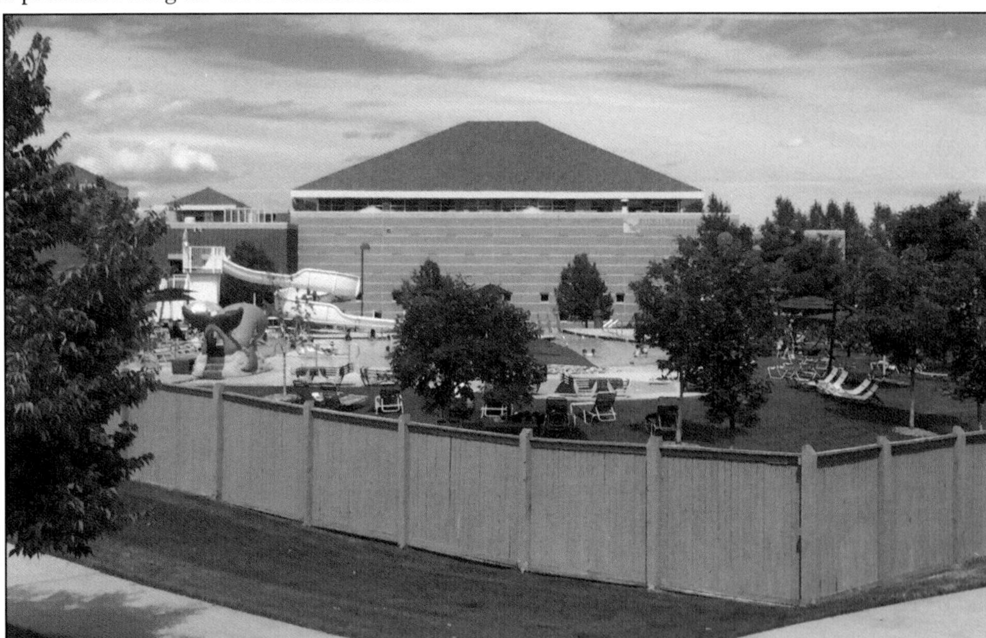

Westridge has the most popular outdoor pool for parents, which is sometimes called "the whale pool" because of the kids' whale slide. Like the Eastridge pool, the water depth is zero to three feet, and it also hosts a larger water slide for older kids. People driving by can look over and see families hanging out around the pool.

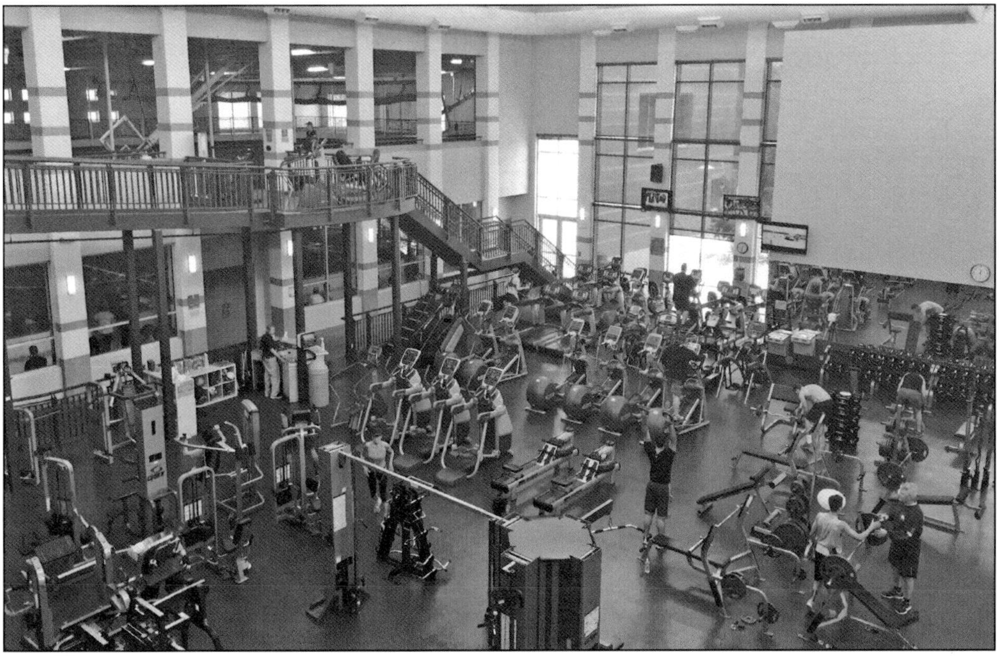

As the recreation centers grew, so did the size and openness of the workout facilities. Westridge has the most-open workout facility, located in the center of the facility with a roof over two stories above. The current workout facility is normally a combination of weights and aerobic like stationary bikes, elliptical machines, and treadmills.

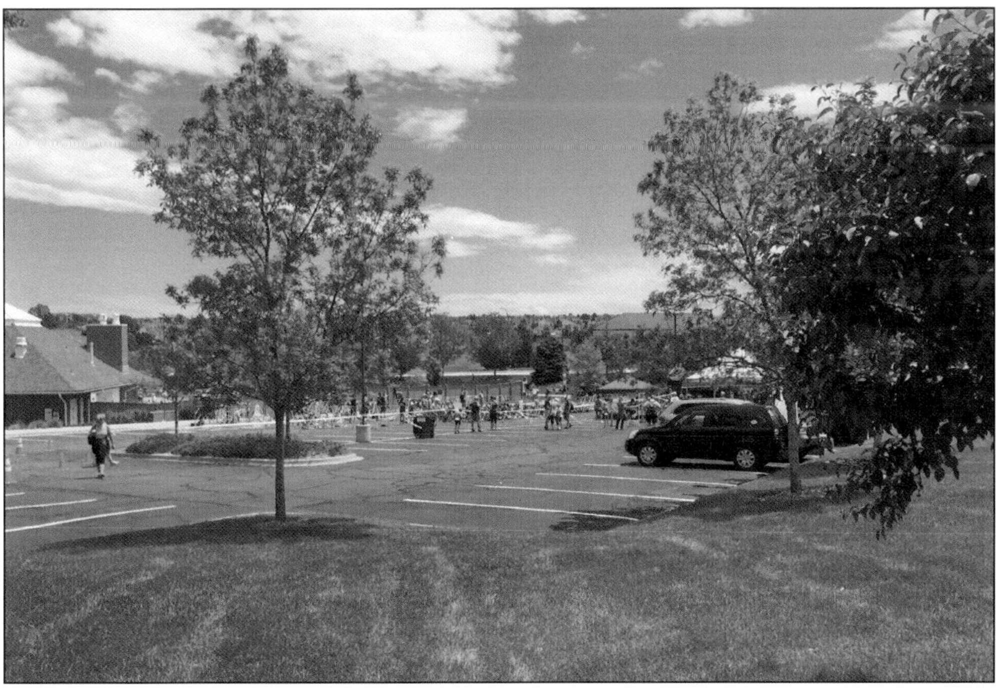

Westridge also uses its indoor and outdoor facilities along with the connected Marcy Gulch trail system to host outdoor events, like this kids' triathlon. Adult triathlons are also hosted at Westridge. (Courtesy of Highlands Ranch Metro District.)

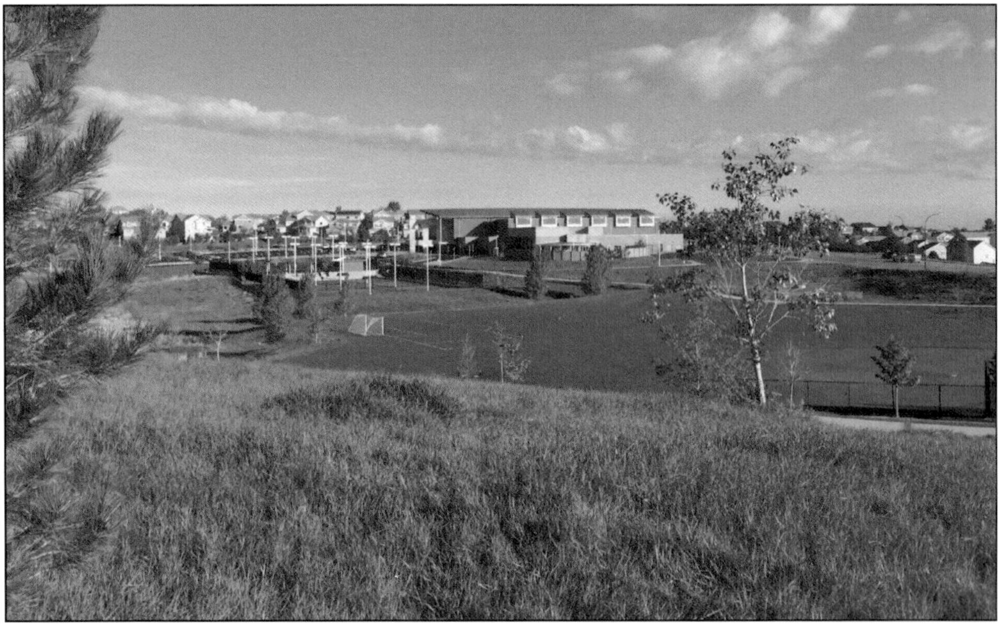

The fourth (and expected to be last) recreation center is Southridge, which opened in 2005. Southridge contains tennis courts, pools, workout facilities, a running track, multiuse indoor gym, a fitness studio, art rooms, a senior lounge (used mainly by the Highlands Ranch Senior Club), small and large meeting rooms, a pottery studio, and the Debus Wildcat Mountain Auditorium. It is the only recreation center in Highlands Ranch that has a large commercial kitchen.

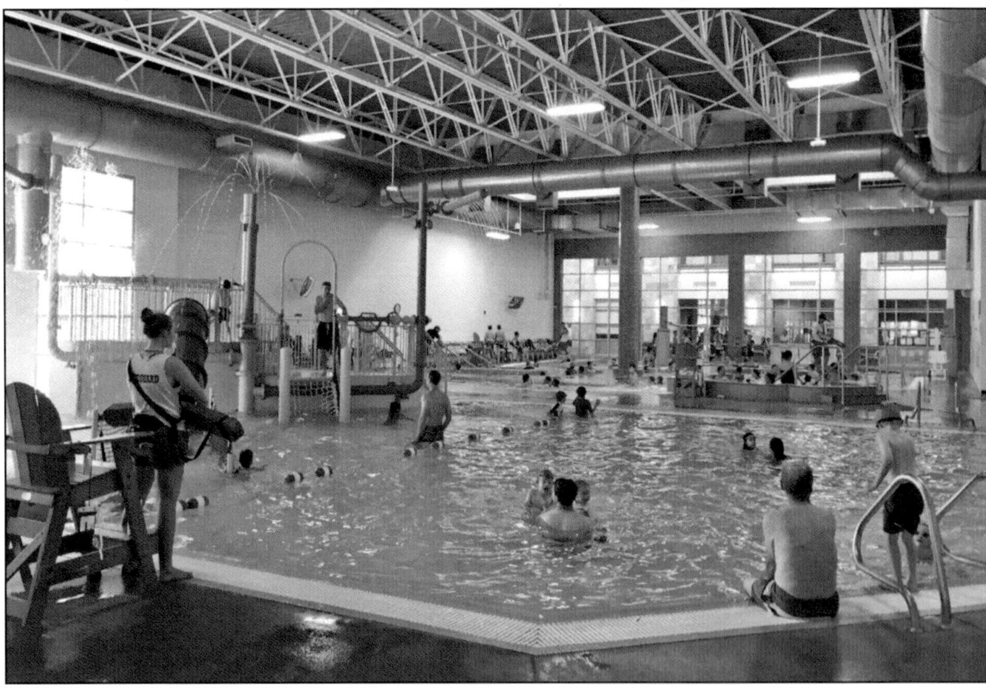

Southridge is the only recreation center that does not have a lap pool; its pools are more social pools. The indoor pools include a zero-to-three-foot-depth pool with play structures, a lazy river, a hot tub, a log cross, and a warmer therapy pool.

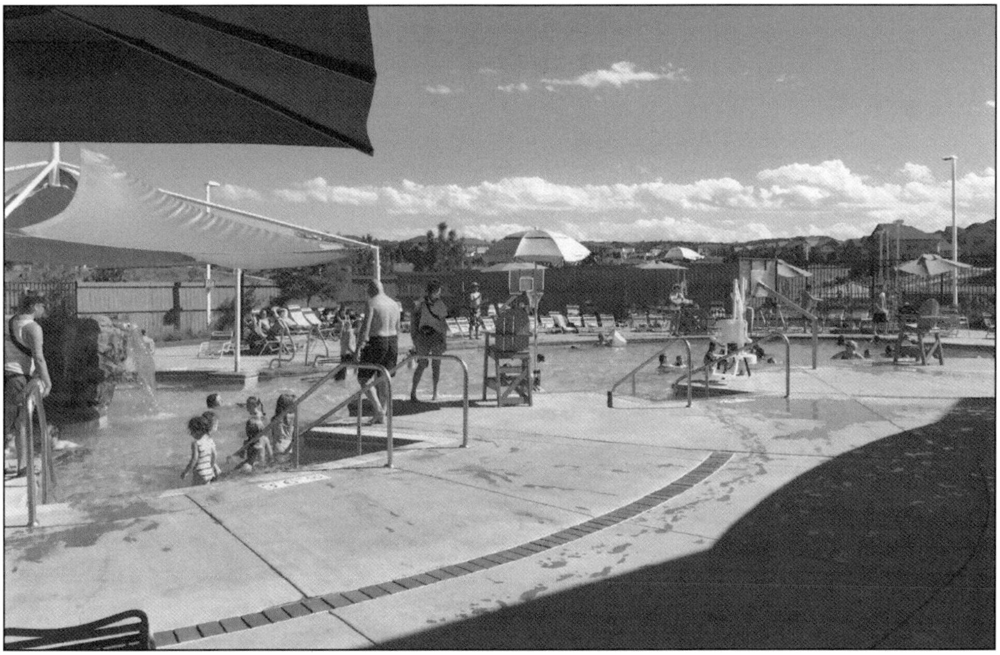

The outdoor pool at Southridge was also designed to tie into the social aspect of pool life. The irregular-shaped pool contains a rock waterfall and has basketball hoops. The pool is mostly two to three feet deep but has a deeper end that is five feet.

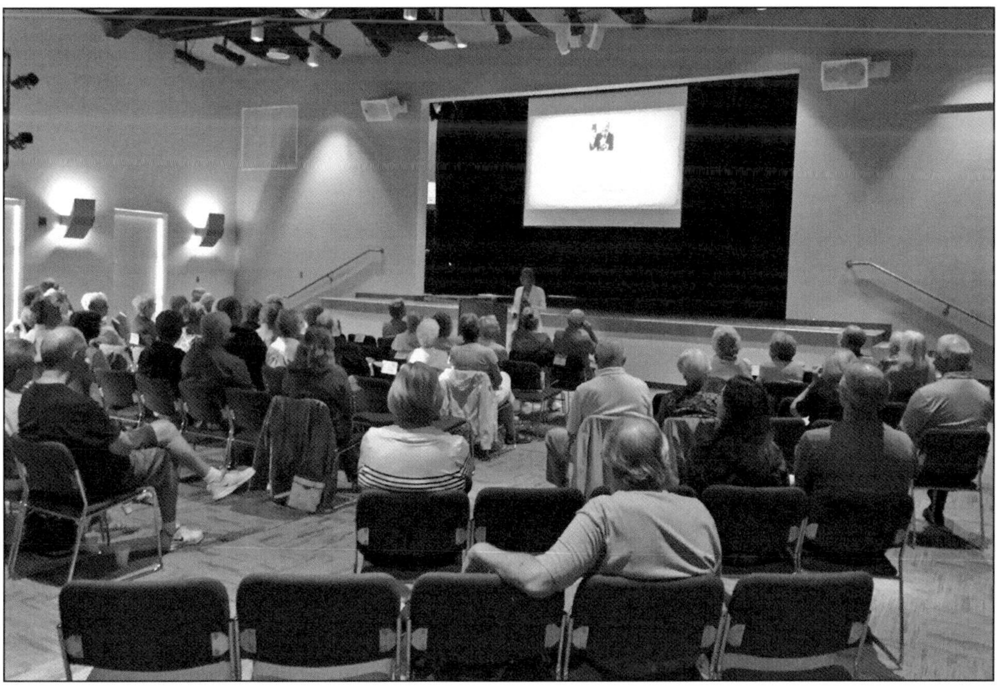

Southridge has also become the regular host site for the Highlands Ranch Historical Society (HRHS). The HRHS provides educational and entertaining programs. The society has regular meetings every third Monday to share the history of Highlands Ranch, regional history, and even national history.

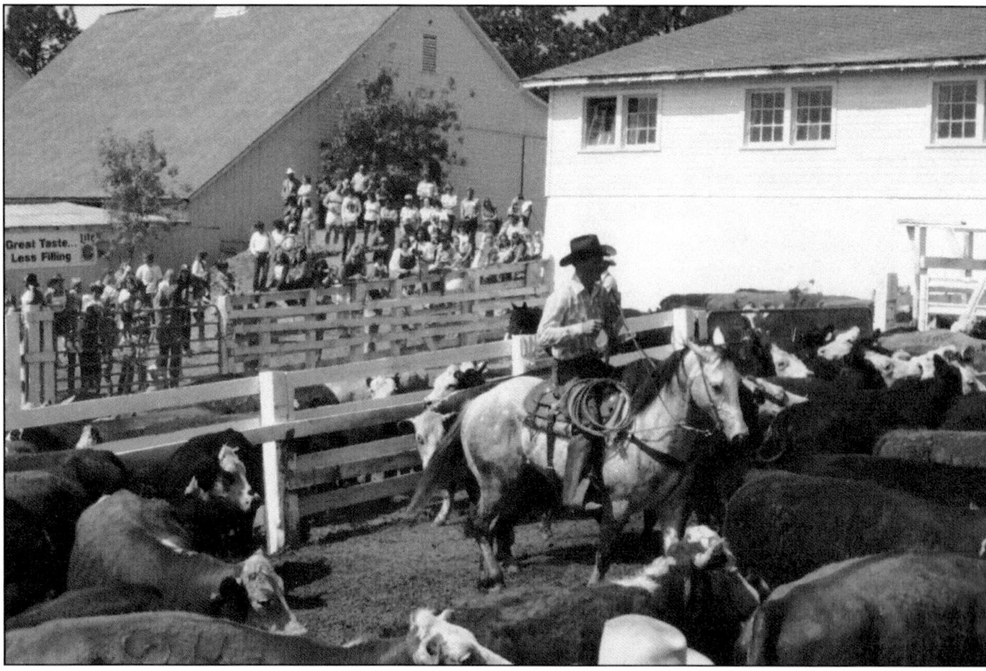

In 1984, people were also encouraged to learn more about the ranch's operations and watch the cattle handling. (Courtesy of the Douglas County History Research Center, Douglas County Libraries, 2011.008.0001.)

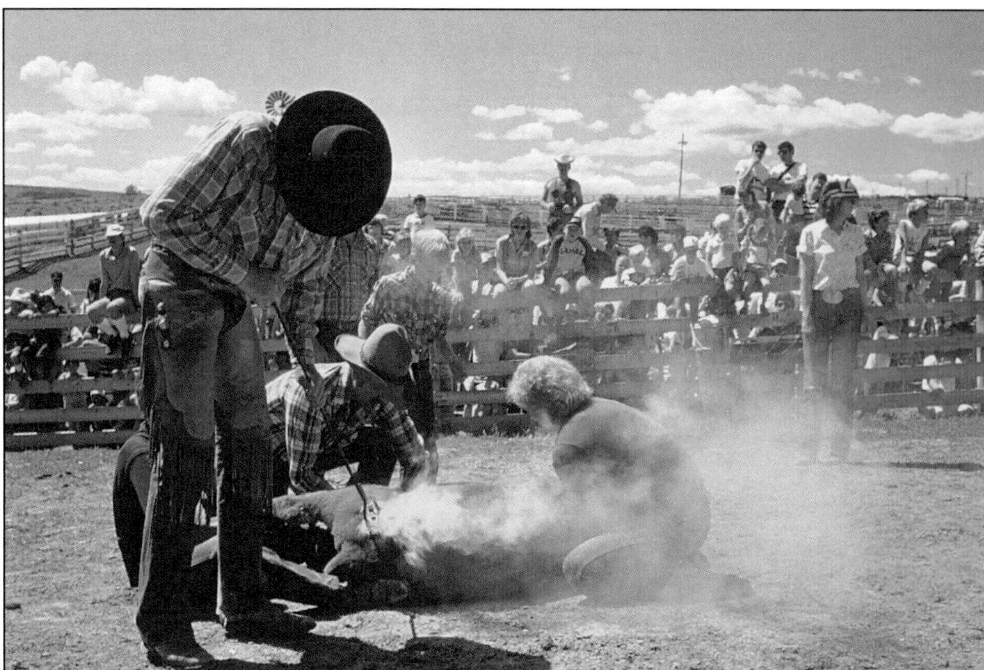

The Highlands Ranch Community also enjoys its ranching traditions including the annual branding of the new cattle on the ranch. Here, a cow is branded with the Highlands Ranch brand while a crowd of residents looks on. (Courtesy of Highlands Ranch Metro District.)

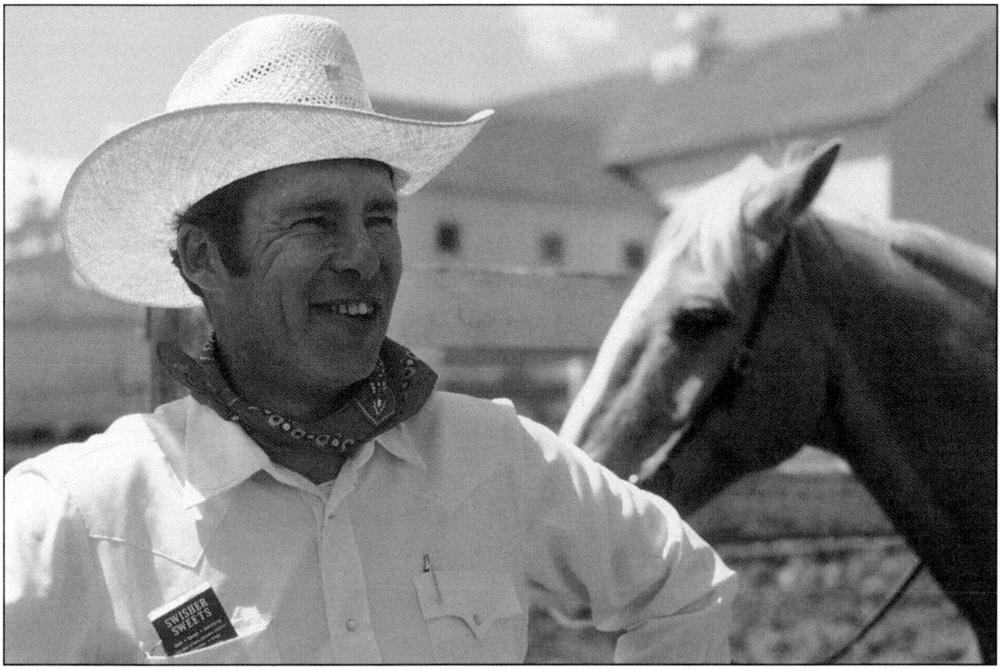

Art Cook ran ranching operations for the Mission Viejo Company. He was known at the "Voice of Highlands Ranch." Cook was also known for his work on community events and building a sense of community. (Courtesy of Highlands Ranch Metro District.)

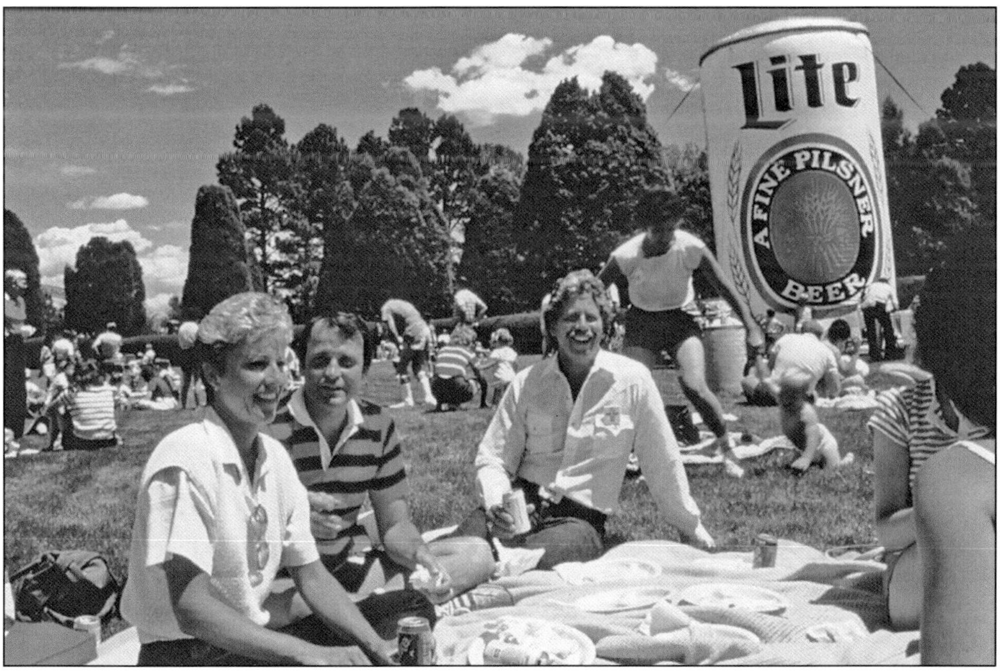

Community gatherings are held at the mansion for people to get together and socialize. One major sponsor of early Highlands Ranch events was Philip Morris. Philip Morris had also owned the Mission Viejo Company since 1972. Note the large inflatable Miller Lite can. (Courtesy of Highlands Ranch Metro District.)

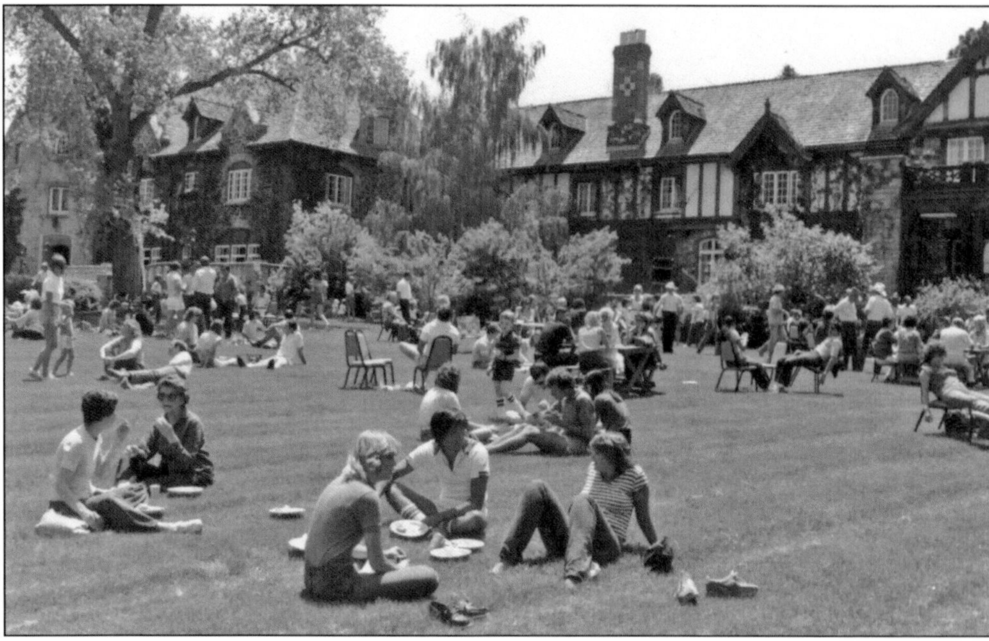

The community used the grounds of the mansion to gather for special events. Today, the mansion is maintained by Highlands Ranch Metro District, and the grounds are kept as a park. (Courtesy of Highlands Ranch Metro District.)

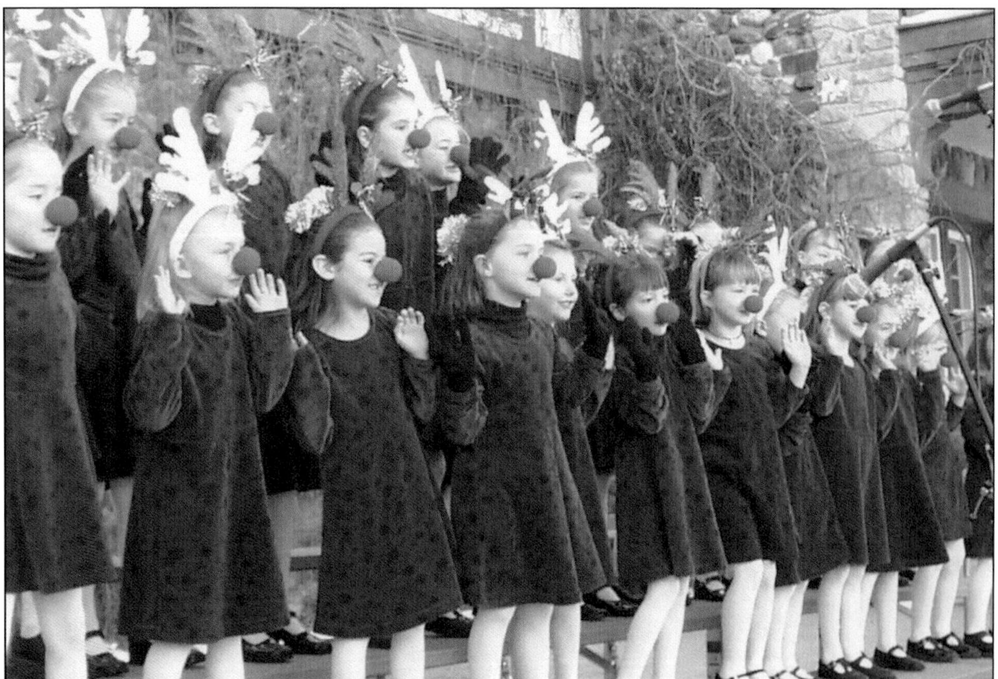

Another festival at the mansion is the holiday party. Choirs from many schools have taken part, including some that dressed the part. Prior to the renovation, the children normally sang out front. Since the addition of the great hall, they can now come out of the cold. (Courtesy of Highlands Ranch Metro District.)

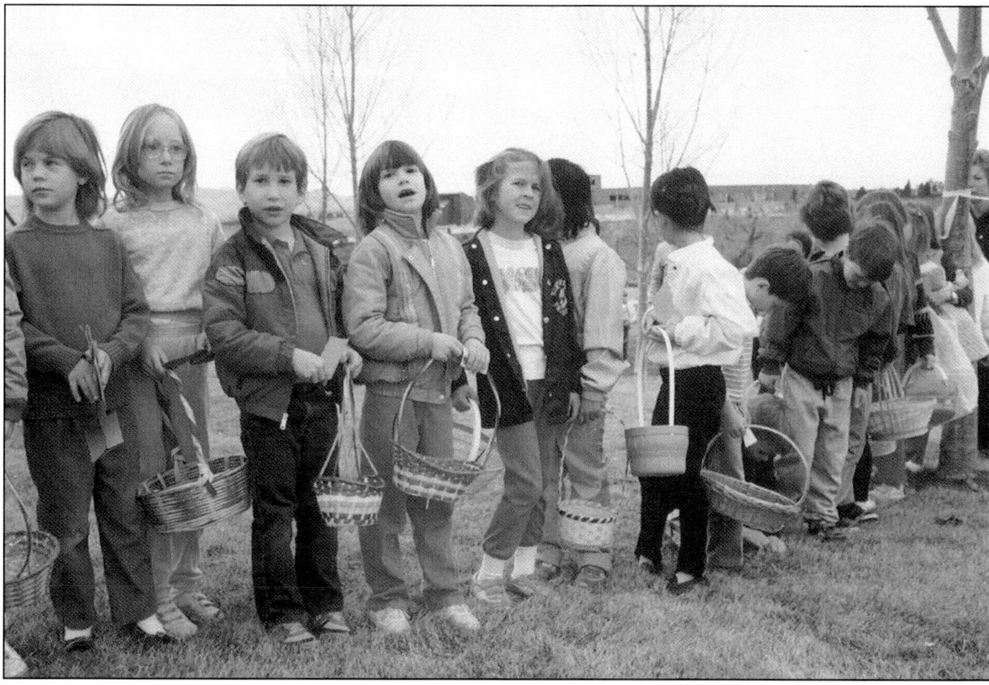

One of the traditions of Highlands Ranch has been an Easter Egg Hunt at Northridge Park. The kids are all lined up to run into the field and collect as many Easter eggs as possible. This event continues today. (Courtesy of Highlands Ranch Metro District.)

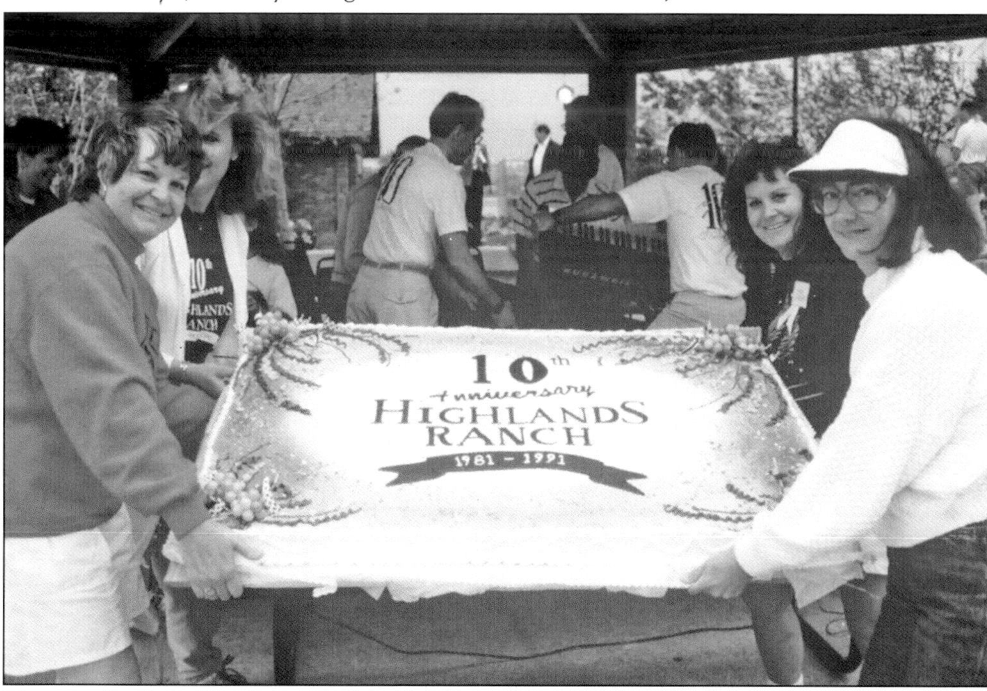

The people of Highlands Ranch are essential to this successful community. Highlands Ranch has celebrated many milestones like its 10th anniversary, which included the giant sheet cake shown here. (Courtesy of Highlands Ranch Metro District.)

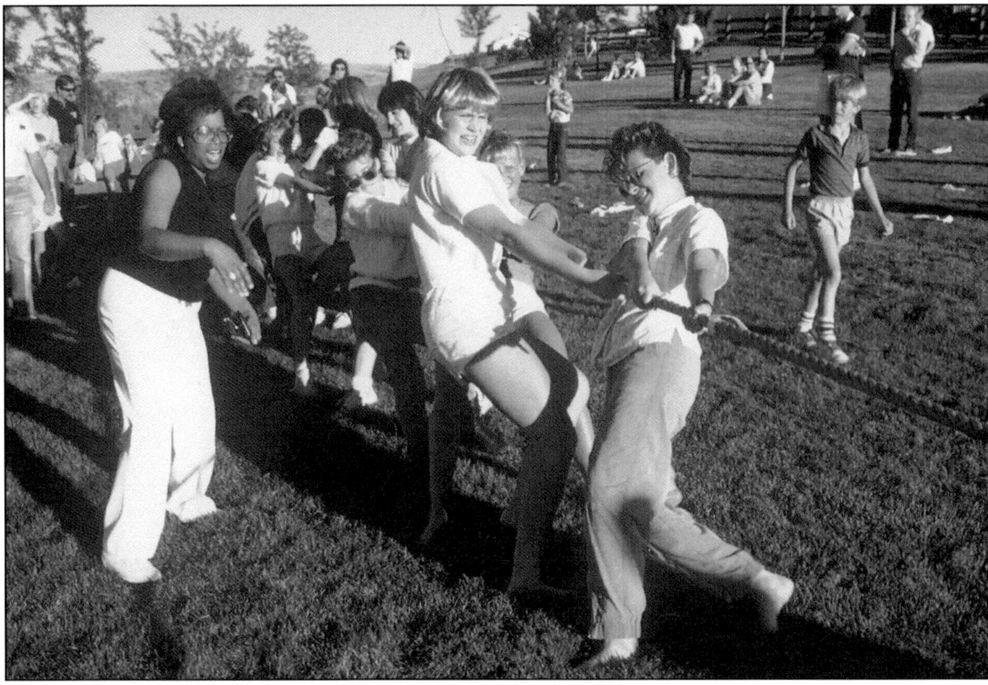

For years, children have been the focus of Highlands Ranch, so much so that comedians have even joked that kids are what is truly grown on the ranch. Here, children expend their energy while playing tug-of-war. (Courtesy of Highlands Ranch Metro District.)

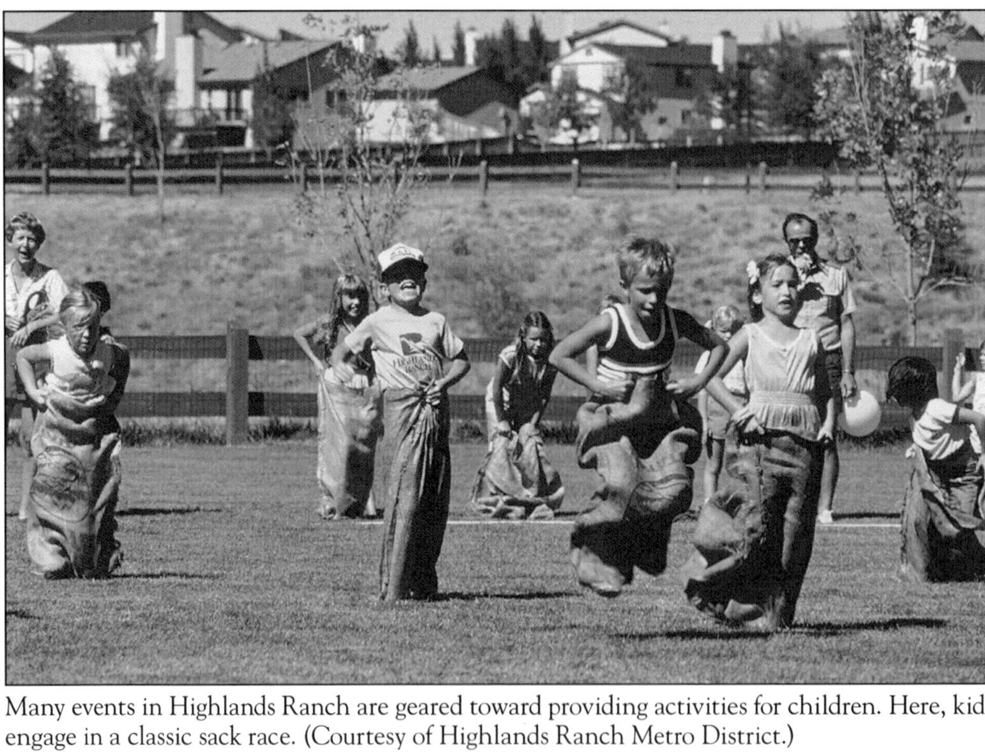

Many events in Highlands Ranch are geared toward providing activities for children. Here, kids engage in a classic sack race. (Courtesy of Highlands Ranch Metro District.)

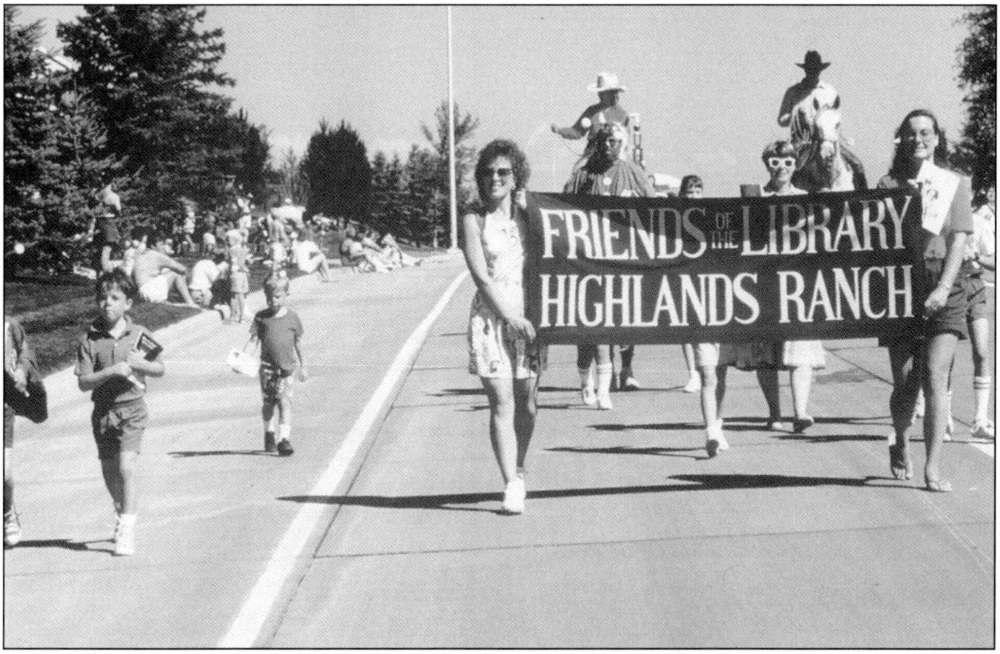

The 10th anniversary also included a parade where people could come out and show their appreciation for the community and for causes dear to their hearts. Note that the ranching spirit is still alive; the parade photograph shows at least two people on horseback. (Courtesy of Highlands Ranch Metro District.)

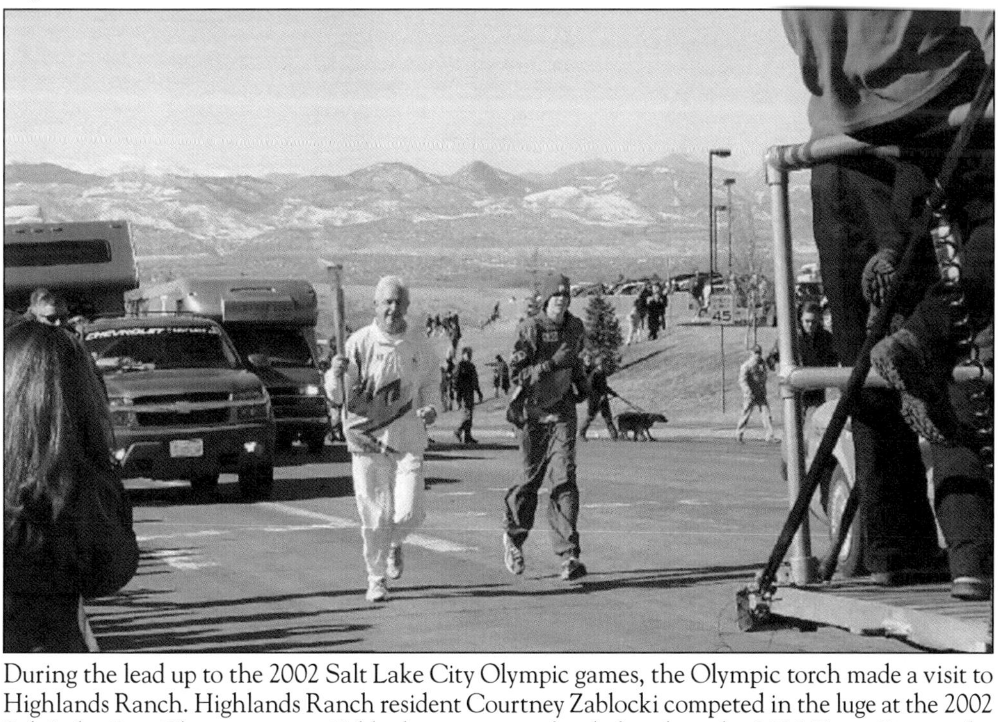

During the lead up to the 2002 Salt Lake City Olympic games, the Olympic torch made a visit to Highlands Ranch. Highlands Ranch resident Courtney Zablocki competed in the luge at the 2002 Salt Lake City Olympic games. Zablocki went on to finish fourth at the 2006 Turin Games, the highest finish ever for an American woman. (Courtesy of Highlands Ranch Metro District.)

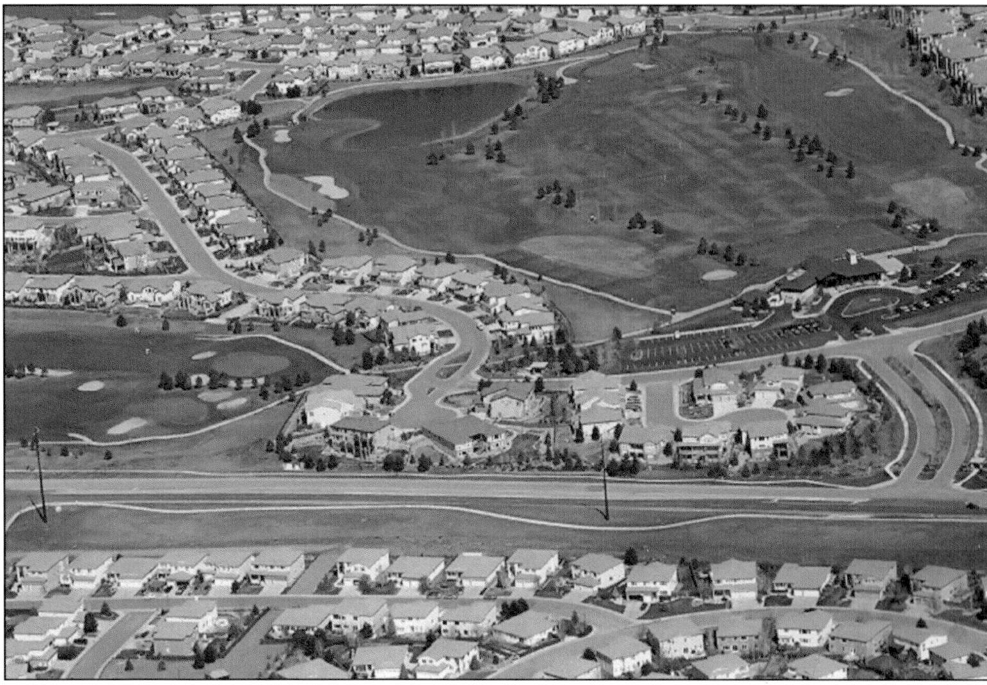

The Highlands Ranch Golf Club is an 18-hole, semiprivate golf club, designed by three-time US Open champion Hale Irwin. The golf course provides a great balance of holes that run along and between the homes. The course also has many areas that are surrounded by nature and the Highline Canal. There are also several holes that provide magnificent views of the Rocky Mountain Front Range. Today the golf course is owned and operated by the University of Denver. (Courtesy of Highlands Ranch Metro District.)

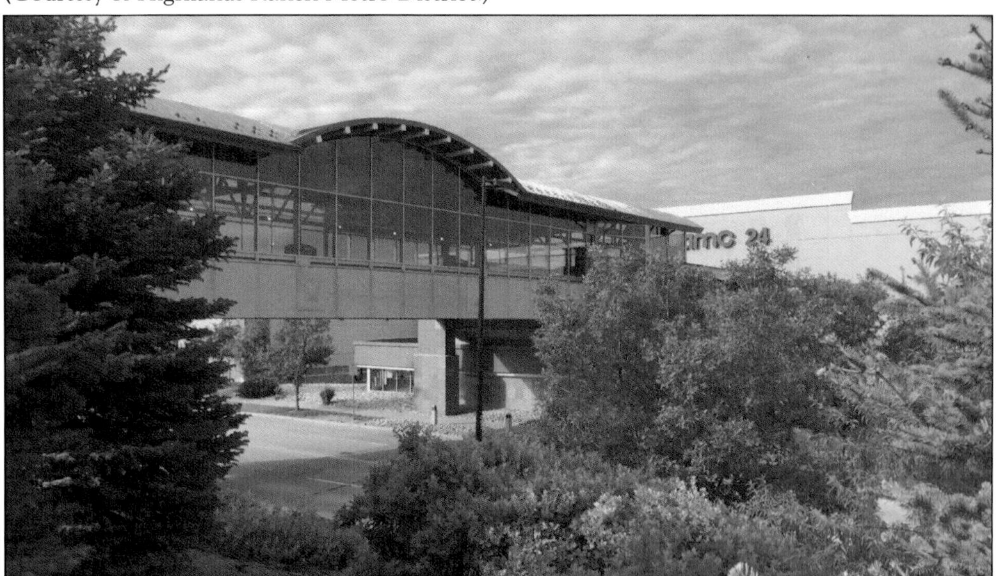

The first major regional entertainment attraction in Highlands Ranch was the addition of the AMC 24 Movie Theater. With 24 screens (including two IMAX screens), it can carry more movies than any of the theaters around and draws people from all across the southern metro area.

Four

OUTDOOR ACTIVITIES

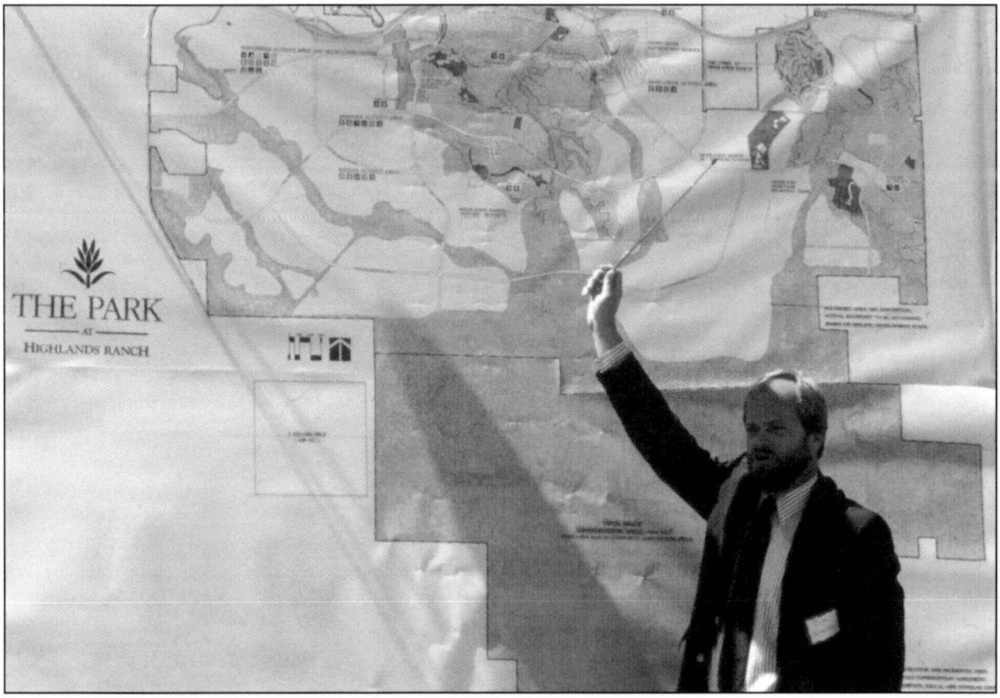

Highlands Ranch's early planning of the parks and connected open spaces throughout the community has secured a high quality of life for residents. The original plan called for 60 percent of Highlands Ranch to remain open space. Jim Worley is shown presenting the plan. Almost four decades later, with the major build-out coming to an end, this goal continues to be met. (Courtesy of Highlands Ranch Metro District.)

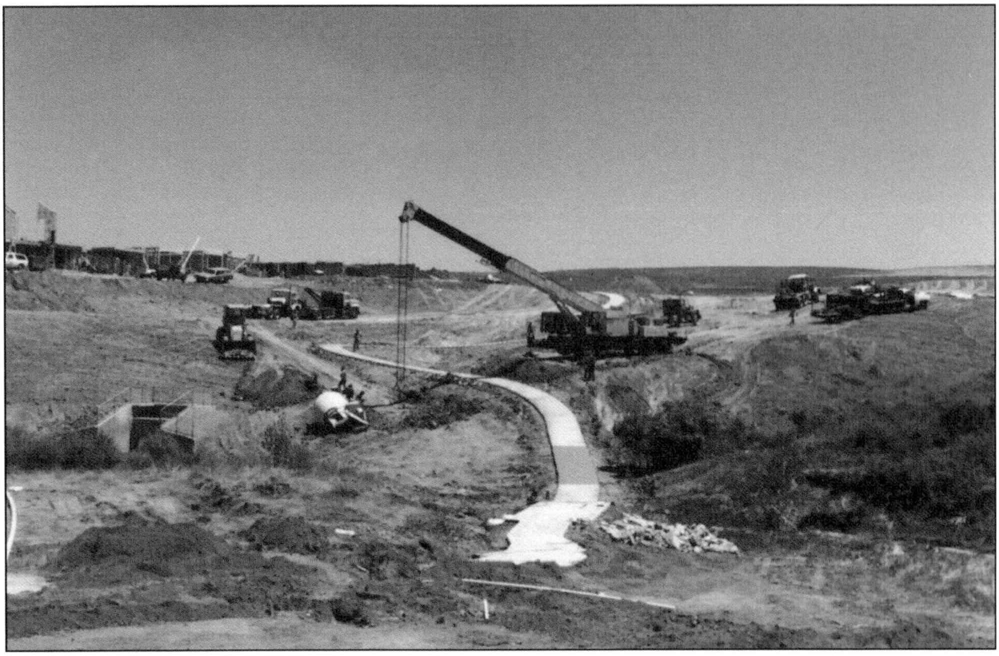

The construction of trails through the open spaces often occurred before the homes in the area were constructed. The forethought of parks, roads, and open space led to interconnected paths that are great for moving around Highlands Ranch without being on the major roadways. (Courtesy of Highlands Ranch Metro District.)

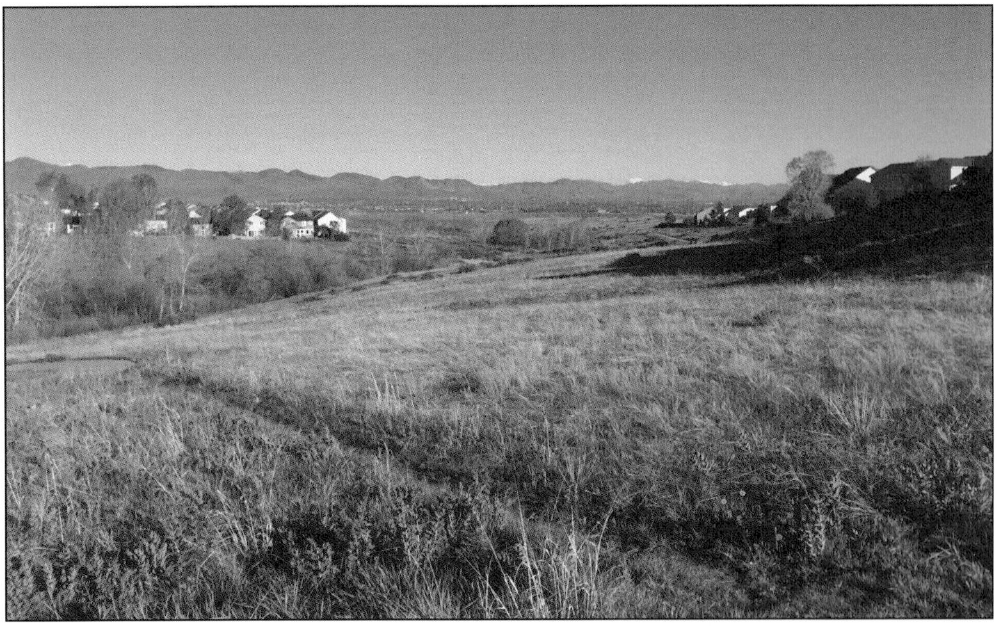

The connected open spaces like Spring Gulch not only join the trails together, but also serve as beautiful separations between the different neighborhoods of Highlands Ranch. In addition, the open space serves as the extended backyard for the many homes that back up to the many open spaces throughout Highlands Ranch. The open spaces also provide a natural home for many rabbits, foxes, and coyotes that call Highlands Ranch home.

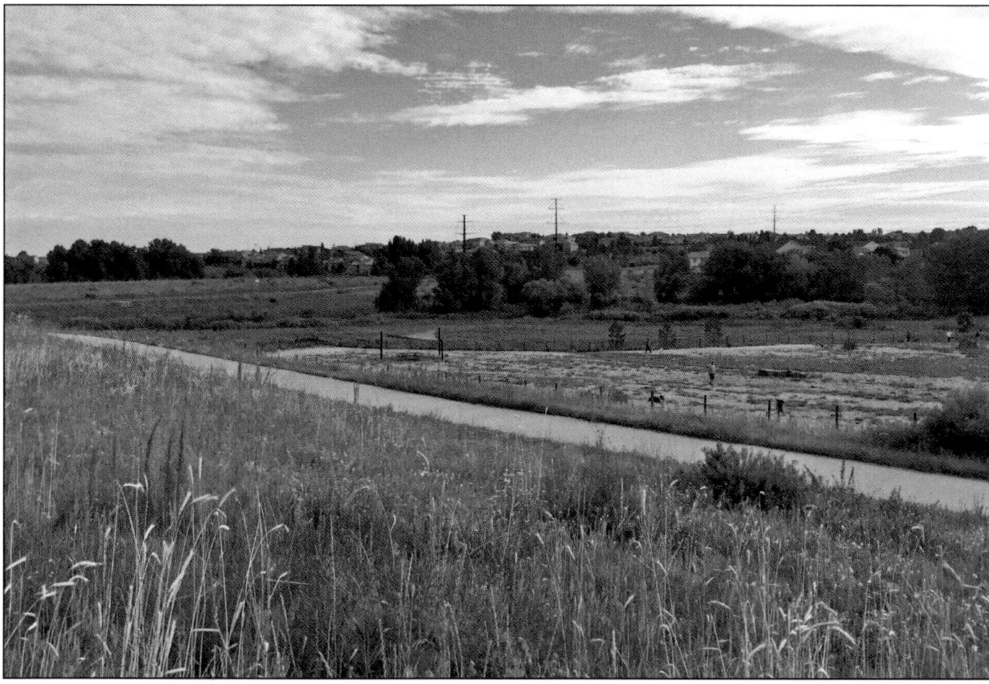

These open spaces provide an area for pets to walk and play. Rover's Run at Redstone Park is one of four dog parks within Highlands Ranch. The other parks are Hound Hill at Highlands Heritage Park, Digger's at Dad Clark Park, and Fido's Field at Foothills Park.

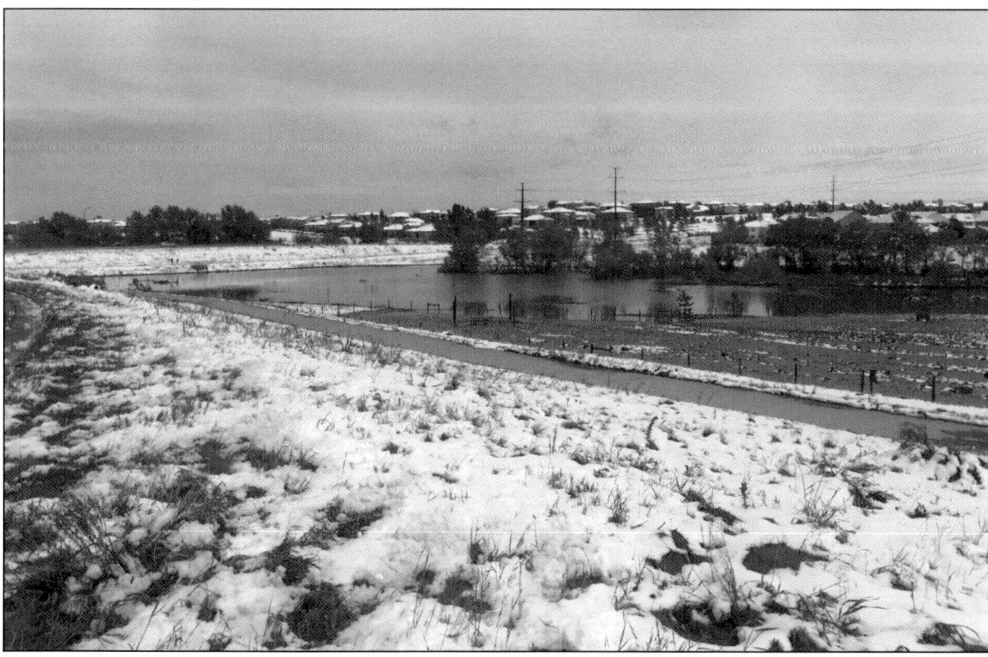

Additionally, the open spaces also serve a more functional role as a tool to manage water flow and runoff. The spring of 2015 was extra wet, with many snowstorms and rainstorms. On several occasions every year, Marcy Creek near Redstone Park fills, slowing the flow of water heading downstream to reduce flooding.

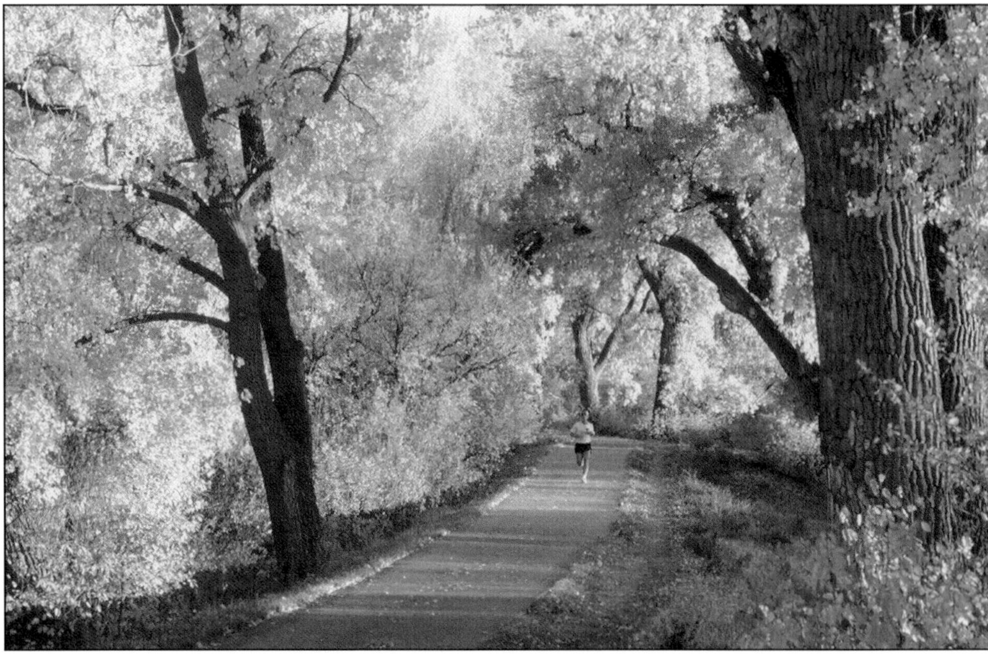

A runner makes his way along the Highline Canal Trail between Broadway and Santa Fe Drive on a beautiful fall day. The trail system is another great aspect of being outdoors in Highlands Ranch. The Highline Canal itself has been providing water along the northwest corner of Highlands Ranch for over 100 years. (Courtesy of Highlands Ranch Metro District.)

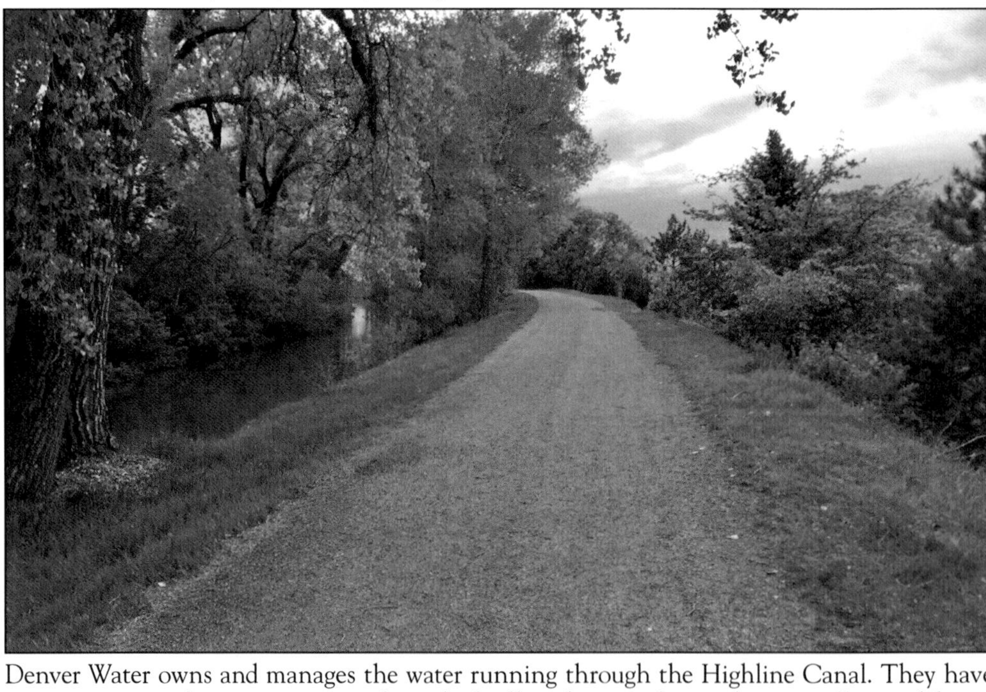

Denver Water owns and manages the water running through the Highline Canal. They have spent many years buying up water rights, which allow them to choose the most efficient delivery methods to customers. As the Highline Canal winds for miles through cities and towns, flowing water provides life for the trees and other vegetation along the canal.

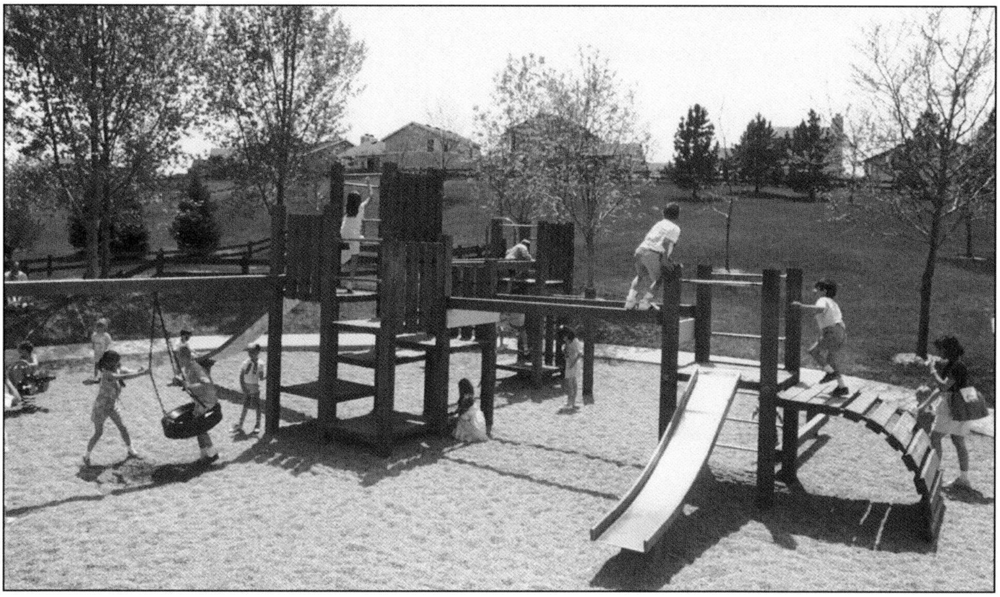

All kids big and small love a trip to the playground. Pictured is the original playground at Northridge Park full of kids that called Highlands Ranch home in the early days. Northridge Park was the start of the Highlands Ranch's master plan that always called for many parks. Today, Highlands Ranch Metro District manages 26 parks, which include 22 playgrounds for today's Highlands Ranch kids to enjoy the outdoors. (Courtesy of Highlands Ranch Metro District.)

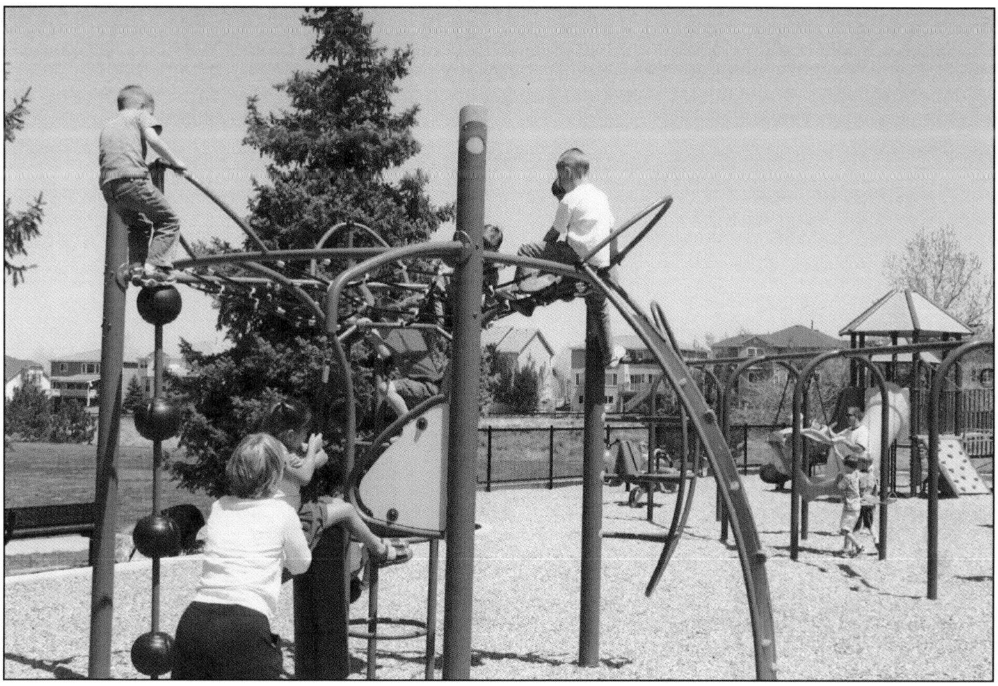

Over the years, the type of construction materials for playgrounds has changed from wood frames and metal slides to metal frames with plastic slides. The equipment has also gotten more colorful, as seen here at the Falcon Park playground. The primary purpose, though, entertainment for Highlands Ranch children, remains the same. (Courtesy of Highlands Ranch Metro District.)

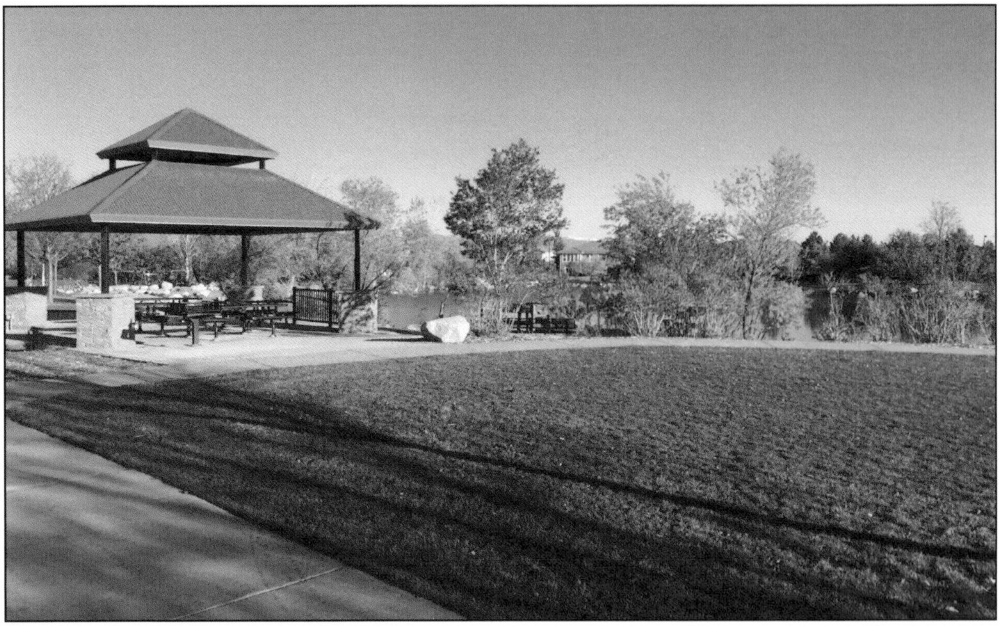

The parks of Highlands Ranch are also gathering places where family and friends can share special events. Almost all of the parks throughout Highlands Ranch feature picnic shelters where people can throw a party or just relax. The shelters also provide protection from both sun and rain.

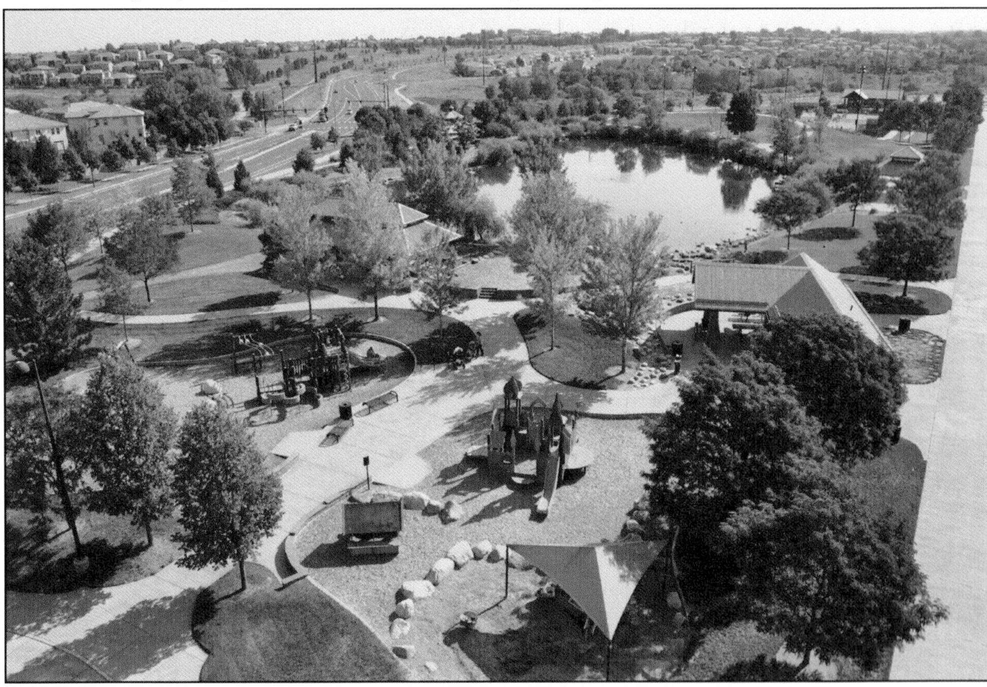

The pond at Redstone Park provides a unique feature in Highlands Ranch where natural water is scarce. The pond provides a good area for reflection in the middle of the soccer fields, tennis courts, and the playground. Near the playground, kids normally go to the water's edge or play in the little creek that starts next to the playground and flows into the lake. (Courtesy of Highlands Ranch Metro District.)

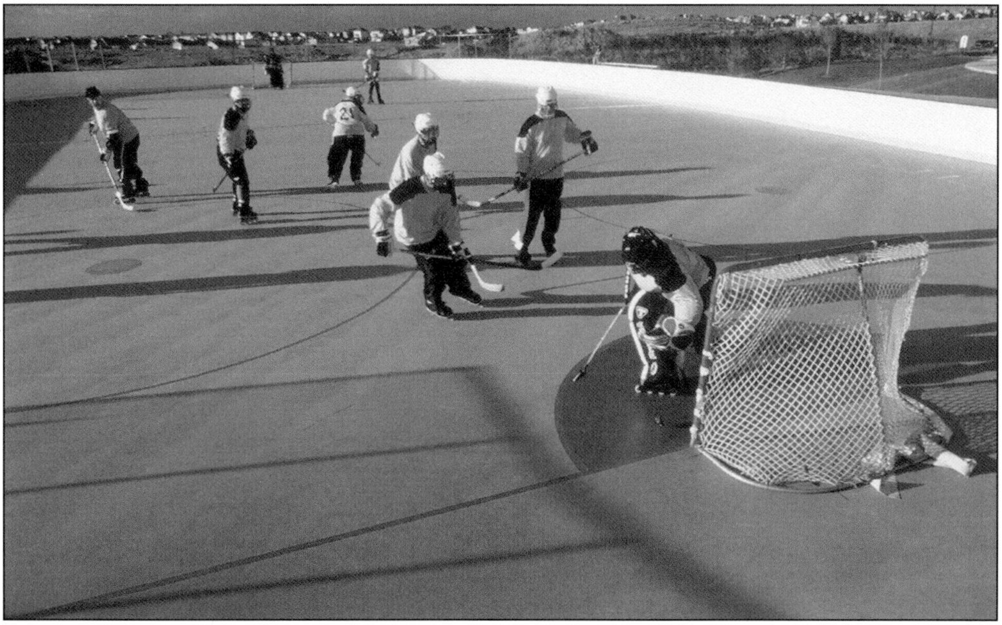

Highlands Ranch has also found unique uses for the water storage tanks. The Tanks Park was built on the large concrete lids of the tanks. The Tanks Park is used for skateboarding, rollerskating, and roller hockey. In 2015, four pickleball courts were added at the park with funding from the Highlands Ranch Park and Recreation Foundation. (Courtesy of Highlands Ranch Metro District.)

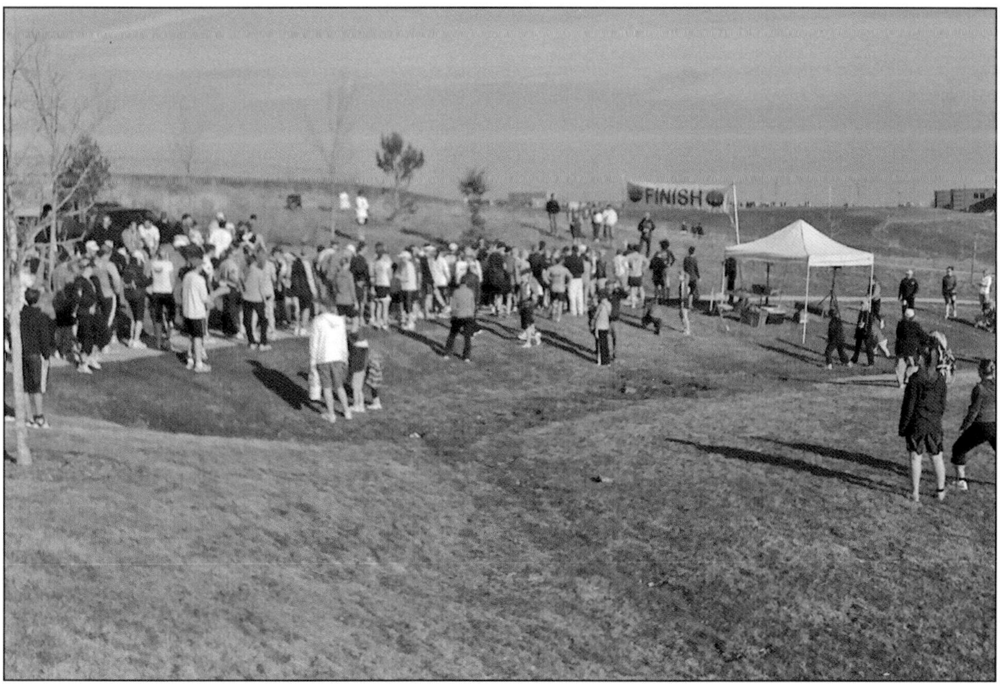

The open spaces of Highlands Ranch provide areas for many activities. The Highlands Ranch Community Association (HRCA) gets the residents and visitors to Highlands Ranch in motion by holding a run series every year. The run series is well respected and can be used to register qualifying times for many runs in the region.

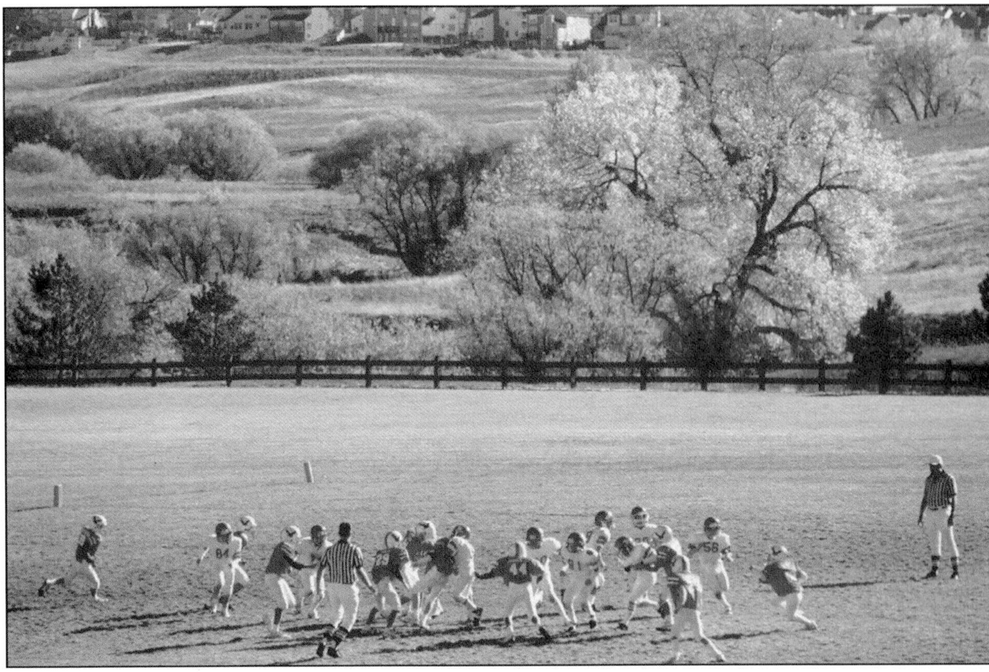

The kids of Highlands Ranch have always been into participating in sports. Twenty of the parks have sport fields. This picture shows a youth football game being played at Northridge Park. (Courtesy of Highlands Ranch Metro District.)

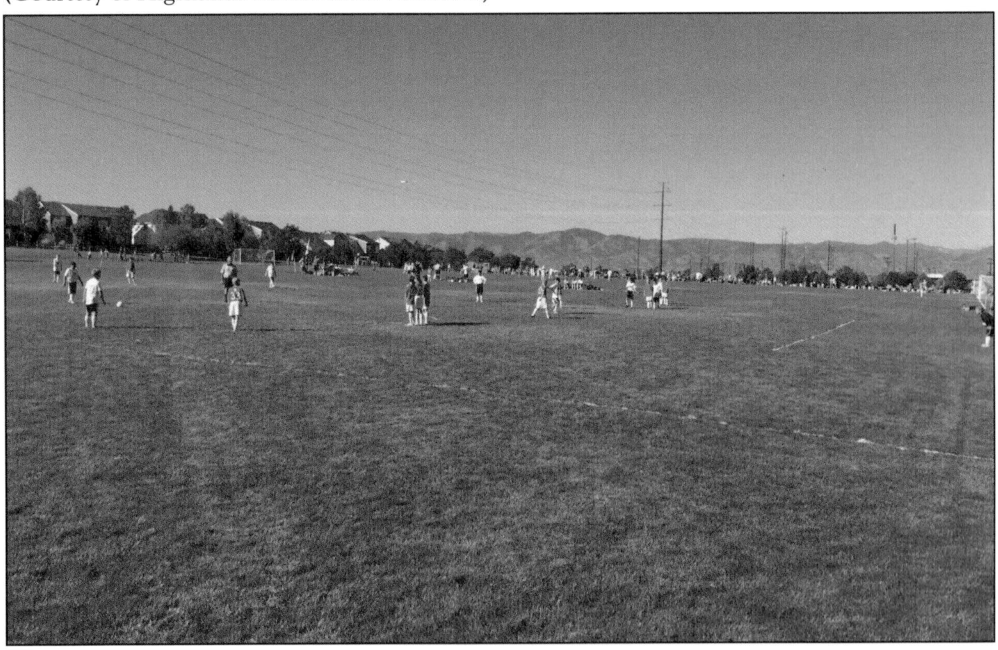

Soccer, the largest sport in the world, also plays a major role in the lives of the kids in Highlands Ranch. The game and the term "soccer moms" became synonymous with life in the suburbs at the end of the 20th century. The largest sports park today is Redstone Park with four soccer fields, four baseball diamonds, six tennis courts, fishing, a skate park, a batting cage, and Shea Stadium, which is used for football, soccer, and lacrosse.

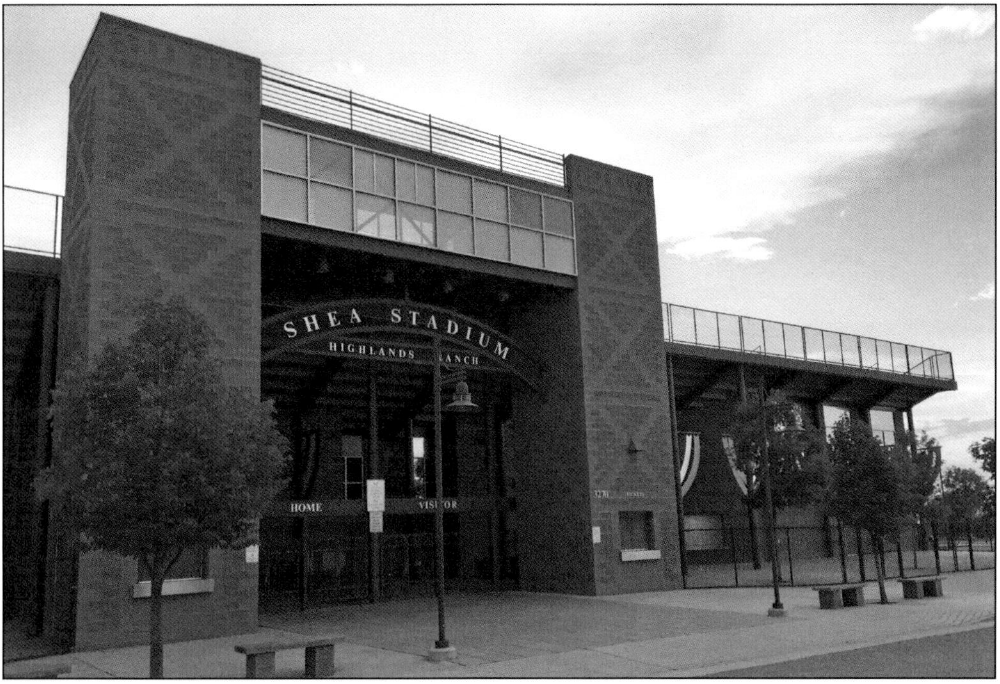

For the largest sporting events in Highlands Ranch, the metro district has Shea Stadium on the west side. For those who attend, the stadium provides great views of both the game and the mountains beyond.

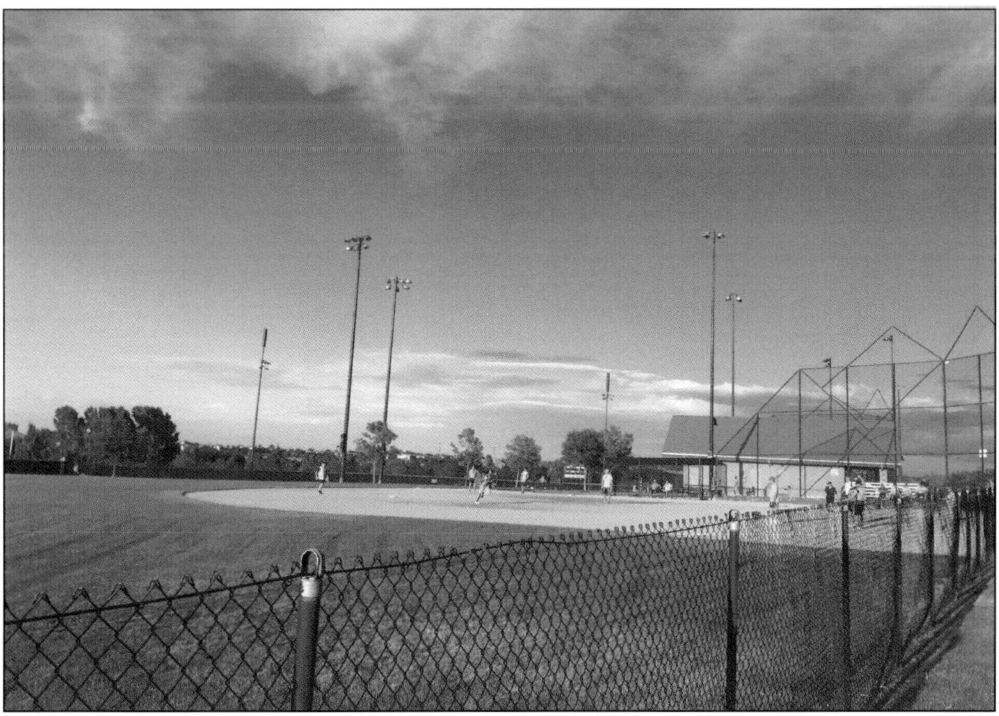

America's favorite pastime continues to flourish in Highlands Ranch, where leagues play both during the day and night at Redstone Park.

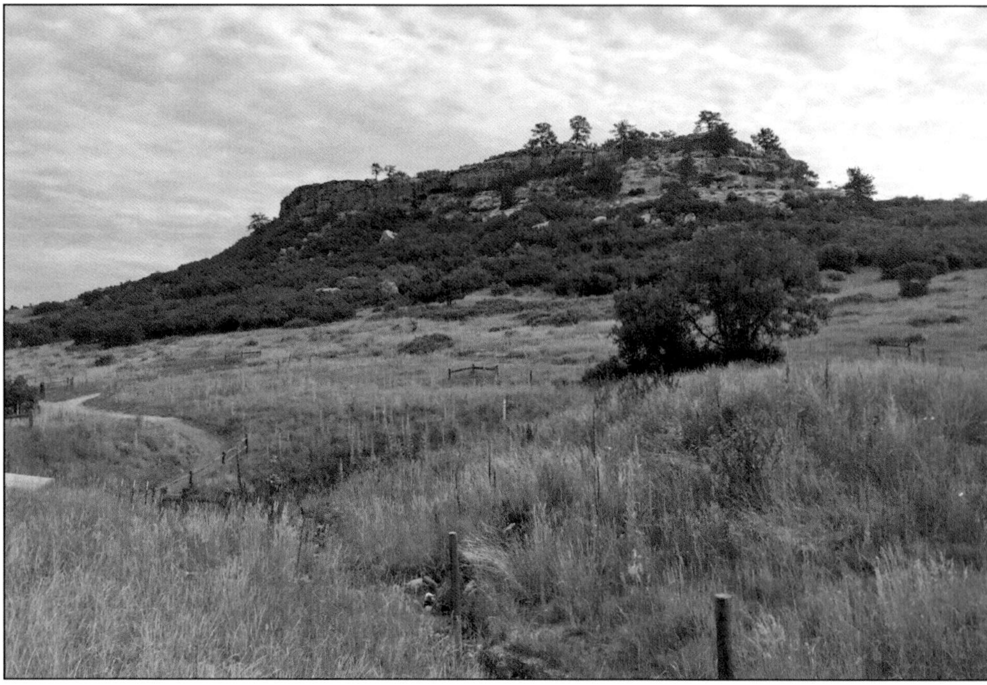

Wildcat Mountain, on the east side of Highlands Ranch provides a great location to escape into nature. The mountain also provides a natural barrier between Highlands Ranch and Castle Pines to the southeast.

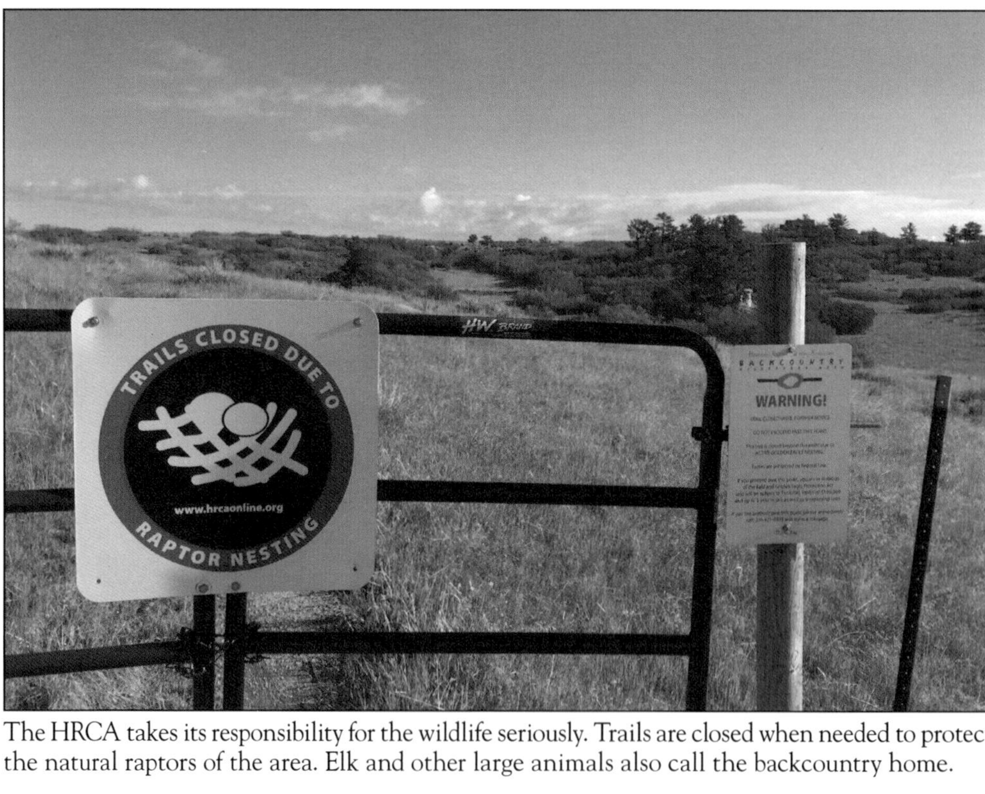

The HRCA takes its responsibility for the wildlife seriously. Trails are closed when needed to protect the natural raptors of the area. Elk and other large animals also call the backcountry home.

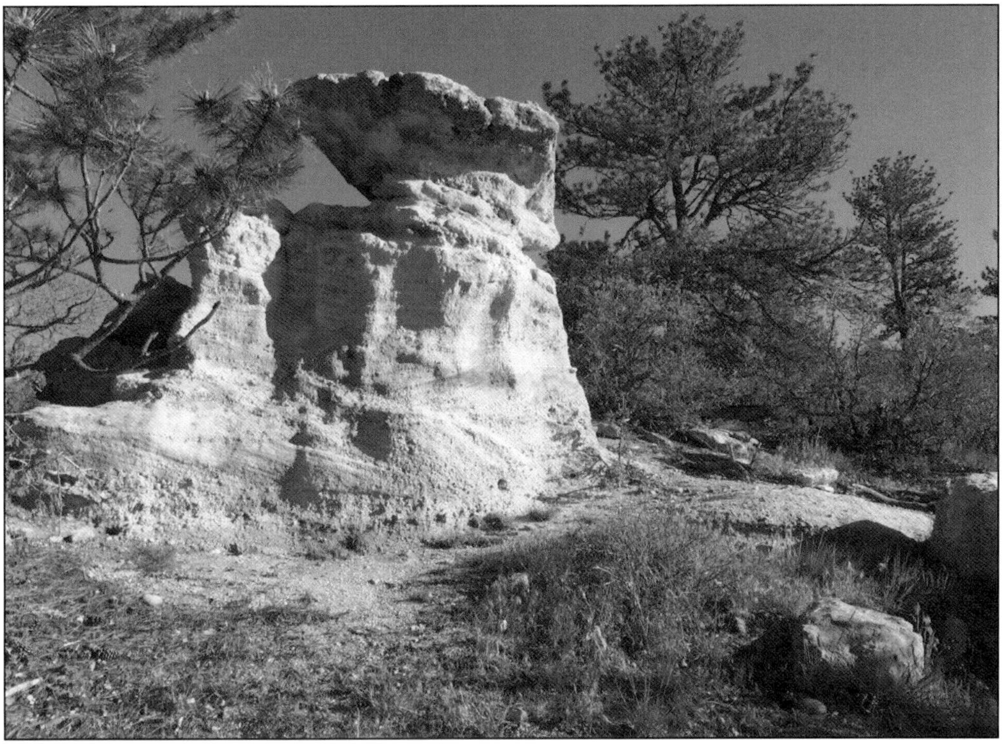

The Wildcat Mountain area also provides beautiful views of the geological history of the area.

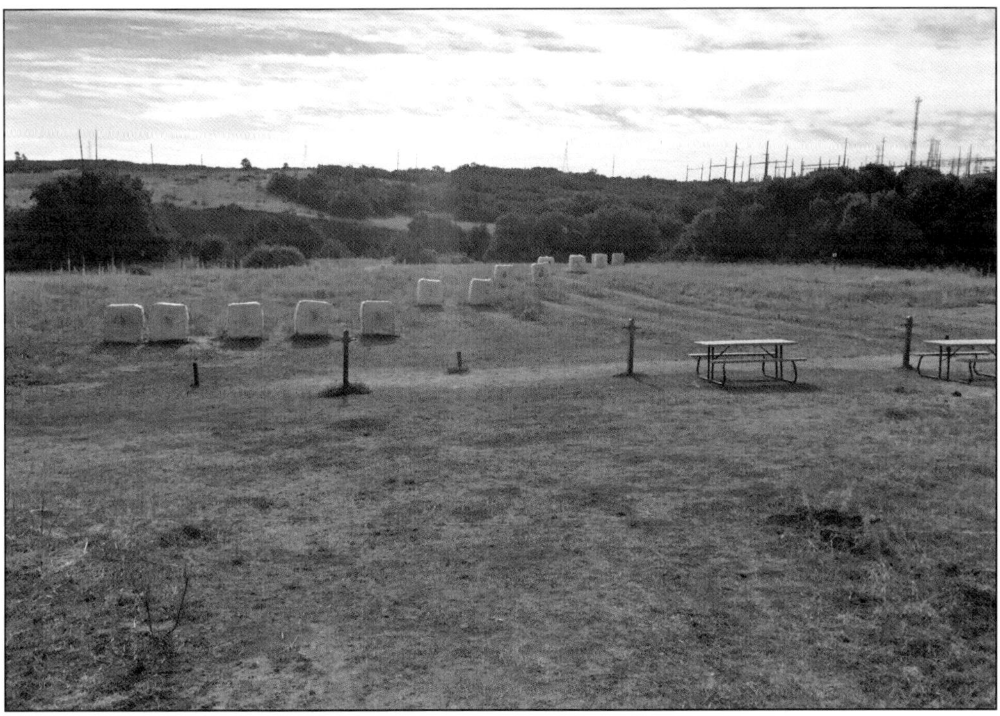

An archery range is one of the many activities with ties to the past. In the background on the right, a major power substation that serves the community of Castle Pines to the south is visible.

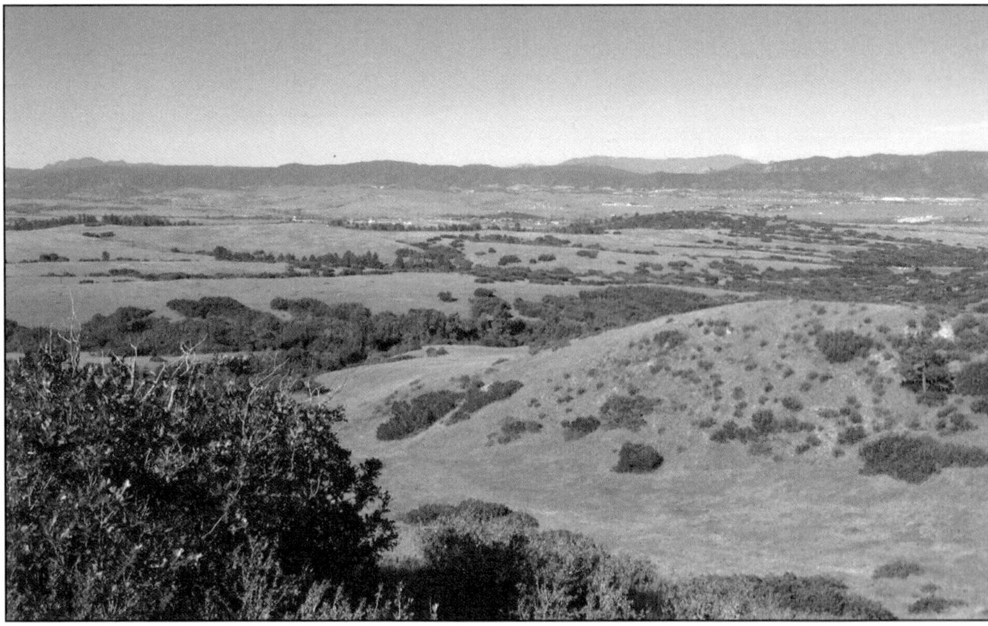

The largest block of open space is not actually within Highlands Ranch's parks; it's the 8,200-acre Backcountry Wilderness Area, located south of the area homes. The Highlands Ranch Community Association (HRCA) manages this space. The Backcountry will continue to serve as a major natural division between Highlands Ranch and the communities of central Douglas County, like Castle Rock and Sedalia, for generations to come.

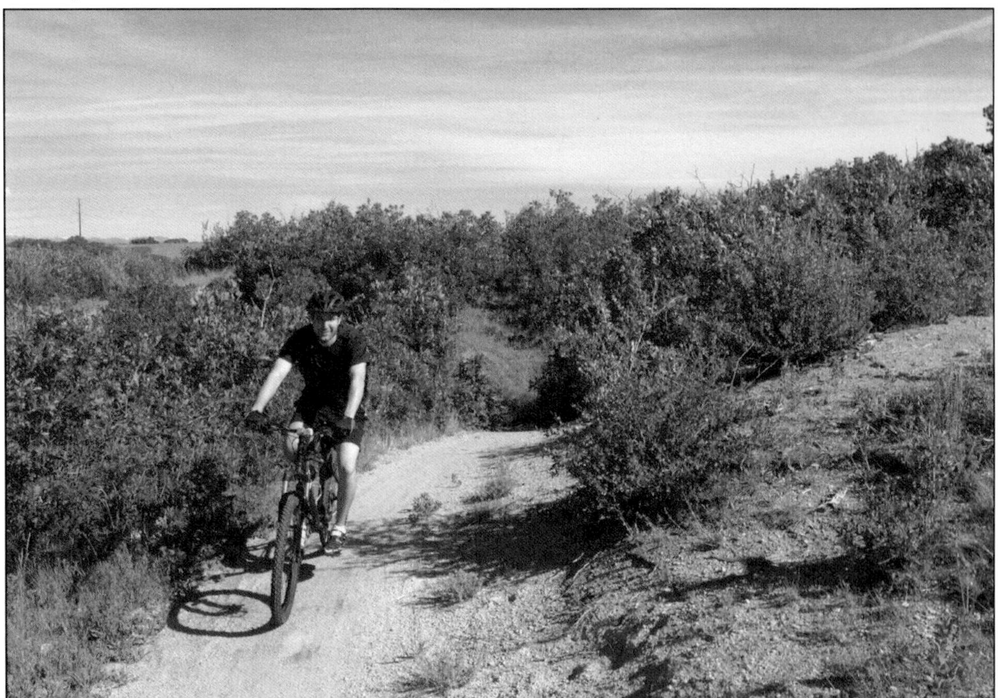

HRCA provides and maintains miles of mountain-biking trails for the residents of Highlands Ranch. In just minutes, one can travel from the city to the country by biking the trails.

Five

Getting That Town Feel

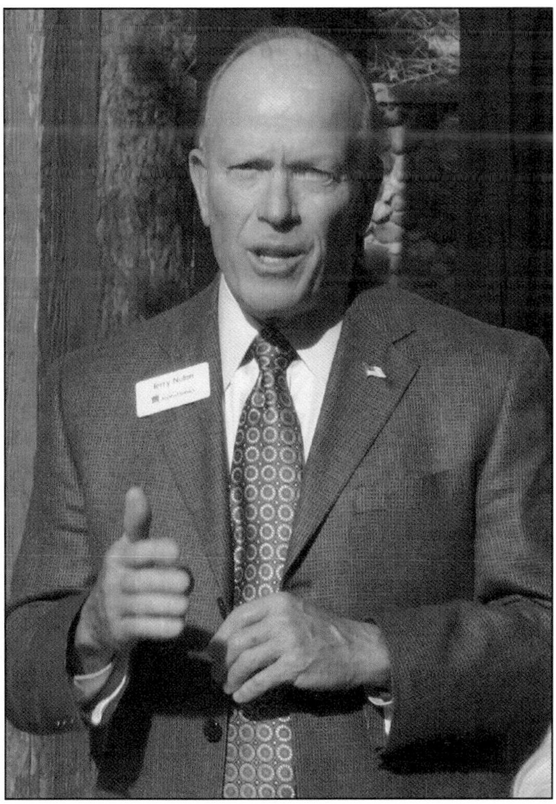

By the mid-1990s, Highlands Ranch had established itself, and a new phase began with two major changes. The first was when Terry Nolan became the new general manager of Highlands Ranch Metro District, a position he has continued to hold for almost two decades. Before coming to Highlands Ranch, Nolan spent 24 years in the Navy as an A-7 pilot, retiring as a captain in 1995. (Courtesy of Highlands Ranch Metro District.)

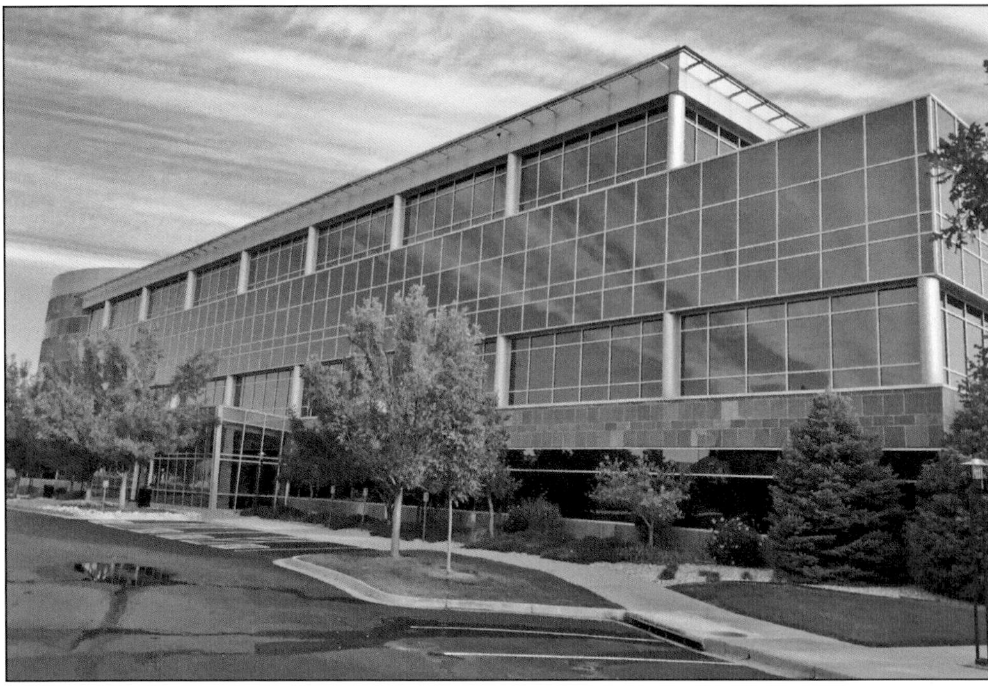

The second major change was when Mission Viejo sold the remaining development of Highlands Ranch to Shea Homes in 1997. Shea Homes, like Mission Viejo, continued the planned vision for the build-out of Highlands Ranch. The Shea Homes' offices in Highlands Ranch are pictured here.

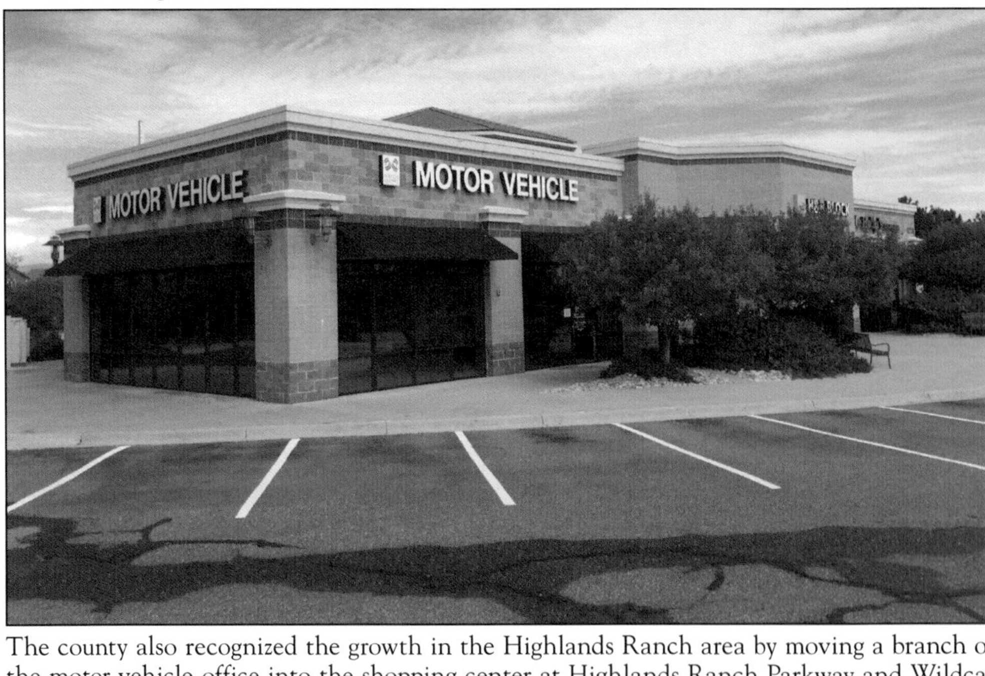

The county also recognized the growth in the Highlands Ranch area by moving a branch of the motor vehicle office into the shopping center at Highlands Ranch Parkway and Wildcat Reserve Parkway to assist residents in registering their cars. Continual improvements allow most residents to renew their licenses without needing to come to the office in person, thus helping to keep the lines shorter.

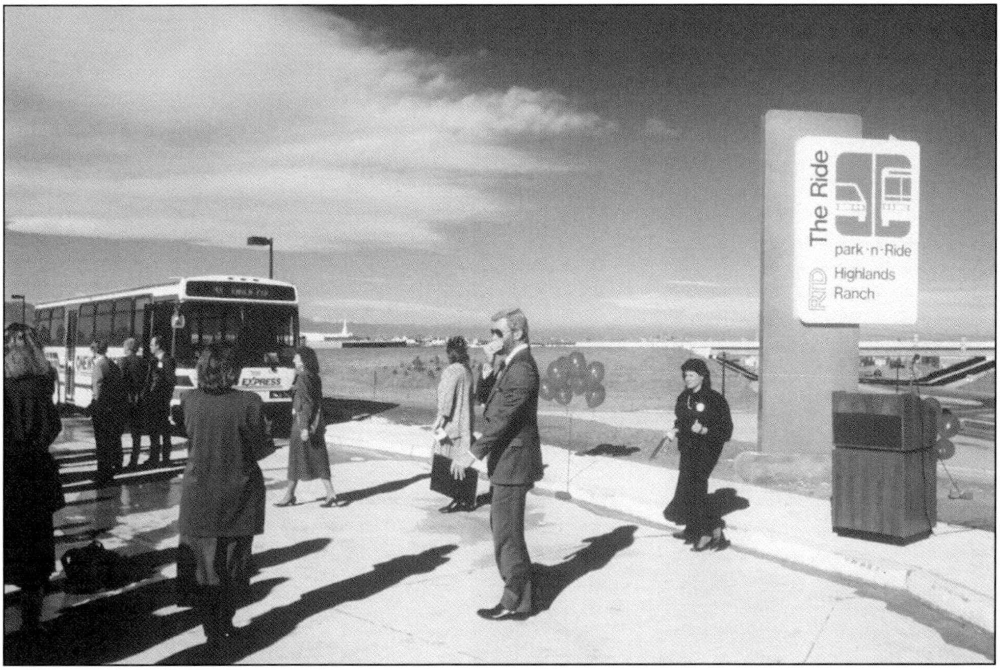

The Regional Transportation District (RTD) serves Highlands Ranch and the Denver area. The opening of the Highlands Ranch park-n-ride at C-470 and University Boulevard was the subject of celebration. (Courtesy of Highlands Ranch Metro District.)

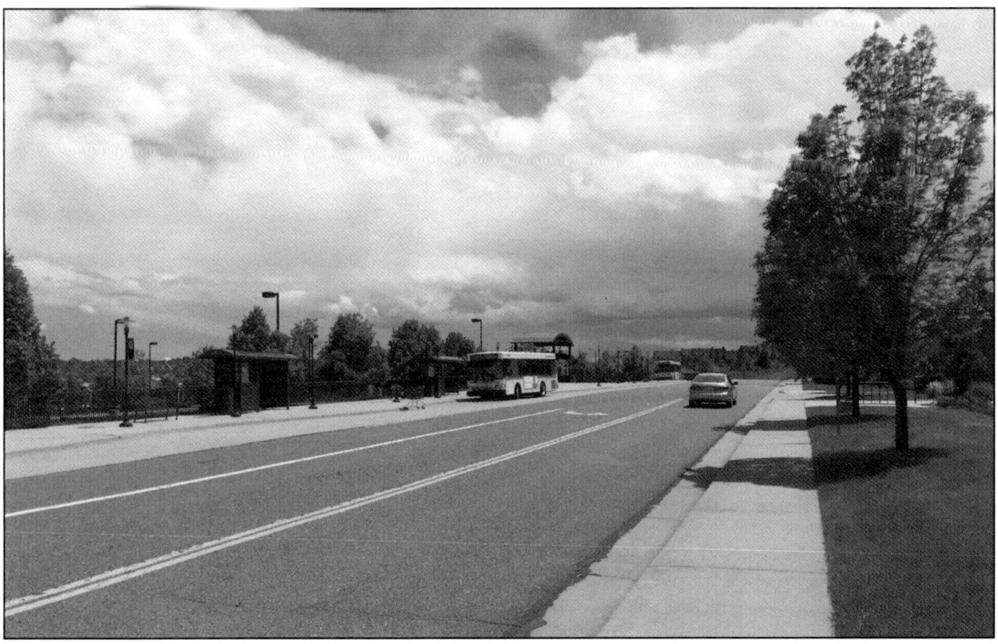

Today, Highlands Ranch is served primarily by three east-west routes—the 401, 402L, and 403—all of which stop at the RTD Town Center park-n-ride. Routes go from the light rail stop at the Mineral station in Littleton to the light rail stops on I-25, including Lincoln and Park Meadows. The Town Center is also the end point of the 0 bus route that travels north on Broadway to downtown Denver.

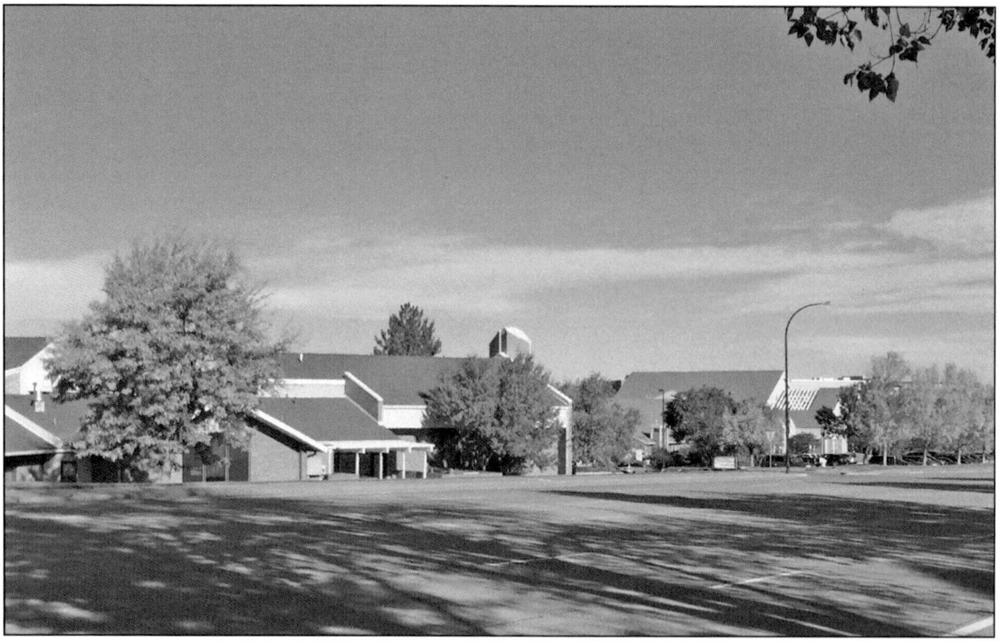

Churches make a community feel like home, and there are many scattered around Highlands Ranch. Due to the master plan, some of the churches found themselves grouped together. Two of the early churches located along Broadway are St. Luke's United Methodist Church and Christ Lutheran Church.

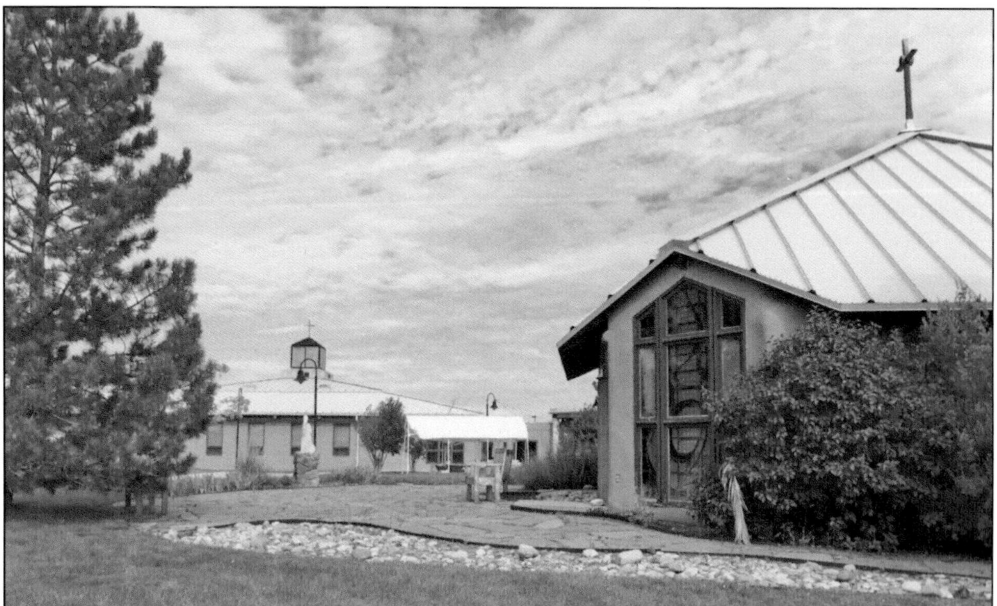

Pax Christi Catholic Church was the first Catholic church in Highlands Ranch. The Catholic Church separated the Archdiocese of Denver and Colorado Springs at the Arapahoe and Douglas County line. Therefore, Pax Christi also provided the citizens of Highlands Ranch with the first local church in the Archdioceses of Colorado Springs. Pax Christi is located on the east side of Highlands Ranch near the corner of South Quebec Street and McArthur Ranch Road.

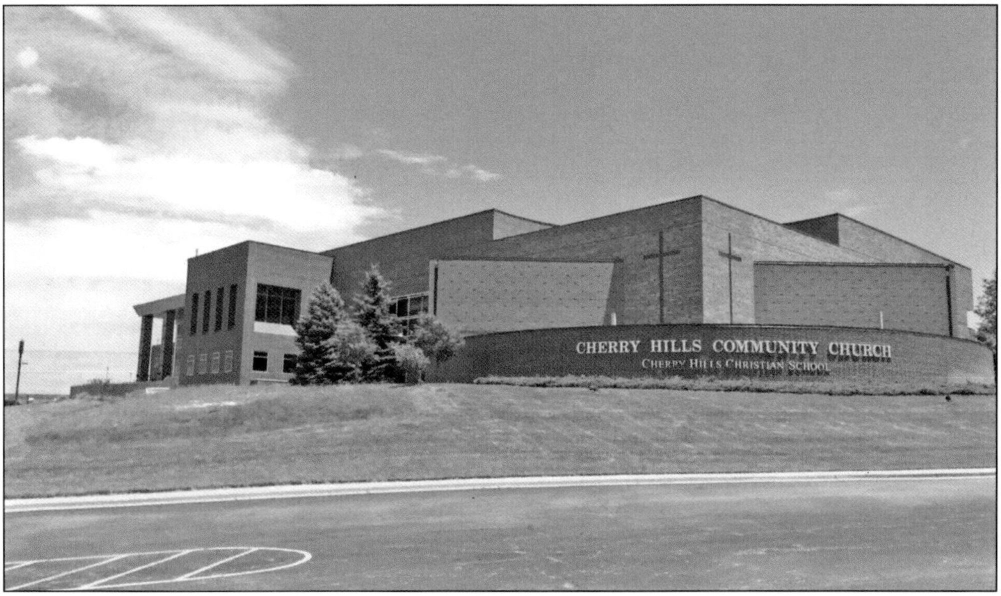

The Cherry Hills Community Church is a mega church in Highlands Ranch. Membership is estimated to be about 6,000. Located in the center of Highlands Ranch, the church is an active member of the community, hosting community events like the HRCA Touch-a-Truck, which lets kids explore police cars, government vehicles, helicopters, fire trucks, and more. The church also joins with the attached Cherry Hills Christian School to provide education and entertainment opportunities to the children of Highlands Ranch.

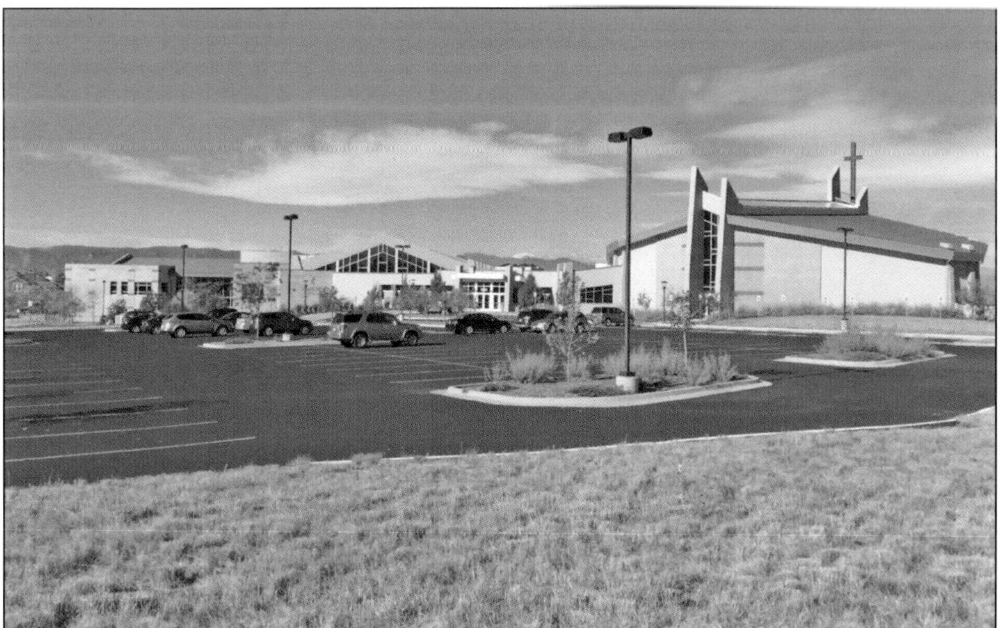

St. Andrew United Methodist Church on University Boulevard is another large draw for the people of Highlands Ranch. The church did not start in Highlands Ranch but moved to this beautiful new home from farther north on University Boulevard near South Suburban's Goodson Recreation Center.

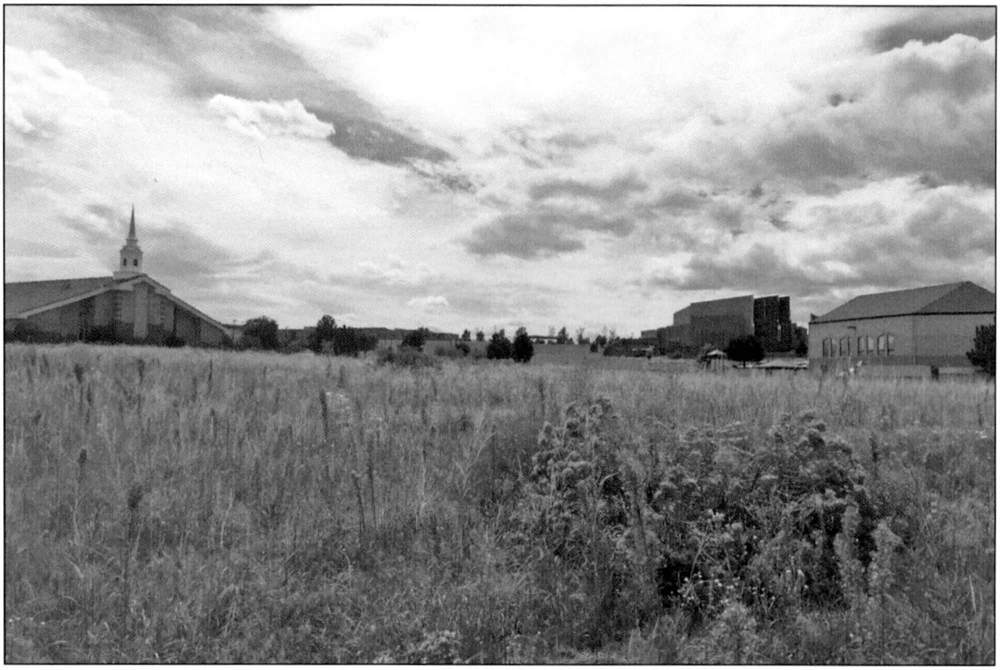

The zoning rules grouped churches together, with the largest single concentration being near the corner of Highlands Ranch Parkway and Foothills Canyon Boulevard. This includes, from left to right, the Church of Jesus Christ of Latter Day Saints, St. Mark Catholic Church, and Holy Cross Lutheran Church.

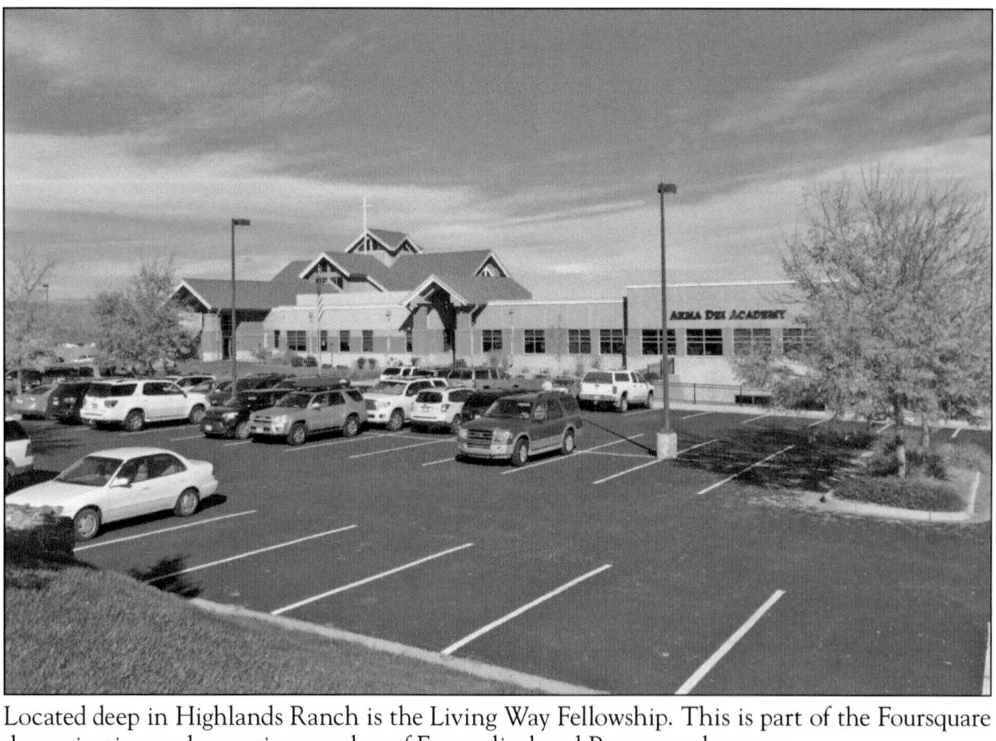

Located deep in Highlands Ranch is the Living Way Fellowship. This is part of the Foursquare denomination and an active member of Evangelical and Pentecostal groups.

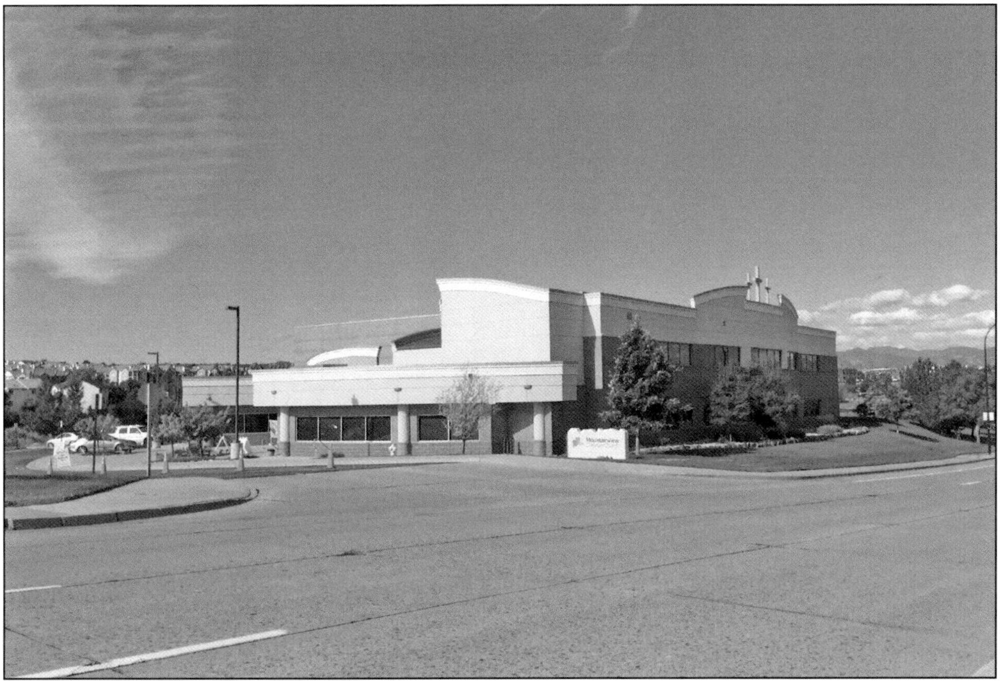

The Mountainview Christian Church is located near the Town Center of Highlands Ranch. Mountainview provides a casual and contemporary, nondenominational church for the citizens of Highlands Ranch.

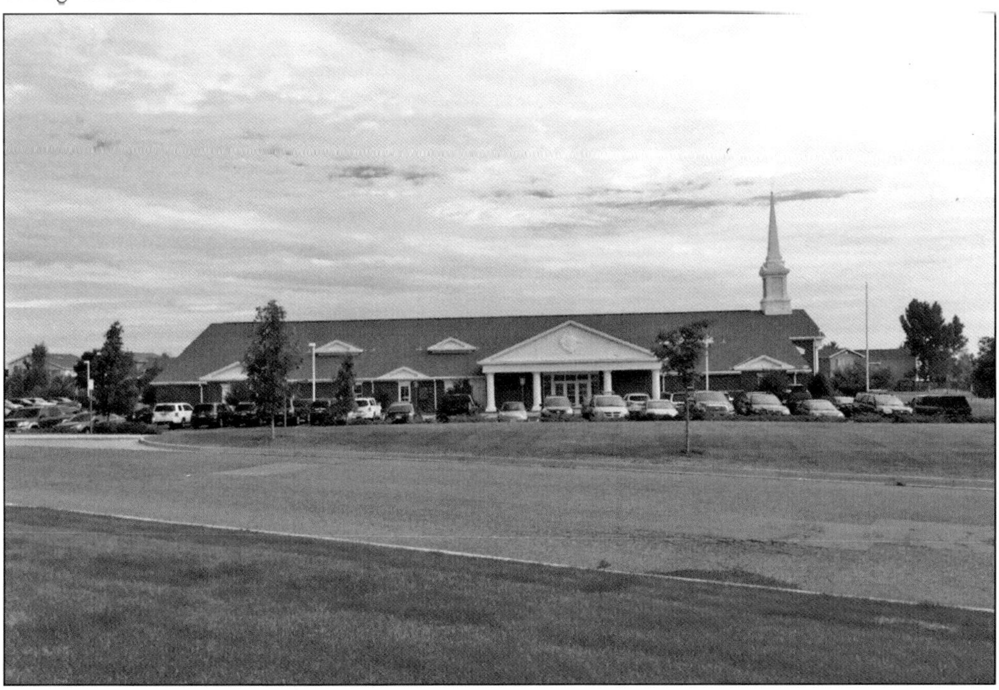

The Church of Jesus Christ of Latter-Day Saints, also known as the LDS Church or the Mormon Church, has a second location for its active members near the intersection of Wildcat Reserve Parkway and Fairview Parkway.

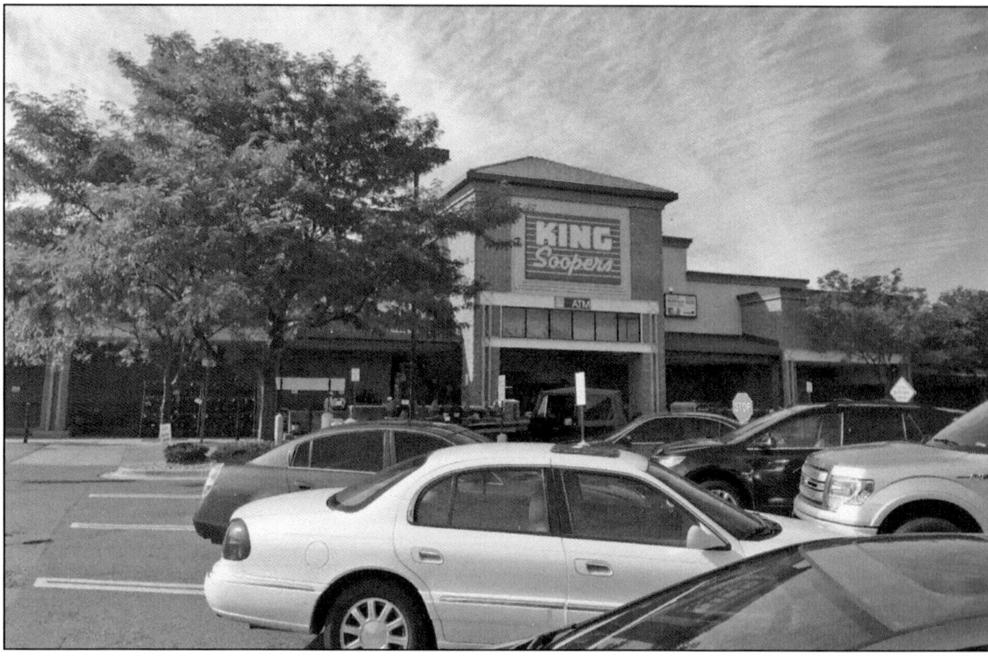

A modern suburban shopping center started growing in Highlands Ranch around the intersection of University Boulevard, Colorado Boulevard, and Highlands Ranch Parkway. The anchor of a shopping center is often the grocery store, and the main grocery store at this intersection is King Soopers.

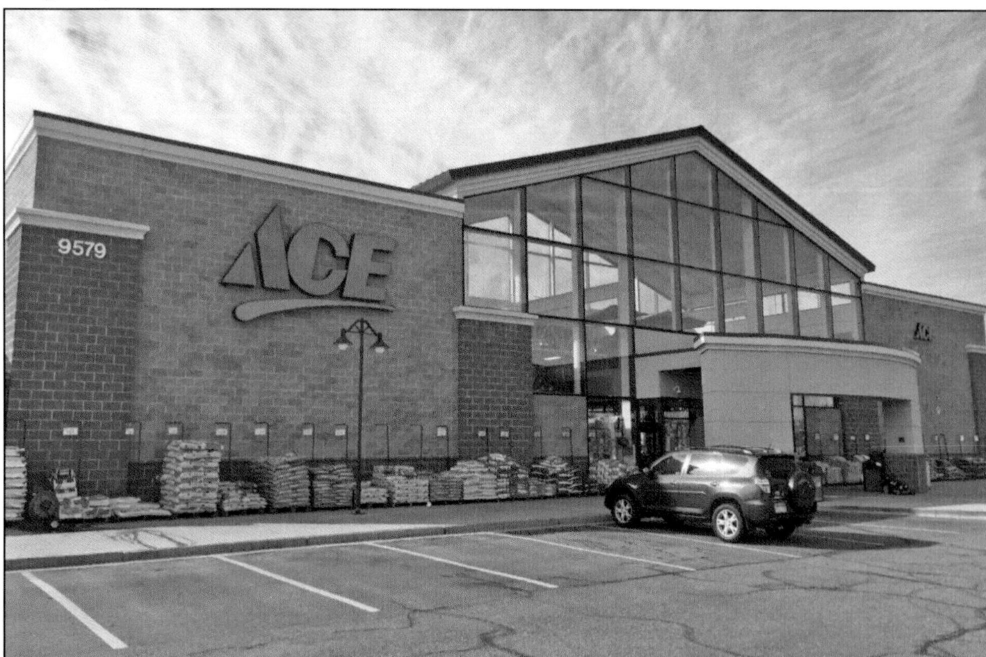

For many years, the residents of Highlands Ranch have looked to the Ace Hardware, located at the eastern end of the complex, for home maintenance. The Ace Hardware provides the tools and supplies needed to turn a standard suburban house into a home.

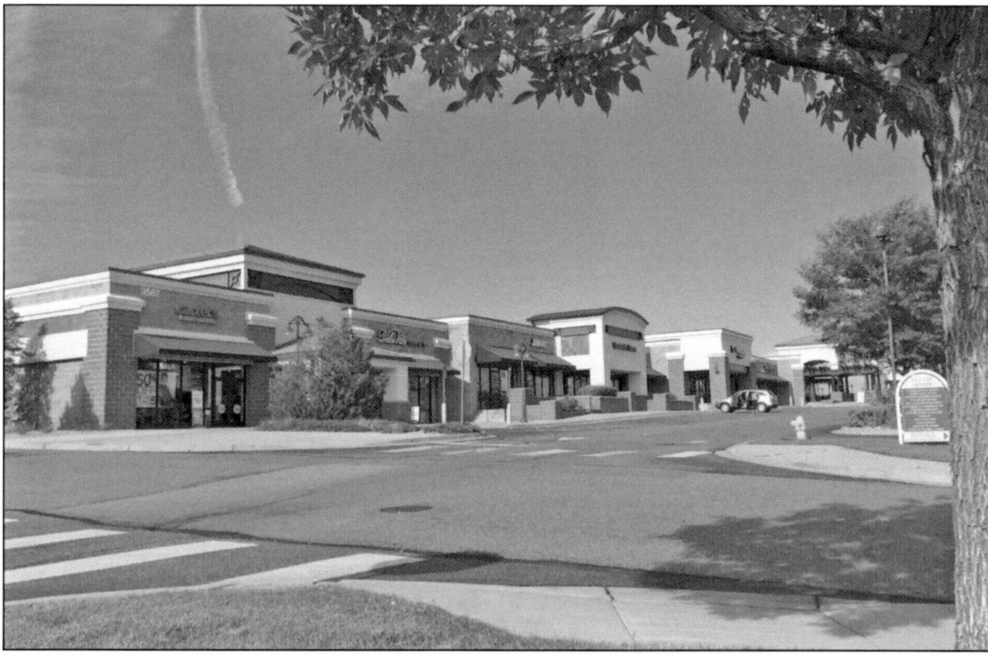

The Highlands Ranch Village Center is a good example of a modern suburban shopping center. It has many supporting stores both attached to the anchor store and in a variety of buildings throughout the parking lot.

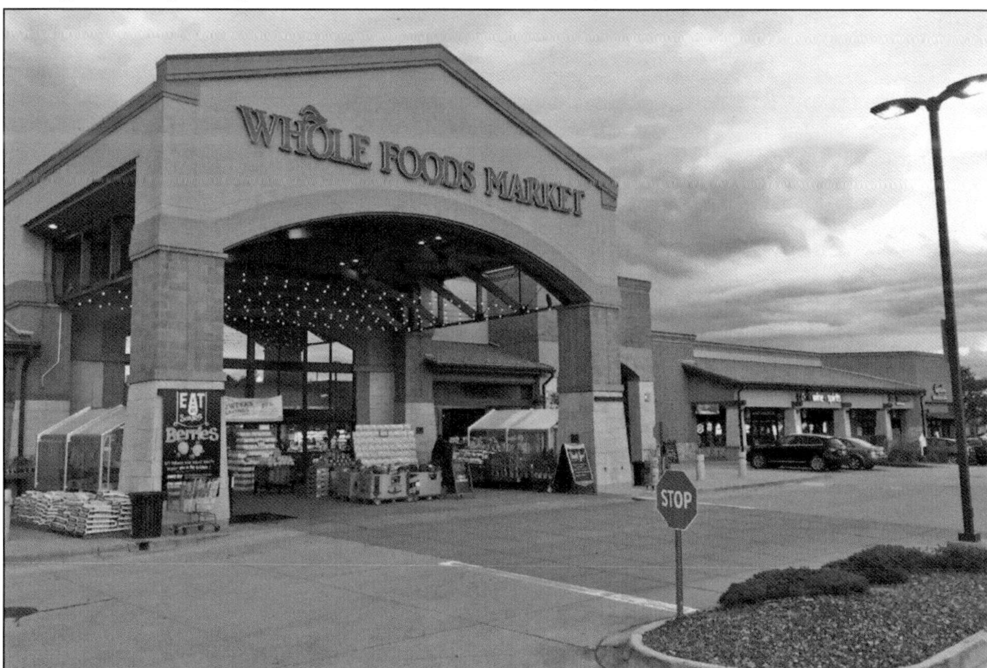

The 1990s and 2000s were also marked by a shift in people wanting more organic, natural, and less processed foods. To meet this demand, Whole Foods Market moved in across the street from the King Soopers. The high-quality food found a market with the residents of the more affluent Highlands Ranch.

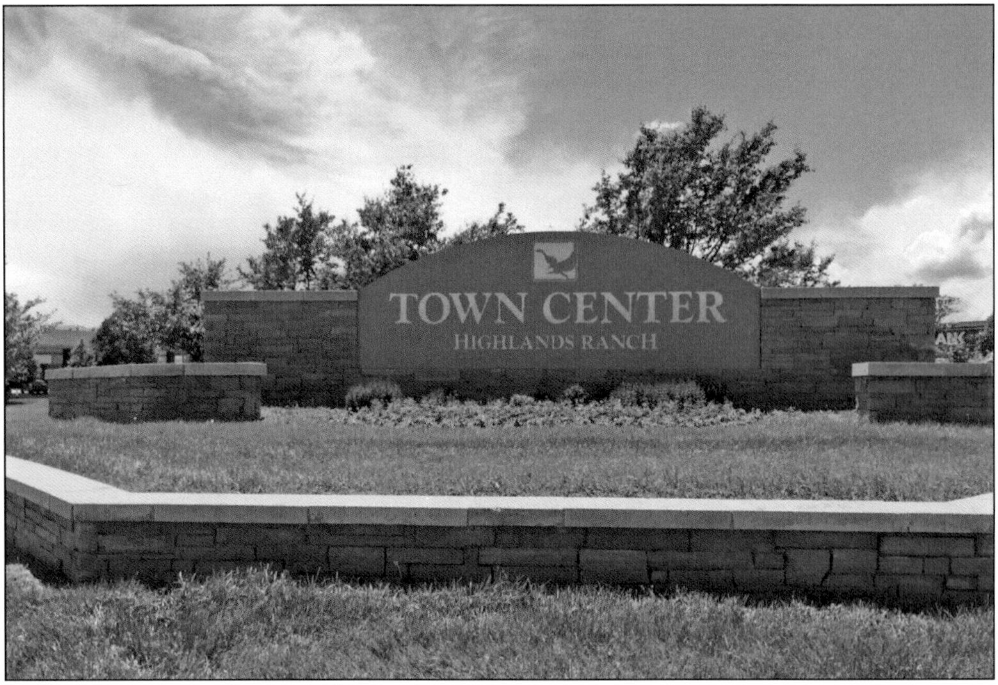

To get the "town feeling," Highlands Ranch also started to build up Town Center, which started at Broadway and Highlands Ranch Parkway and then spread west along Highlands Ranch Parkway to Lucent Boulevard.

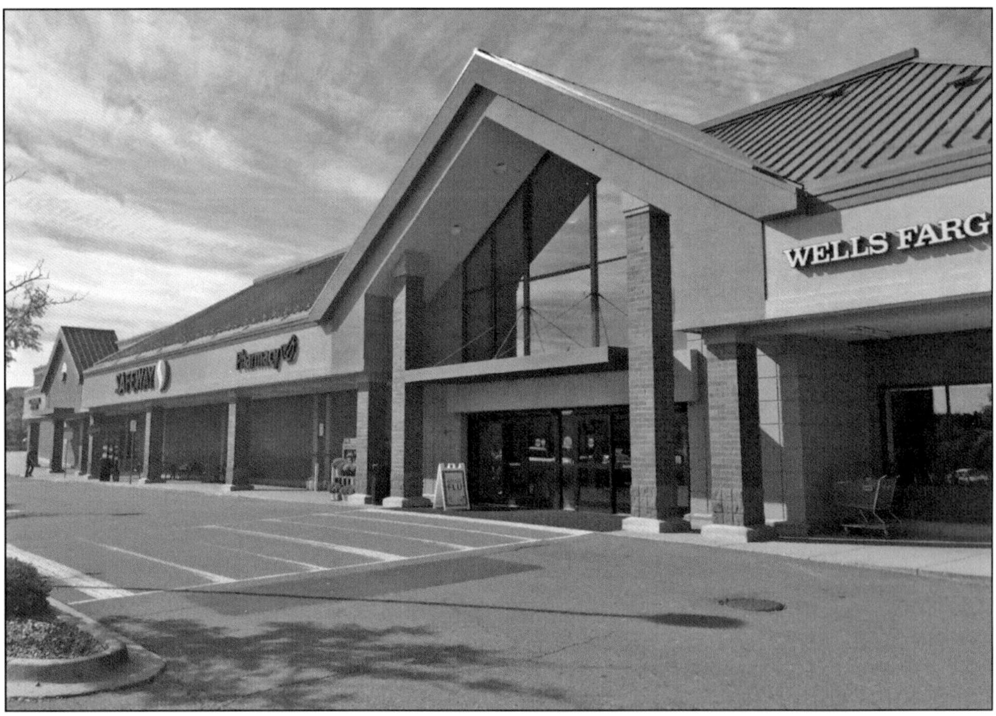

The first main anchor and shopping area built was the Safeway Shopping Center. Like other shopping centers, the complex is anchored by the grocery store and contains many other smaller stores.

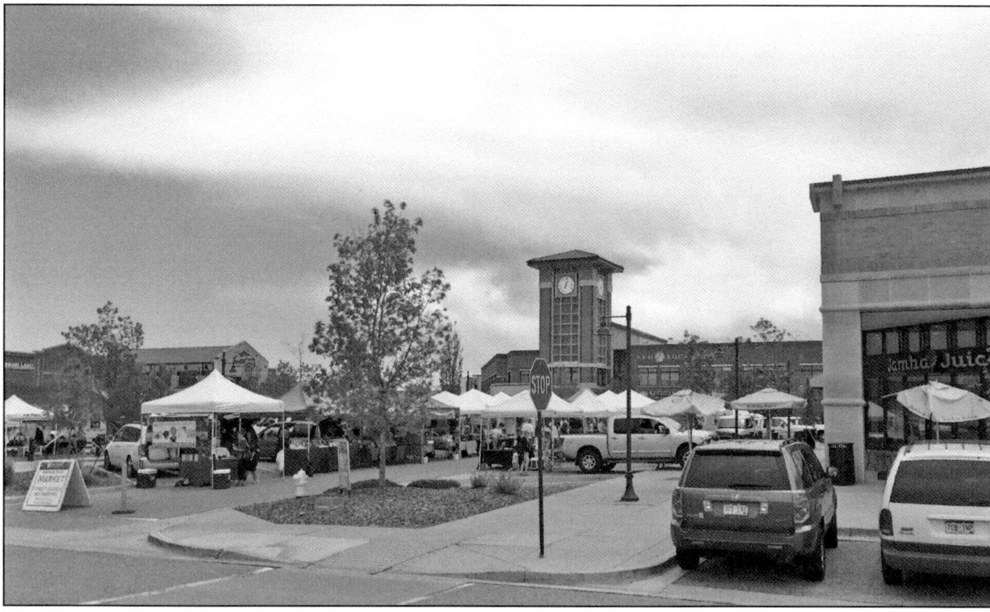

The heart of Town Center was opened in 2005. The opening also provided Highlands Ranch with a new iconic image of the clock tower that was placed in the center of Town Center. The Town Center serves as the home of a farmers' market every Sunday from the spring into the fall. Town Center became known as the heart of Highlands Ranch and provides the community with unique character.

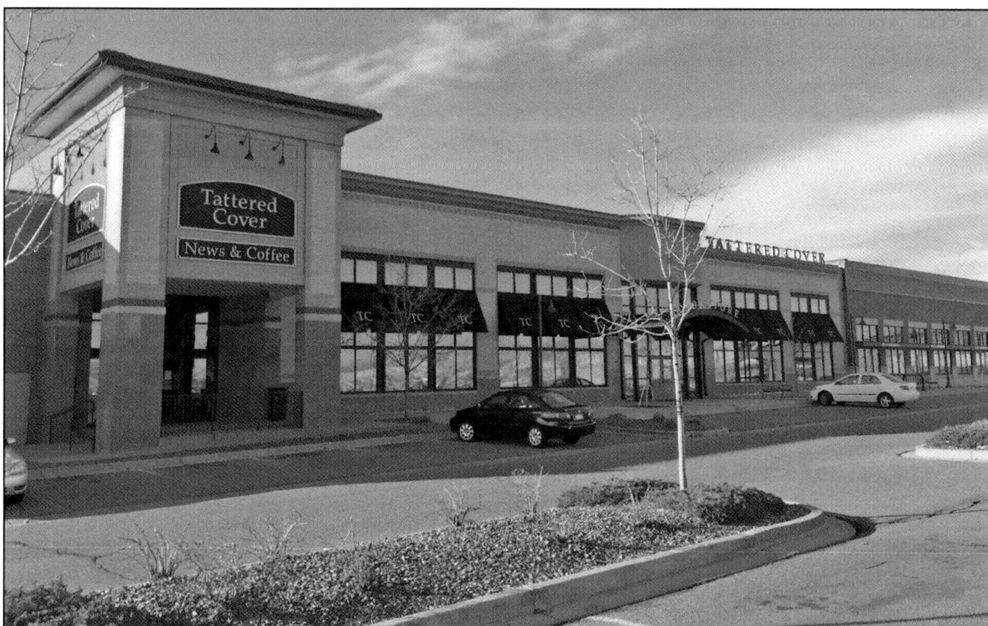

The residents of Highlands Ranch were excited when the Tattered Cover opened in Highlands Ranch Town Center. The Tattered Cover has previously proven to be a popular independent bookstore in the Cherry Creek area, and Highlands Ranch was a great place for them to try a first expansion into the suburbs. The store remained an icon of Town Center from its opening in 2005 until it moved 10 years later in 2015.

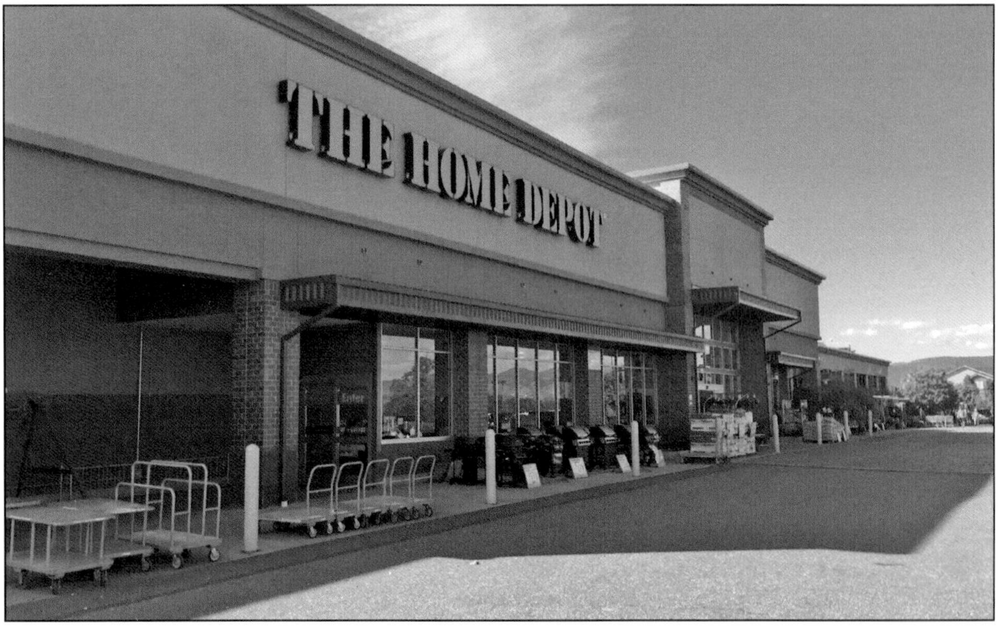

The first controversial development in Town Center occurred when the large home improvement retailer, Home Depot, moved in. Many residents were unhappy that a large box store was being built in Town Center instead of smaller, independent stores. After this initial controversy, Home Depot has played a major role in providing building supplies and knowledge to the community for the continued development, improvement, and maintenance of the homes in Highlands Ranch.

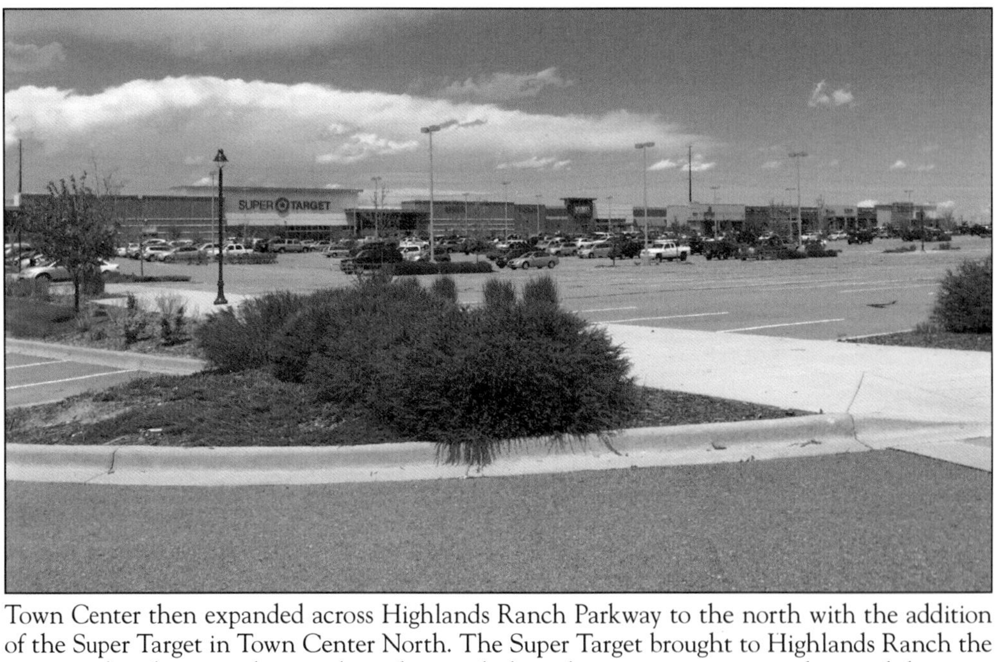

Town Center then expanded across Highlands Ranch Parkway to the north with the addition of the Super Target in Town Center North. The Super Target brought to Highlands Ranch the next trend in shopping that combines home, clothes, electronics, grocery, and general shopping all in one large store. Larger stores also brought about the need for even larger parking lots for the customers. The parking lots of Town Center serve a civic service providing parking during parades and Fourth of July fireworks celebrations.

Several shopping centers also brought art into their design. The Super Target parking lot runoff ponds are the home of several concrete gorillas. It is clear after a rainstorm that these "mountain gorillas" have not taken swimming lessons.

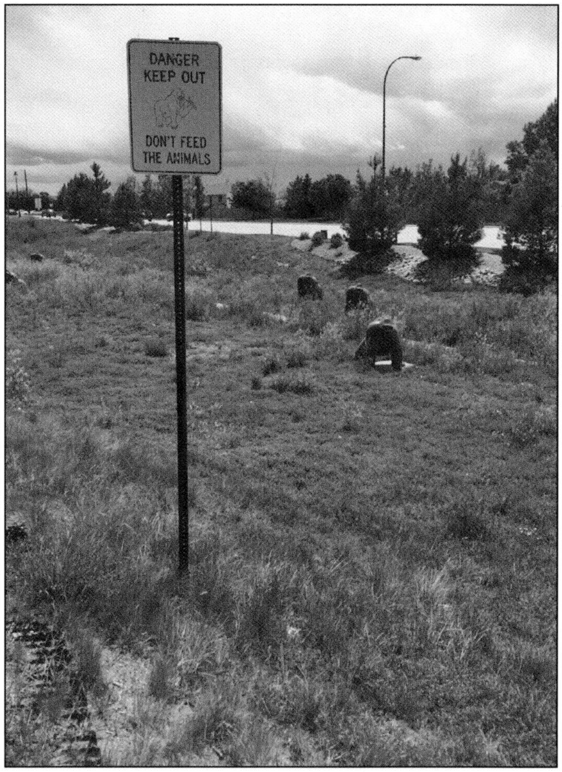

The story of retail in the 1990s would not be complete without Starbucks. Starbucks opened independent coffee shops as well as those found inside grocery stores and other retail locations.

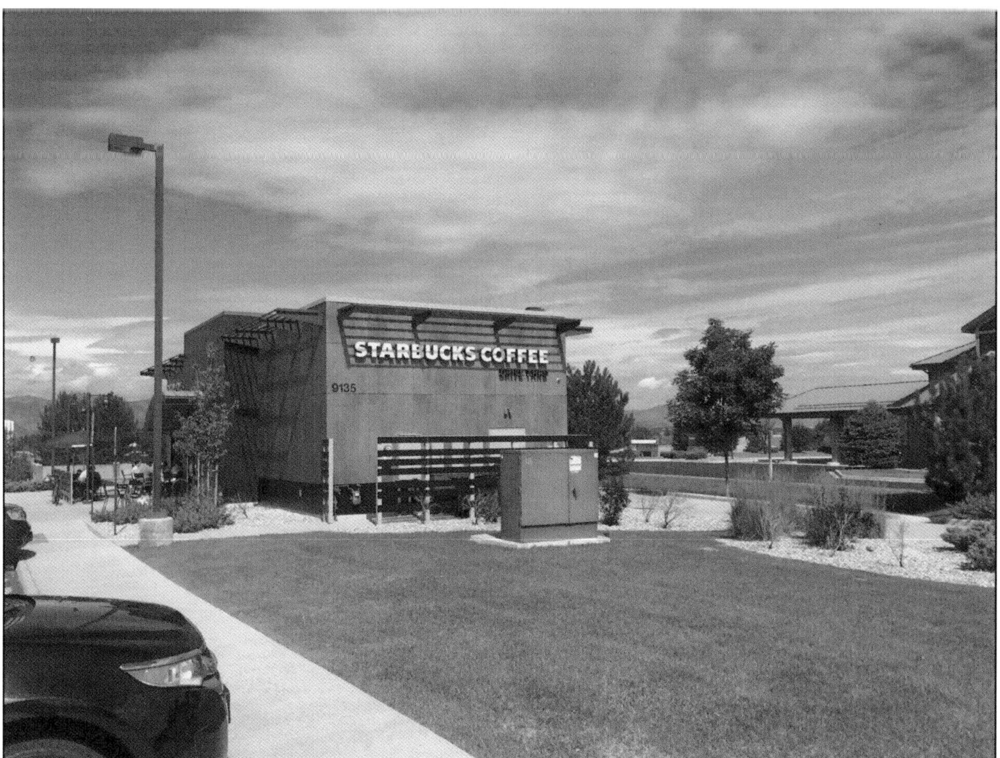

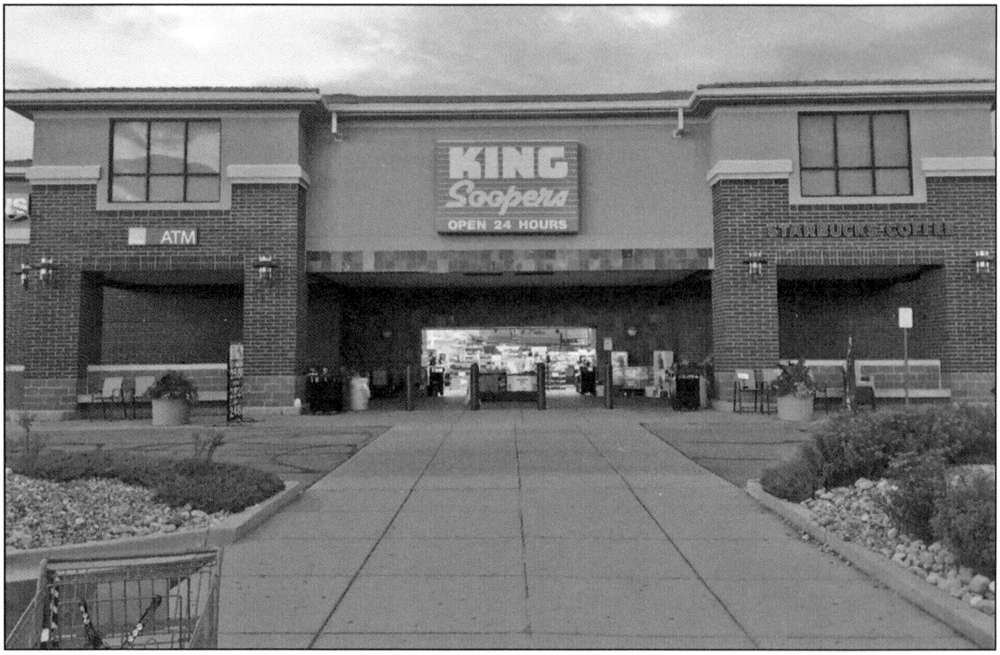

As Highlands Ranch continued to expand to the west, the residents on the west side needed better access to a grocery store. King Soopers opened a store at Highlands Ranch Parkway and Wildcat Reserve Parkway. Many grocery stores started to stay open 24 hours a day to meet the need of customers both day and night.

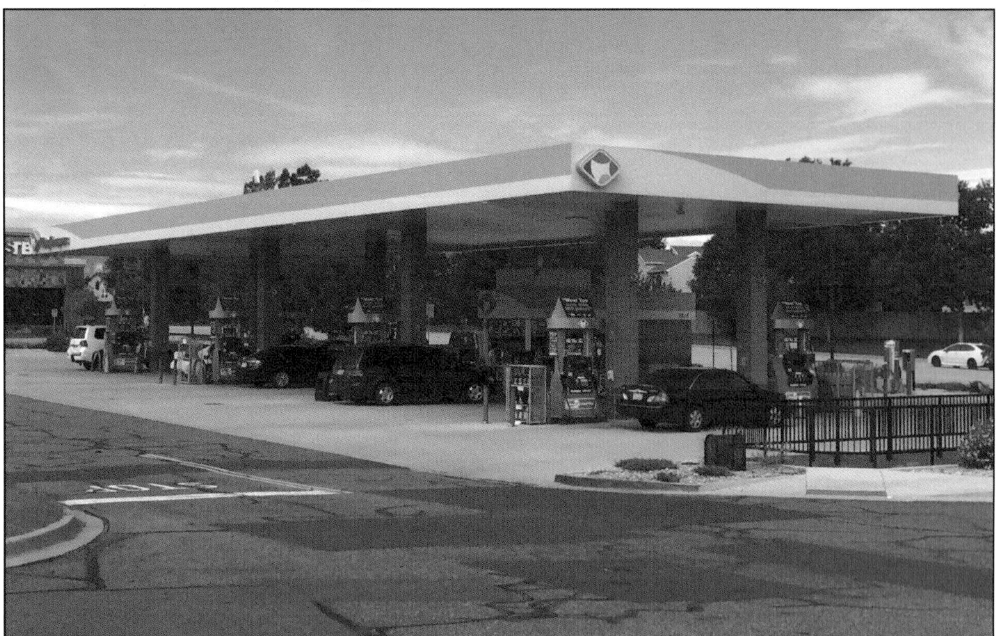

As area grocery stores looked at additional ways to provide service to customers, they added gas stations at some of their stores in the 2010s. King Soopers started providing this service for the residents of Highlands Ranch and regularly offered discounts on the price of gas based on the amount of groceries and other services that have been purchased at their stores.

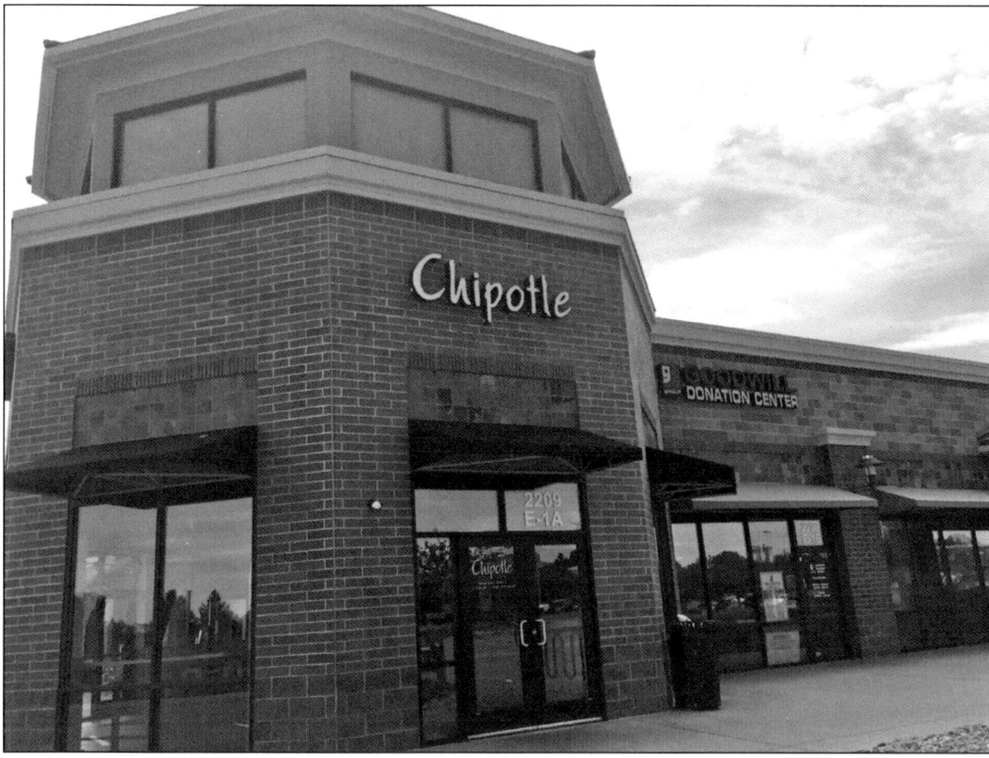

Pictured are Chipotle and Goodwill. Chipotle is a regional success story, starting in Denver at a location by the University of Denver. The chain makes fresh burritos and tacos using socially responsible ingredients made to order in front of the guests. Goodwill also helps the socially conscious of Highlands Ranch give their excess possessions. Goodwill provides jobs and training to those who are in need of them.

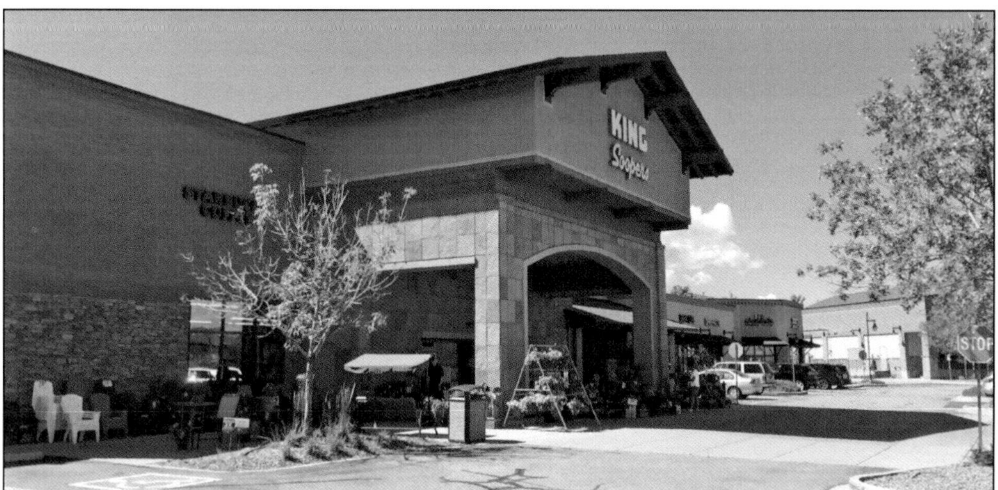

The last major direction for retail development was to support the communities to the south. This was accomplished with the development of another modern suburban shopping center at East Wildcat Reserve Parkway and McArthur Ranch Road. Once again, King Soopers serves as the anchor grocery store.

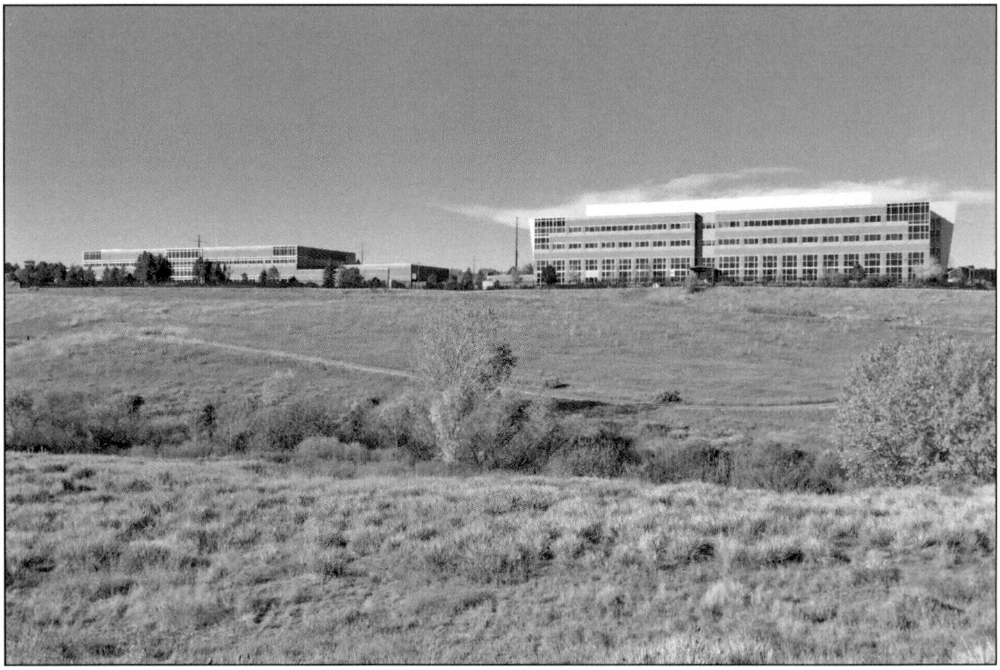

Several large office buildings are found along the open space near Broadway. The businesses that fill these buildings make up the eastern border of the Highlands Ranch Business Center.

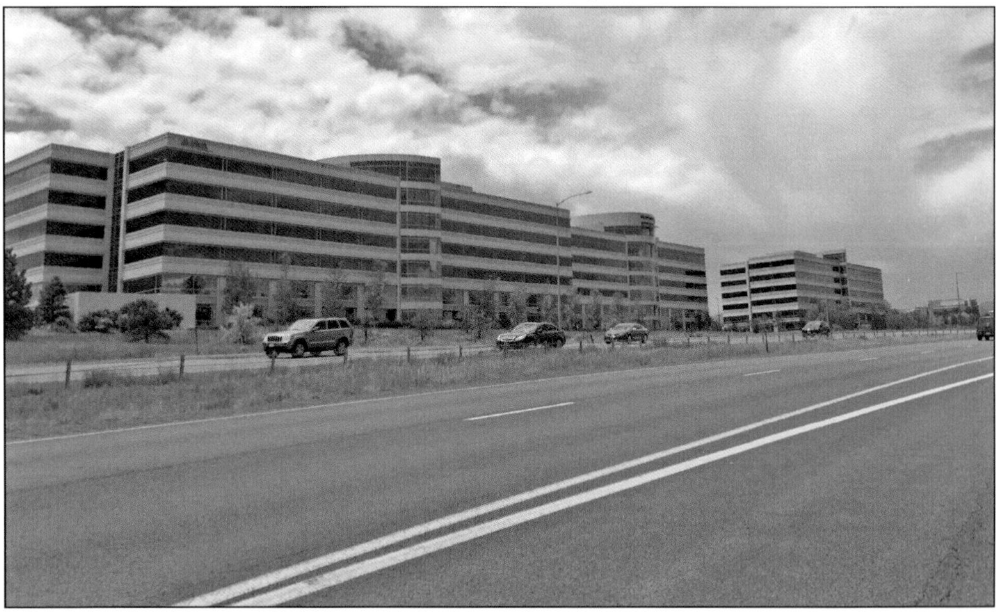

Approximately 25,000 people leave Highlands Ranch each workday morning for professional jobs mostly located in Downtown Denver and in the Tech Center along I-25 to the east. As the final phase of the Highlands Ranch build-out, the Highlands Ranch Business Center is being built and is expected to continue to expand over the next decade. The most noticeable office buildings in the area are the three Lucent and Avaya Technology buildings, located along C-470 at the Lucent exit. Note that the off-ramp was named after the first major company to build in the new Highlands Ranch Business Center.

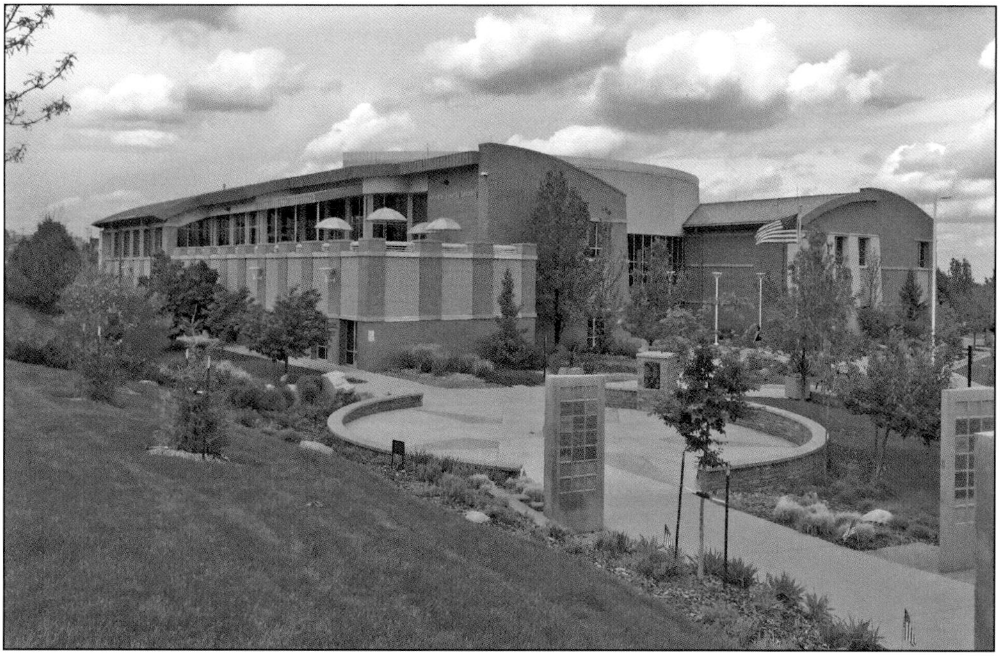

The citizens of Highlands Ranch along with Douglas County Libraries created a great library in the heart of Highlands Ranch between Town Center and Civic Green Park. The library serves thousands every year. In 2007, Douglas County Libraries received the John Cotton Dana Award, the American Library Association's "most prestigious award."

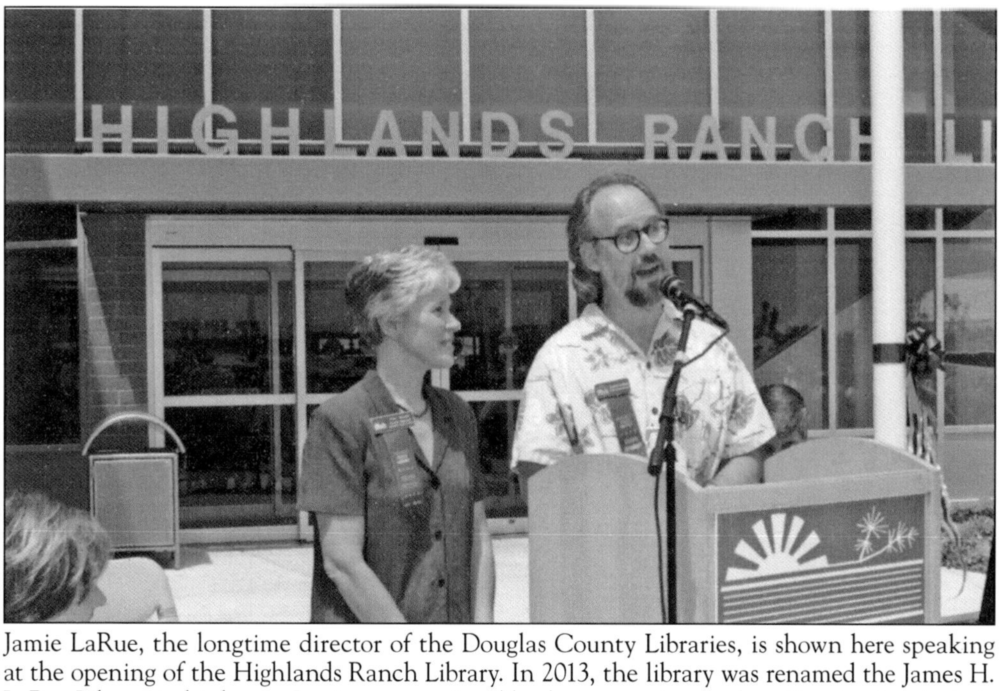

Jamie LaRue, the longtime director of the Douglas County Libraries, is shown here speaking at the opening of the Highlands Ranch Library. In 2013, the library was renamed the James H. LaRue Library in his honor. Jamie was a national leader in creating modern libraries that include space for not only books, but also eBooks, CDs, and other media formats. (Courtesy of Douglas County History Research Center, Douglas County Libraries.)

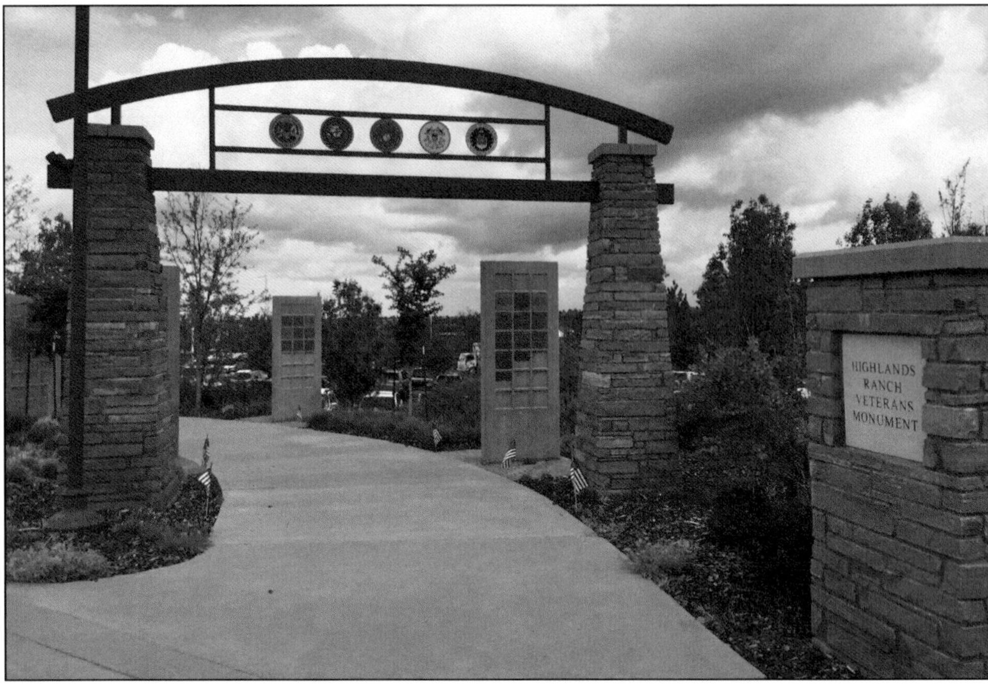

Outside the library is the Highlands Ranch Veterans Monument, dedicated July 1, 2009. Many members of the Highlands Ranch community have served their country in the Armed Forces. Some have even made the ultimate sacrifice, giving their lives in defending freedom.

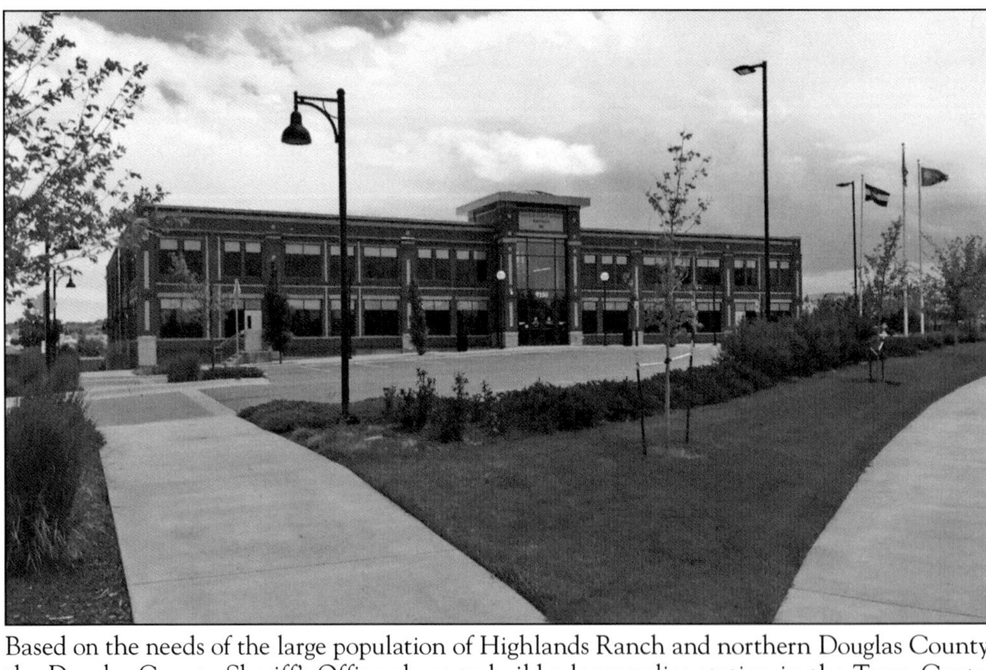
Based on the needs of the large population of Highlands Ranch and northern Douglas County, the Douglas County Sheriff's Office chose to build a large police station in the Town Center area for better service, lower response times, and reduced transportation costs. The Douglas County sheriff has served Highlands Ranch very well, and the residents have turned down talk of incorporation because they are happy with these county services.

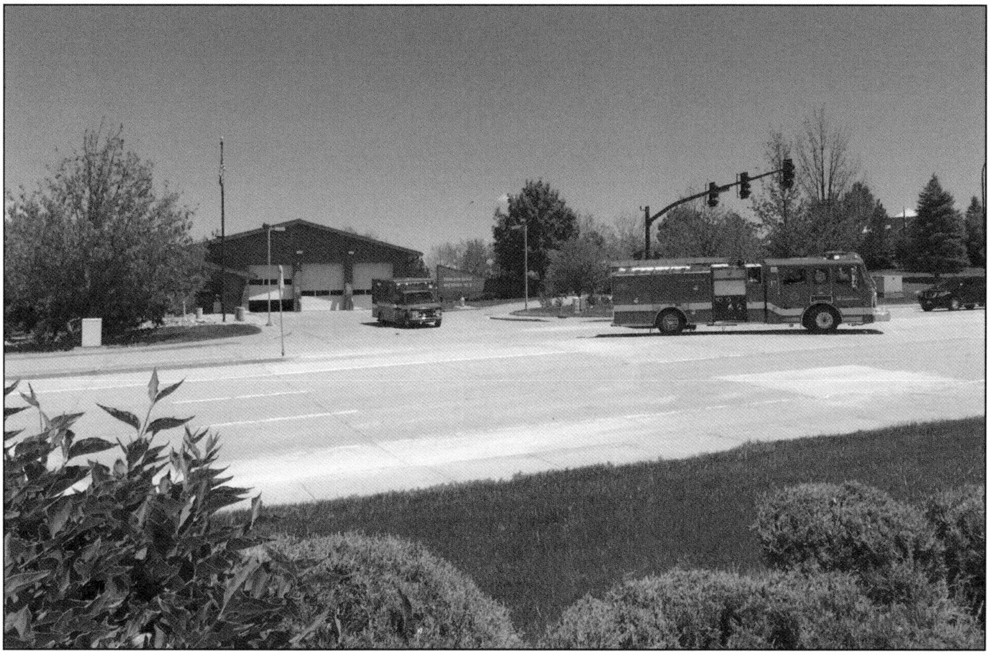

Fire services for Highlands Ranch are contracted by Highlands Ranch Metro District from the Littleton Fire Department. Fire Station No. 17 is located on University Boulevard near the Eastridge Recreation Center and supplies services to most of the east and north side of Highlands Ranch.

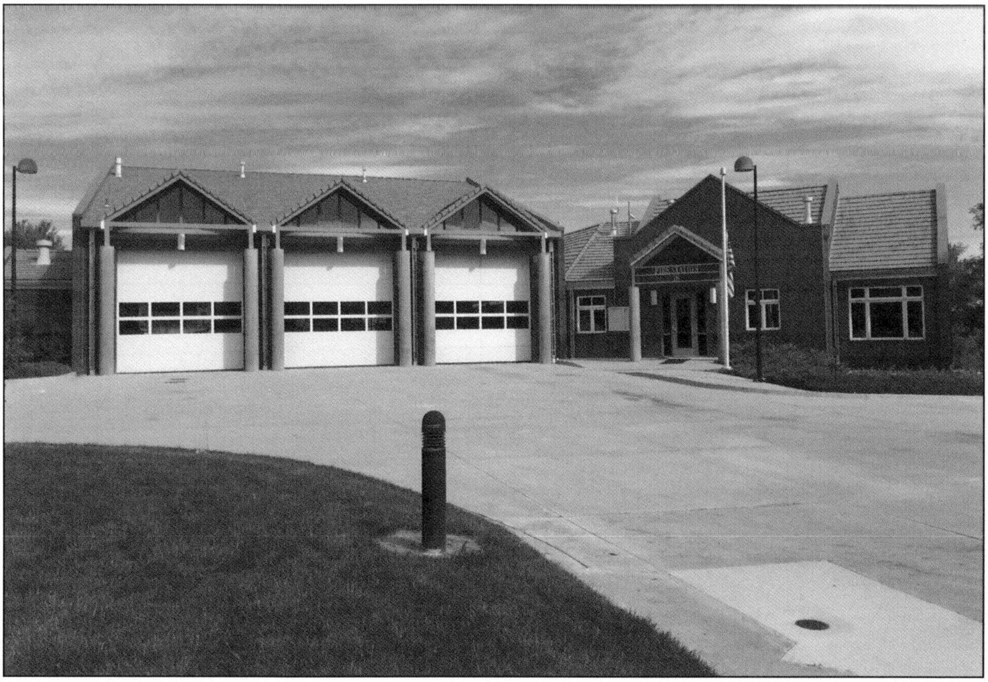

Fire Station No. 18 is located south of Town Center and is the most central to the whole Highlands Ranch area. Fire Station No. 16 is located just outside Highlands Ranch along Santa Fe Drive and provides services to the western side of Highlands Ranch.

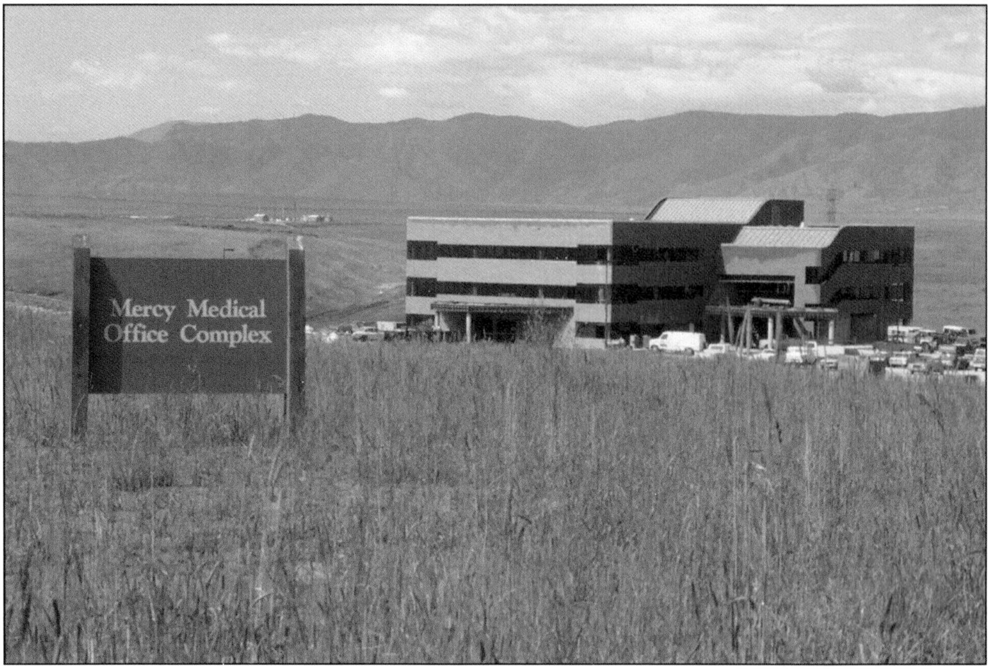

The first medical building in Highlands Ranch was the Mercy Medical Office Complex. This early picture helps show what is not there yet, which includes C-470 and the western side of Highlands Ranch. (Courtesy of Highlands Ranch Metro District.)

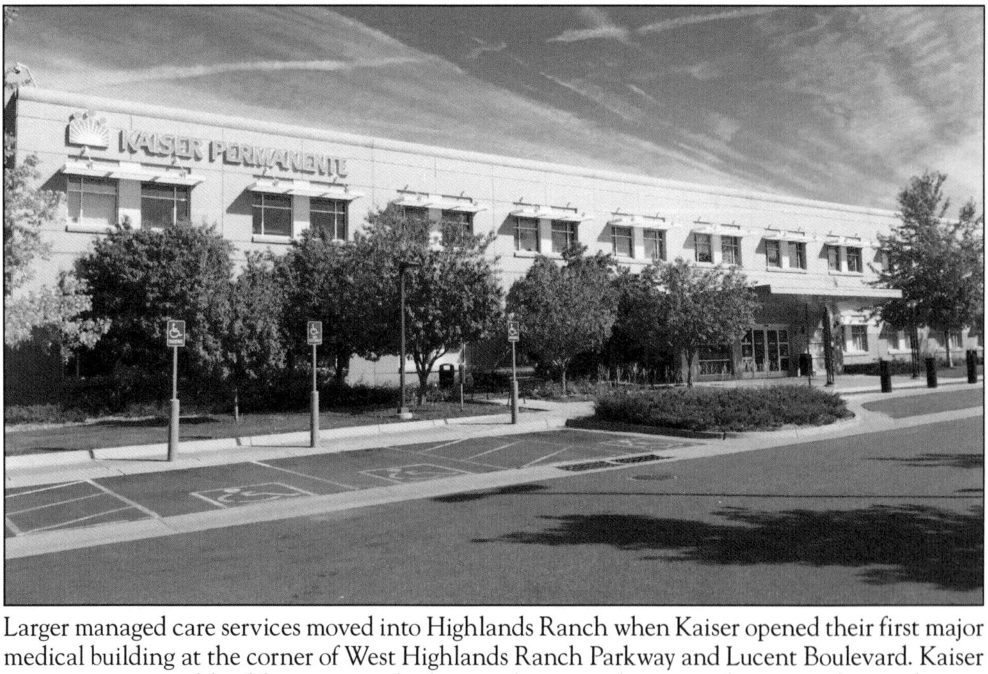

Larger managed care services moved into Highlands Ranch when Kaiser opened their first major medical building at the corner of West Highlands Ranch Parkway and Lucent Boulevard. Kaiser is a major national health-care provider known for using their own doctors and specialists to keep costs down. Another added advantage is that the customer knows that Kaiser covers all the doctors in the building. Based on growth in Highlands Ranch, Kaiser has spread into other nearby buildings.

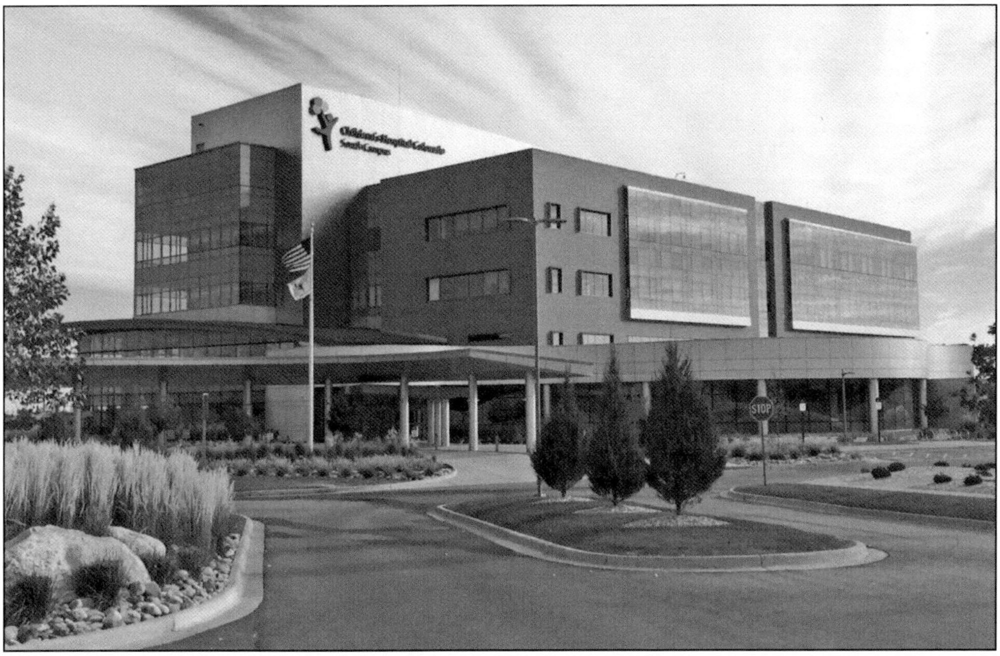

The Children's Hospital Colorado South Campus, Highlands Ranch, opened December, 19, 2013, at the corner of C-470 and Lucent Boulevard. It provides the highest-quality medical care to the children of Highlands Ranch. The location provides quick access and shorter travel times compared to the Children's Hospital in Aurora.

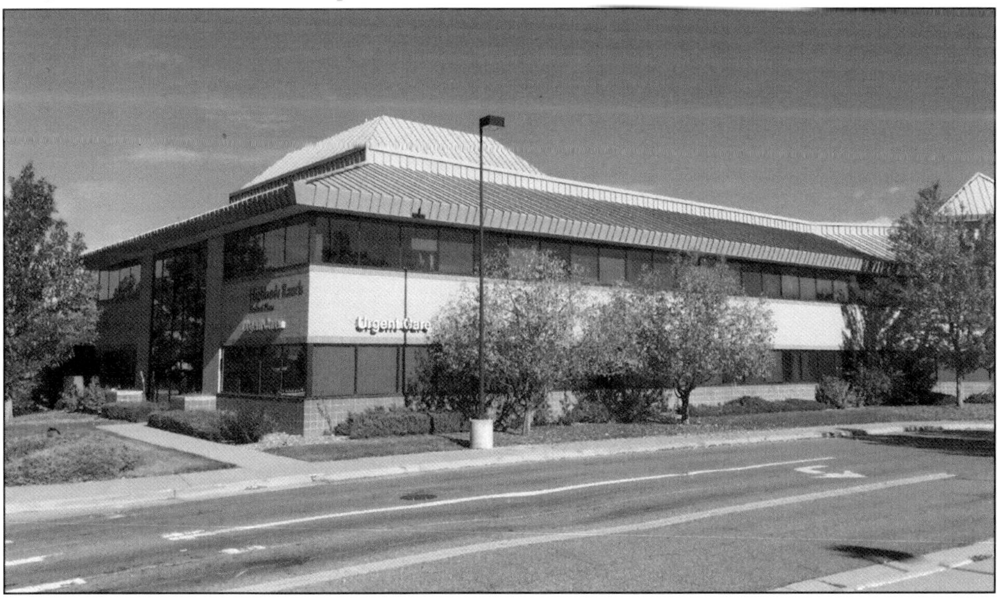

Another major change in health care taking hold in the 2000s was the rise of urgent care facilities. Urgent care provides medical service in an on-demand style for conditions ranging from the common cold to broken bones. Urgent care facilities normally have extended hours of service into the evening and on weekends, providing better access than traditional doctors' offices. They are usually cheaper and less crowded than emergency rooms, which continue to provide service to the most critical medical conditions.

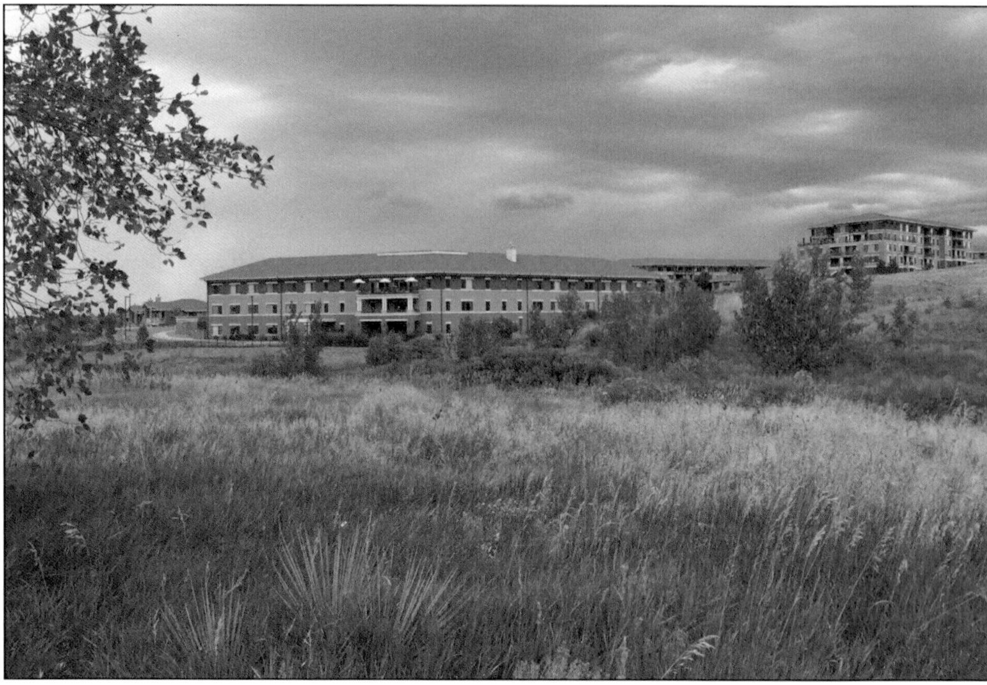

Vi Senior Living on University Boulevard provides active, independent, and assisted living experiences to members of Highlands Ranch. Vi is one of two major senior living options with the other being Wind Crest in the northwest corner of Highlands Ranch.

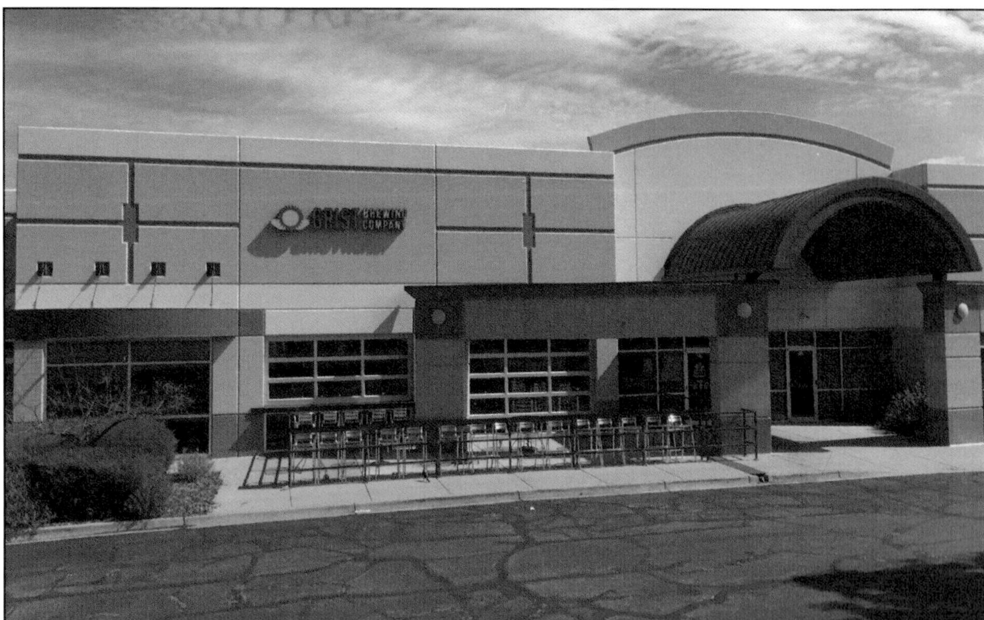

One of the newest attractions is Highlands Ranch's first production brewery, the Grist Brewing Company, located on the west side near Santa Fe Drive and Town Center Drive. The Grist, which opened in November 2013, is a 20-barrel brew house. Grist craft beers are for sale at most liquor stores around Highlands Ranch.

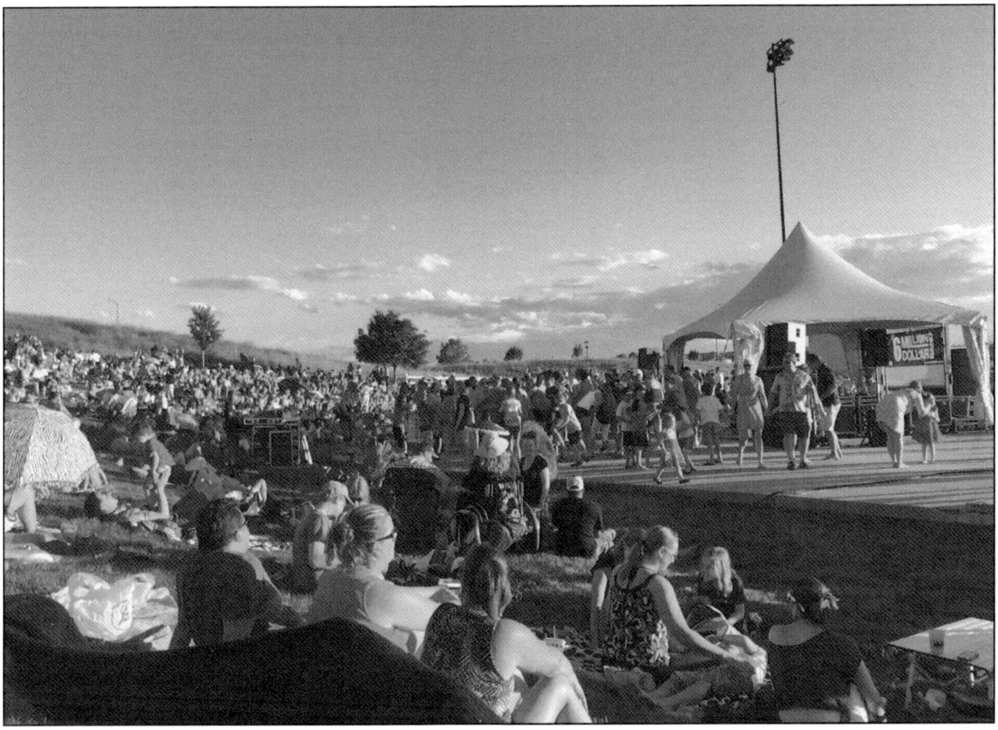

HRCA-sponsored free summer concerts at Highland Heritage Regional Park bring out many residents to enjoy their Thursday evenings. During the concert pictured, the 6 Million Dollar Band performed hits from the 1980s while the crowd watched, listened, and danced.

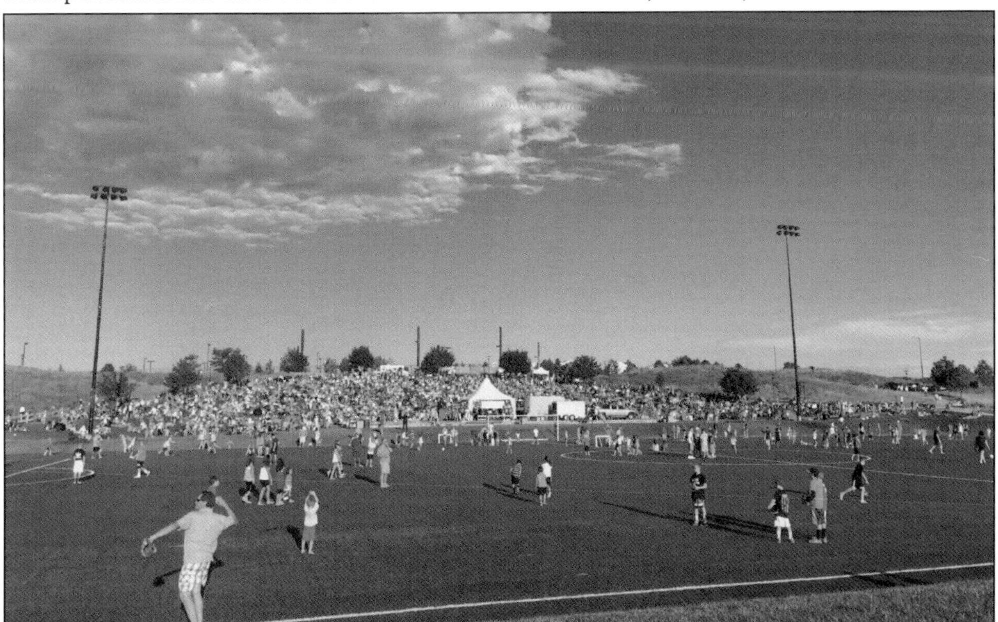

The summer concerts at Highland Heritage Regional Park include more than just music and dancing. The synthetic playing field behind the stage provides a wonderful location for kids to run and play as parents supervise from a distance.

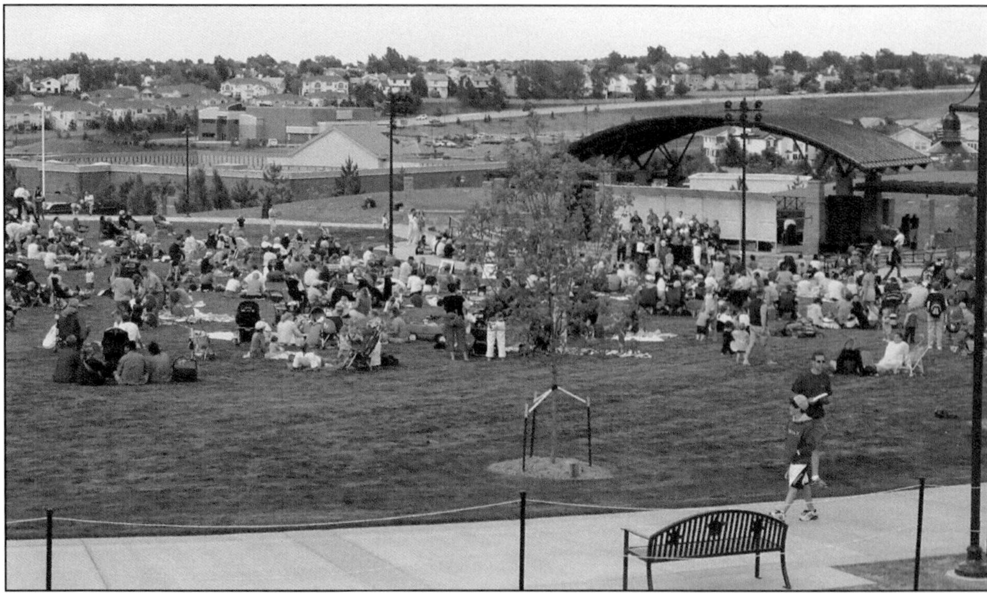

A free concert in Civic Green Park is a wonderful way to spend the evening. Highlands Ranch enjoys the wonderful Colorado weather that makes outdoor concerts enjoyable every summer. Outdoor concerts also provide a fun way for the community to come together. They allow the large community to continue to bond. Civic Green Park is a great park for concerts and also has shelters, playgrounds, a stream, and a water feature. In addition, Civic Green Park has many paved and dirt paths that allow users to stroll through its gardens. (Courtesy of Highlands Ranch Metro District.)

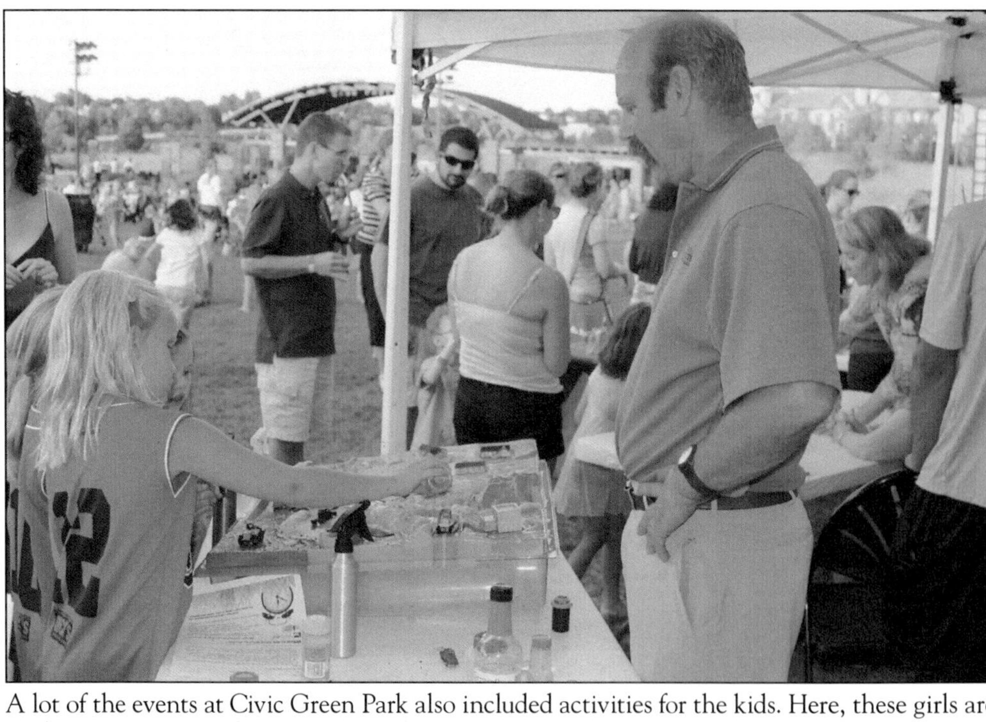

A lot of the events at Civic Green Park also included activities for the kids. Here, these girls are working on a project. (Courtesy of Highlands Ranch Metro District.)

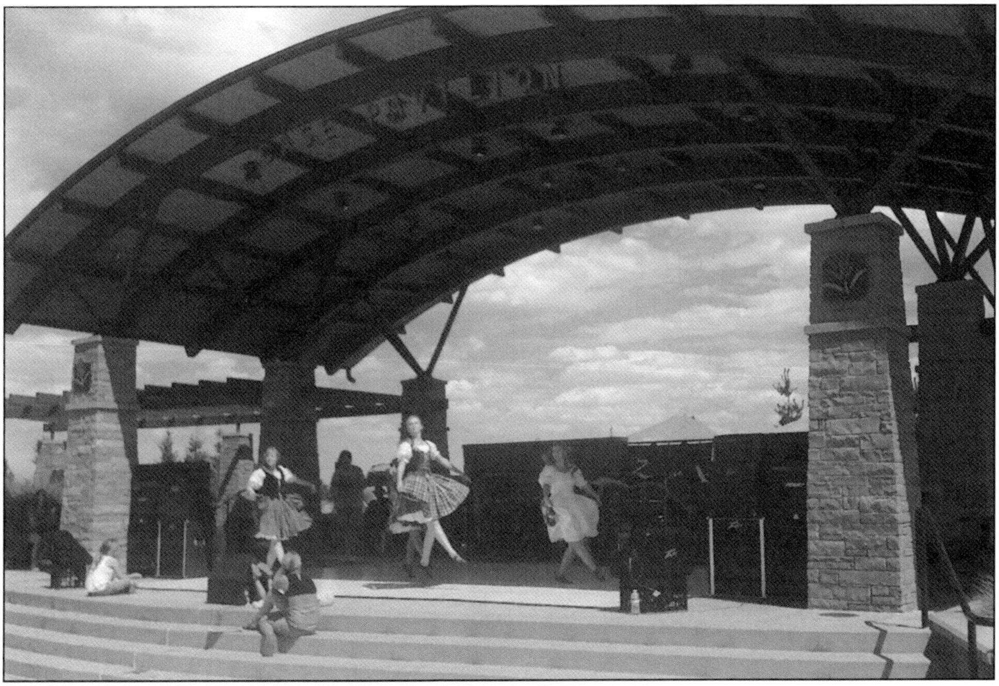

Some of the concerts put on by Highlands Ranch Metro District are themed. Pictured are Irish dancers at an Irish festival. Most of these festivals and concerts feature local acts and performers, which is good exposure to performing in front of a crowd.

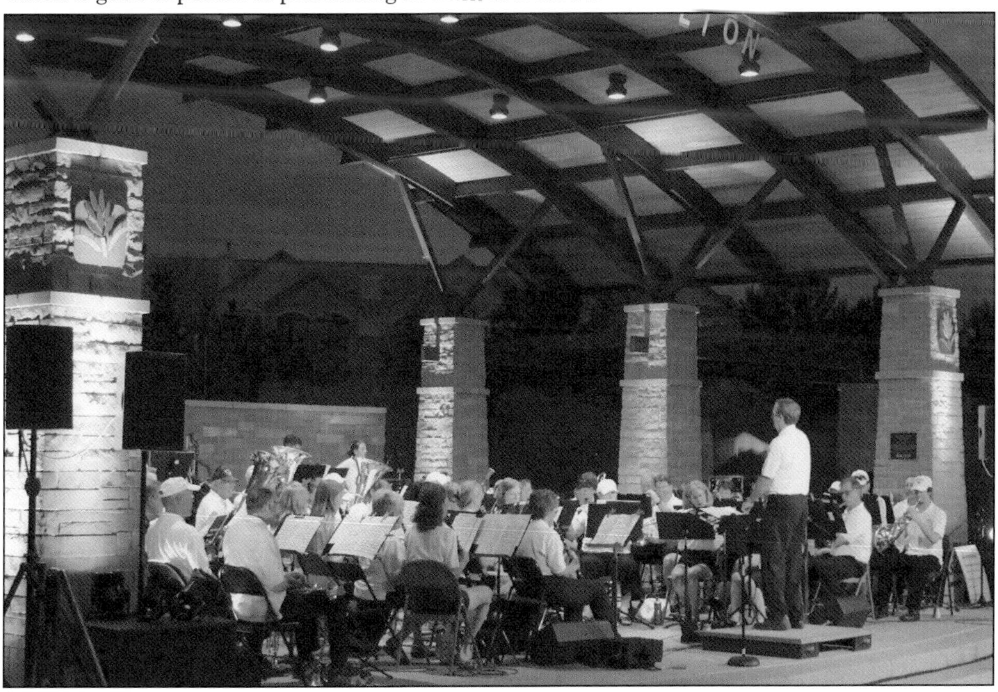

Not all the concerts at Civic Green Park end at nightfall. The lighting on and around the stage allows performances into the early evening. The lights are especially important in the spring and fall when the weather is nice, but the sun disappears as the festivities are going on.

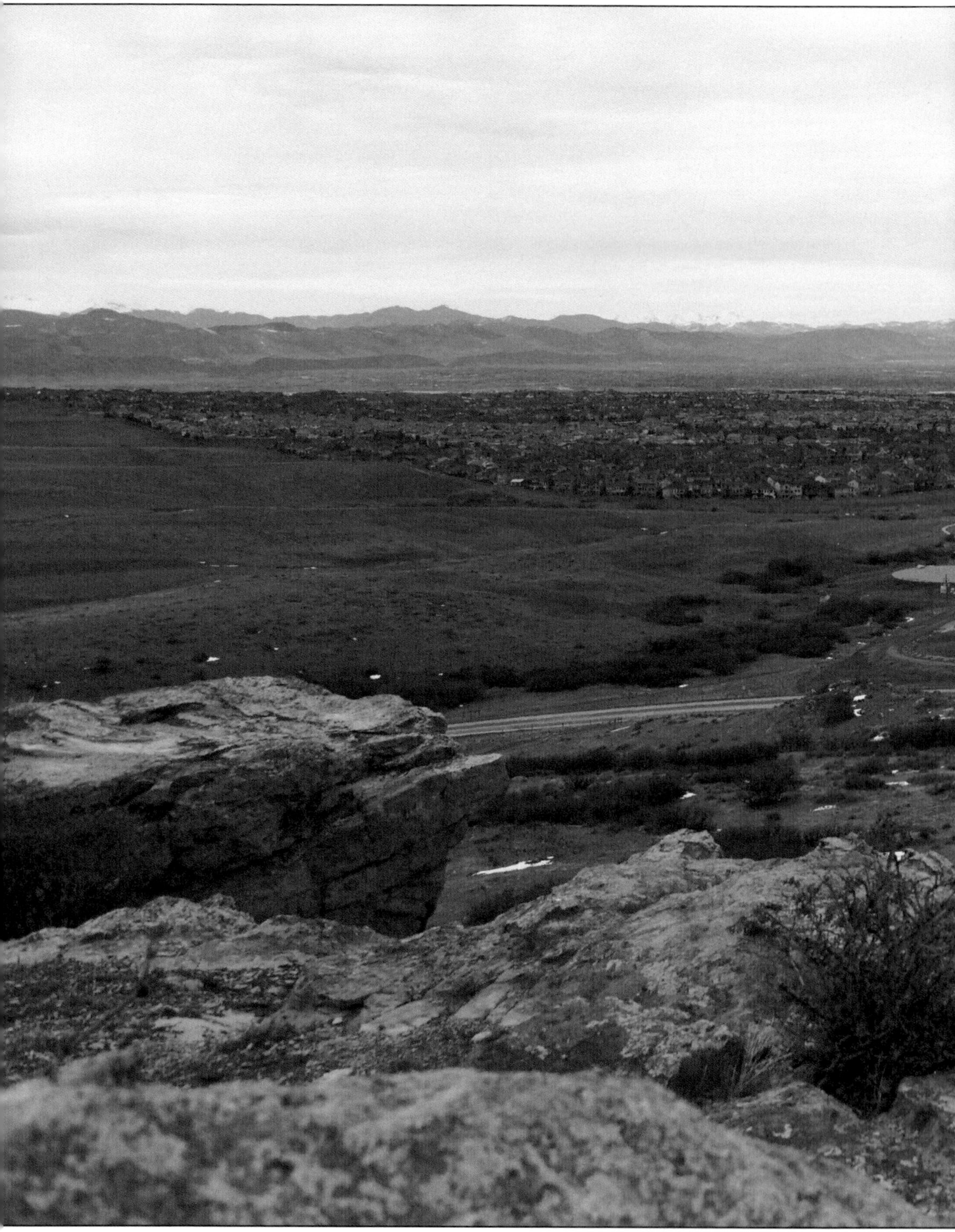

The Highlands Ranch area has grown from the native people of the plains to homesteads to a large ranch, and now to the planned community of Highlands Ranch. While the current build-out phase is almost complete, the future still holds great promise. This view of Highlands Ranch

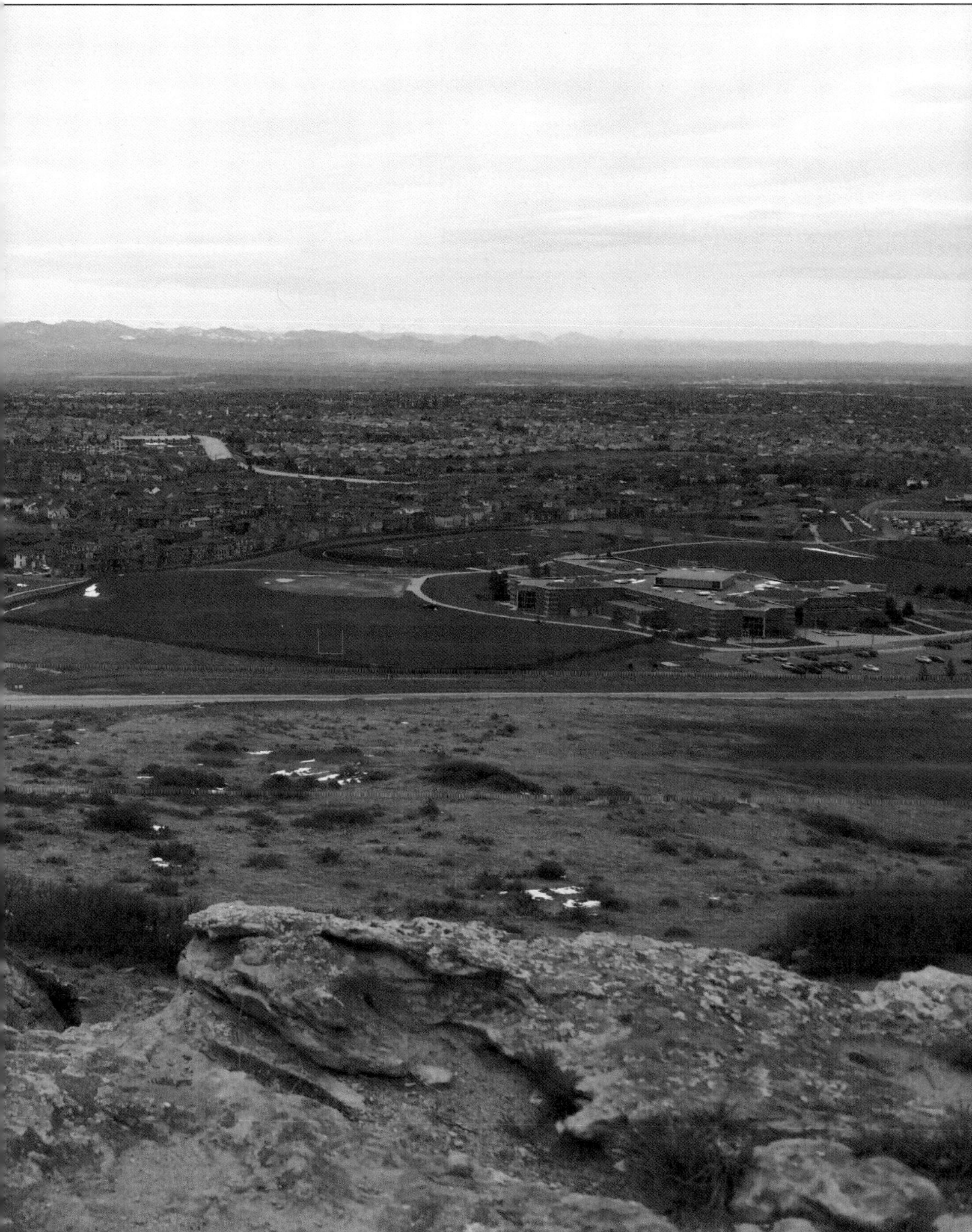

from Wildcat Mountain captures the community's vastness and provides a glimpse of the immense possibilities for the future.